WHY ISLAMISTS GO GREEN

Edinburgh Studies of the Globalised Muslim World

Series Editor: **Frédéric Volpi**, Director, Prince Alwaleed Bin Talal Centre for the Study of Contemporary Islam, University of Edinburgh

This innovative series investigates the dynamics of Muslim societies in a globalised world. It considers the boundaries of the contemporary Muslim world, their construction, their artificiality or durability. It sheds new light on what it means to be part of the Muslim world today, for both those individuals and communities who live in Muslim-majority countries and those who reside outside and are part of a globalised ummah. Its analysis encompasses the micro and the macro level, exploring the discourses and practices of individuals, communities, states and transnational actors who create these dynamics. It offers a multidisciplinary perspective on the salient contemporary issues and interactions that shape the internal and external relations of the Muslim world.

Forthcoming and available titles

A Political Theory of Muslim Democracy
Ravza Altuntaş-Çakır

Salafi Social and Political Movements: National and Transnational Contexts
Masooda Bano (ed.)

Why Islamists Go Green: Politics, Religion and the Environment
Emmanuel Karagiannis

Literary Neo-Orientalism and the Arab Uprisings: Tensions in English, French and German Language Fiction
Julia Wurr

edinburghuniversitypress.com/series/esgmw

WHY ISLAMISTS GO GREEN

Politics, Religion and the Environment

Emmanuel Karagiannis

EDINBURGH
University Press

Edinburgh University Press is one of the leading university presses in the UK. We publish academic books and journals in our selected subject areas across the humanities and social sciences, combining cutting-edge scholarship with high editorial and production values to produce academic works of lasting importance. For more information visit our website: edinburghuniversitypress.com

Edinburgh University Press Ltd
The Tun – Holyrood Road
12 (2f) Jackson's Entry
Edinburgh EH8 8PJ

Typeset in 11/15pt Adobe Garamond Pro by
Cheshire Typesetting Ltd, Cuddington, Cheshire, and
printed and bound in Great Britain

A CIP record for this book is available from the British Library

ISBN 978 1 3995 0622 9 (hardback)
ISBN 978 1 3995 0624 3 (webready PDF)
ISBN 978 1 3995 0625 0 (epub)

CONTENTS

GLOSSARY

adl	justice
akhirah	accountability
al-bi'a	environment
al-din	religion
al-mi'raj	the night journey
Amir al-Mu'minin	Commander of the Faithful
aqida	Muslim creed
bid'a	innovation
Dar al-Harb	Abode of War
Dar al-Islam	Abode of Islam
da'wa	calling others to Islam
fiqh	Islamic jurisprudence
fitra	the primordial nature of purity
hadith	words and teachings of the Prophet Muhammad
hajj	annual pilgrimage to Mecca
halal	permissible
harim	wildlife sanctuary
hijra	the journey of the Prophet Muhammad and his followers from Mecca to Medina in the year 622
hima	conservation zone
hizba	accountability

hudna	truce
iftar	the evening meal for breaking fasting during the Islamic month of Ramadan
ihsan	perfection or excellence
ihya' al-mawat	cultivation of barren land
ijtihad	independent reasoning
ijma'	consensus
iqta	land revenue
jahiliyya	pre-Islamic ignorance
jizya	a poll tax paid by non-Muslims
Ka'ba	a cubic stone monument at the centre of the Great Mosque in Mecca
khalifa	vicegerent
kharaj	property tax
Khulafa al-Rashidun	Rightly Guided Caliphate
madhahib	schools of Islamic jurisprudence
mafsada	harm
Majelis Ulama Indonesia	Indonesian Council of 'Ulama
maqasid	objectives of Shari'a
marja' al-taqlid	highest-ranking religious-legal authority
maslaha	public interest, benefit
mizan	balance
murshid	Sufi teacher
mustad'afin	oppressed
mustakbirin	oppressors
qibla	direction of prayer
rahman	mercy
rawafid	rejectionists
sadaqa	voluntary act of charity
Sahaba	Companions
Shari'a	Islamic law
shura	consultation
Sunna	the Prophet Muhammad's way of life and legal precedent
tahara	cleanliness

tafsir   exegesis
taqwa   God-consciousness
tawhid   unity of God
'ulama   religious scholars
umma   the community of believers
'ushr   tithe
waqf   charitable endowed land
wasatiyya   middleness
wudu   ablution
zakat   alms-giving

TRANSLITERATION

Most Arabic terms have been italicised to indicate that they have not yet become part of the English language. Transliteration of Arabic is always a compromise. The book has used a simplified version of the conventions used by the *International Journal of Middle Eastern Studies*. Therefore, words appear without diacritical marks for long vowels and consonants. Moreover, I have used common spellings of names (e.g., Khomeini, Osama bin Laden, Hizbullah). The spelling of Turkish names has been preserved as it is. All dates are common era (CE). It should be noted that the book uses Muhammad Ali's English translation of the Qur'an.[1]

Note

1. *The Holy Qur'an*, tr. Muhammad Ali, 4th ed. (Lahore: Ahmadiyya Anjuman Isha'at Islam, 1951).

SERIES EDITOR'S FOREWORD

Edinburgh Studies in the Globalised Muslim World is a series that focuses on the contemporary transformations of Muslim societies. Globalisation is meant, here, to say that although the Muslim world was always interacting with other societal, religious, imperial or national forces over the centuries, the evolution of these interconnections constantly reshapes Muslim societies. The second half of the twentieth century has been characterised by the increasing number and diversity of exchanges on a global scale bringing people and societies 'closer', for better and for worse. The beginning of the twenty-first century confirmed the increasingly glocalised nature of these interactions and the challenges and opportunities that they bring to existing institutional, social and cultural orders.

The series is not a statement that everything is different in today's brave new world. Indeed, many 'old' ideas and practices still have much currency in the present, and undoubtedly will also have in the future. Rather, the series emphasises how our current globalised condition shapes and mediates how past worldviews and modes of being are transmitted between people and institutions. The contemporary Muslim world is not merely a reflection of past histories, but is also a living process of creating a new order on the basis of what people want, desire, fear and hope. This creative endeavour can transform existing relations for the better, for example by reconsidering the relations between society and the environment. It can equally fan violence and hatred as illustrated in the reignition of cycles of conflicts over sovereignties, ideologies or resources across the globe.

The Globalised Muslim World series arrives at a challenging time for any inquiry into Muslim societies. The new millennium began inauspiciously with a noticeable spike in transnational and international violence framed in 'civilisational' terms. A decade of 'war of terror' contributed to entrenching negative mutual perceptions across the globe while reinforcing essentialist views. The ensuing decade hardly improved the situation, with political and territorial conflicts multiplying in different parts of the Muslim world, and some of the most violent groups laid claim to the idea of a global caliphate to justify themselves. Yet, a focus on trajectories of violence gives a distorted picture of the evolution of Muslim societies and their relations with the rest of the world. This series is very much about the 'what else' that is happening as we move further into the twenty-first century.

Emmanuel Karagiannis's *Why Islamists Go Green* places at the forefront of the debate the issue that has acquired an increasing prominence in Muslim communities around the world in the first decades of this century: environmentalism. The book shows how the relationship between the Islamic doctrine and the natural world is an eminently political topic that has been taken up by diverse Islamist organisations and shaped to respond to a variety of contemporary predicaments. While militant movements may seem unlikely proponents of a 'green' agenda, Karagiannis's work reveals how their articulation of political Islam includes traditional views of the relations between the Muslim community and the environment, as well as creating new connections and synergies. He illustrates that by differentially including religious, scientific and political sources, Islamists reframe for themselves and their audience the place of green issues in Muslim communities at the local, glocal and global level.

Considering the discourses and practices of the Egyptian Muslim Brotherhood, of Hizb ut-Tahrir, of Hizbullah, of Hamas and of jihadi-Salafi groups like al-Qaeda and ISIS, the analysis presented in the book uncovers some important trends in the interactions between Islamism and the environment. Karagiannis invites the reader to think past the mere notion of an instrumentalisation of green issues to encourage social and political mobilisation by actors who do not necessarily have much of an environmentalist agenda. The work details the ways in which these issues are anchored in a global vision for a 'good' Muslim society and indicate a recognition that addressing worsening environmental conditions is increasingly an important dimension of governance for Islamists. It also shows the different prioritisations of these green issues in the overall strategic orientations of different Islamist movements, underscoring the diversity of their approaches. Karagiannis's contribution is a most welcome addition to the literature on both Islamism and environmentalism that undoubtedly paves the way for a new wave of studies of these issues across the globalised Muslim world.

Frédéric Volpi
Chair in the Politics of the Muslim World
University of Edinburgh

PREFACE AND ACKNOWLEDGEMENTS

In her widely praised novel *The Kindness of Enemies*, the Sudanese-Scottish writer Leila Aboulela tells a story that takes place in the Caucasus of the mid-nineteenth century. In one of its scenes, the legendary Muslim leader of the anti-Russian resistance Imam Shamil recites for his son Jamaleldin the following Qur'anic verse:

> In the creation of the heavens and the earth, and the alternation of the night and the day, and the ships that run in the sea with that which profits men; and the water that Allah sends down from the sky, then gives life therewith to the earth after its death and spreads in it all [kinds of] animals, and the changing of the winds and the clouds made subservient between heaven and earth, there are surely signs for a people who understand. (2:164)

It is a powerful moment for young Jamaleldin, who comes to realise God's power of creation as manifested through the rain, the wind and the clouds. He walks with his fearsome warrior father around their quiet village in the middle of the night, but he can hear the 'breathing' of stars and forests.[1] He connects with the Creator of the universe because he feels His presence. Here, Aboulela essentially describes the return to *fitra*, the primordial nature of purity whereby humans are born to submit to God's will and follow His commands. This transcendent union between God, man and nature lies at the heart of the Islamic understanding of the cosmos.

At the beginning of the third decade of the twenty-first century, it is becoming clear that humanity and the planet face enormous and potentially catastrophic environmental challenges. The effects of global warming and climate change could devastate countries and destroy communities. Droughts and floods have already resulted in massive loss of life and migration flows. Air pollution has been identified as a cause of cancer and other health problems. The pollution of oceans and other bodies of water has threatened marine life. Many animal species are close to extinction owing to human activities. Indeed, the list of environmental problems is endless.

From North Africa to Indonesia, Muslim communities have struggled to cope with the new environmental realities. Consequently, ecological issues and concerns have been added to the political agenda in most countries. Although the Muslim faith has much to say about the environment and its relationship with humans, the position of Islamist groups is rather unknown. This is probably not a surprise, given that the use of the term *political Islam* can evoke visions of conflict, carnage, patriarchy and oppression. After all, Islamism has often been described as outdated and anti-modern. If political Islam is, as it has often been claimed, a reactionary movement against Western-driven modernity, its adherents must be incapable of tackling contemporary challenges. Yet this stereotypical and Western-centric perspective has ignored the reality of contemporary Islamism. Contrary to perceptions, some Islamists have increasingly discussed environmental and environment-related issues.

This is an understudied phenomenon that social sciences and humanities have almost ignored. The research in this volume focuses on an ostracised segment of political Islam that has been labelled as extremist or militant, with a particular reference to five groups and movements. The Muslim Brotherhood is a former governing party in Egypt which has a long history of clandestine activity. Hizb ut-Tahrir supports non-violent methods but holds extremist views, by Western standards. Hamas and Hizbullah are armed groups-turned-political parties which have acquired power at the local or national level. Finally, al-Qaeda and ISIS are militant organisations with global reach.

These Islamist groups are chosen as representative case studies to demonstrate the depth of Islamist environmentalism. While they have certain similarities, each group has developed its own green agenda in response to different perceptions and priorities. The rise of Islamist environmentalism is an important development because the protection of nature is often understood as a righteous cause without any political strings. The adaptability of these Islamists, deemed to be obstinate, deserves more detailed study. In fact, it is imperative to understand the causes of this new environmentalism as Islamists maintain a claim to authenticity and legitimacy. The interplay between religion and politics is not always self-evident, albeit it is often assumed. The question that arises is whether Islamist environmentalism is motivated by religion, politics or both.

Conducting research on Islamist groups has never been an easy task. Following the 9/11 attacks, there is a prevailing atmosphere of neo-Orientalism and Islamophobia deriving from polarised debates over the West's relationship with the Muslim world. The subsequent securitisation of political Islam has created ethical and practical problems for researchers. Moreover, the pursuit of academic neutrality is a never-ending process for any social scientist. Personal and academic biases are sometimes hard to overcome. Thus, it is important to understand how your own gender, class, ethnicity and education may affect collection and analysis of data.

I would like to thank King's College London's SSPP Publication Subvention Fund for its financial support. Many individuals have assisted in the writing of this book. I am especially grateful to Carool Kersten, whose support and guidance have been of great value in this research. I also extend warm thanks to Michael Northcott and Shuruq Naguib for their constructive feedback. Moreover, I have benefited from interviews with Fachruddin Mangunjaya of Universitas Nasional in Jakarta, Nurdeng Deuraseh of Sultan Sharif Ali Islamic University in Brunei, Osman Bakar of Universiti Brunei Darussalam, and Ibrahim Özdemir of Åbo Akademi University in Turku. I am grateful to the anonymous reviewers for their feedback that helped improved the manuscript considerably. I am also grateful for the critical discussion of a previous version of Chapter 2 which was presented at the annual conference of the International Studies Association in March 2019 in Toronto. Also, I would like to thank my editors at Edinburgh University Press, Emma House and Louise Hutton, and their team for their support and encouragement. My family was, as usual, a source of great strength during the period I was conducting the research. I dedicate this book to the memory of my loving uncle Dimitris Afentakis.

Structure of the Book

The book comprises an introduction, seven chapters, and a conclusion summarising the key findings. The introduction briefly examines contemporary Muslim environmentalist debates and the state of environmentalism in the Muslim world. Then it unpacks the phenomenon of Islamist environmentalism by setting two research questions: what is the environmental policy or approach of Islamist groups, and what role does religion play in Islamist environmentalism? Finally, the introduction describes the methodology of the research.

Chapter 1 provides an overview of the relationship between Islam and the environment by examining Islamic eco-theology as a distinct sub-category of theology. It discusses four themes: land and water, trees, animals, and pollution and energy. The chapter also examines what Shari'a prohibits and permits regarding the environment.

The next five chapters explore five Islamist groups and movements, chronologically ordered. The chapters do not have an identical thematic structure because these actors have different priorities. Chapter 2 considers the oldest group, the Muslim Brotherhood of Egypt. First, it describes the Muslim Brotherhood's general perspective on the environment based on the writings of Hassan al-Banna, Sayyed Qutb, Yusuf al-Qaradawi, Mohamed Badie and Mohamed Morsi. Additionally, the chapter analyses the Brotherhood's policy regarding water management, animals, pollution and energy. Finally, it examines the role of religion in the formulation of the Brotherhood's environmental policy.

Chapter 3 discusses the environmentalism of Hizb ut-Tahrir based on the writings of its founder, Taqiuddin an-Nabhani. It first describes the group's general perspective on environmental issues. It also investigates the group's understanding of water management. The chapter then examines Hizb ut-Tahrir's view of animal issues, pollution and energy. Lastly, it assesses the role of religion in the group's proposed environmental policy.

Chapter 4 investigates the environmentalism of the Lebanese Shi'i group Hizbullah. It begins with its general perspective on the environment, which has been influenced by Ayatollah Khomeini's political theology. The chapter then considers water management, an issue of growing importance for

Lebanon. It also describes the group's understanding of trees, pollution and energy. Finally, the chapter scrutinises the influence of religion on Hizbullah's environmental policy.

Chapter 5 examines the environmentalism of Hamas. The chapter first describes Hamas's general perspective on the environment, particularly the religious significance of Palestine. It also details the group's understanding of water issues, which have serious political implications in the region. Next, the chapter probes Hamas's understanding of trees, animals, and pollution and energy. Finally, it examines the role of religion in Hamas's environmental policy.

Chapter 6 analyses the environmentalism of two jihadi-Salafi groups, al-Qaeda and ISIS. First, it describes their general perspective on the environment, focusing on different perceptions of territoriality. Then it examines their perspective on water, trees, animal issues, pollution and energy. Lastly, the chapter assesses the role of religion in the formulation of jihadi-Salafi environmentalism.

Chapter 7 offers a comparative analytical discussion of the five Islamist groups and movements. It explains how they relate to each other in terms of similarities and differences. The chapter claims that there are three types of Islamist environmentalism due to different scales of environmental engagement. Moreover, it provides an analysis of three non-religious factors that account for the emergence of Islamist environmentalism: alliance-building, political and military expediency, and ideological realignment.

Note

1. Leila Aboulela, *The Kindness of Enemies* (London: Weidenfeld & Nicolson, 2015), pp. 263–4.

In memory of Dimitris Afentakis

INTRODUCTION

The modern environmental movement was born in the United States and Western Europe in the late 1960s to early 1970s, although its roots lie in the anti-industrial romanticism of the nineteenth century.[1] The environmental movement challenged the postwar capitalist orthodoxy and social conformity. Environmentalists criticised dominant ideas about the relationship between humans and non-humans, the socio-economic organisation of Western societies, and the essence of economic growth.[2] Nature and its beings were not to be treated merely as resources for human advancement. In this climate of fierce anti-capitalism, the movement developed intellectual and activist components that produced a new vocabulary (for example, 'biodiversity', 'conservation' and 'sustainability').

The first generation of environmentalists focused on the use of nuclear energy for both peaceful and military purposes, the extinction of species, air and water pollution, and the overexploitation of resources. More specifically, university students, devout Christians and community activists came together to save the environment. However, the movement gradually developed into a multi-issue coalition of groups. During the early 1980s, the first parties were established in Western Europe to promote a green agenda.[3]

Today, environmentalism can be defined as the promotion of values, attitudes and policies aimed at reaching an accommodation between human needs and the limits of the natural environment.[4] Environmentalism as an ideology has included both ecocentric and anthropocentric views and ethics.[5] The former have sought a preservationist approach to nature that centres on care for biodiversity and wilderness protection, while the latter have supported a conservationist approach that focuses on urban pollution and social justice.

Currently, the environmental movement is divided into different sub-movements. Environmental justice is a spin-off from the movement focusing on underprivileged communities which have experienced racism, exploitation and ecological degradation. In effect, it is preoccupied with the socio-economic consequences of the environmental crisis.[6] The conservation sub-movement calls for the protection of natural areas from pollution and economic development.[7] Advocates of animal rights form another sub-movement seeking to end the exploitation and suffering of animals.[8] While the environmental movement is highly heterogeneous, its sub-movements share a vision of a world in which humans and non-humans can live harmoniously in a protected and sustainable environment.

The urgency of the environmental crisis has also generated a debate about faith-based approaches and solutions. Abrahamic religions have viewed the environment as a manifestation of God's glory and have repeatedly stressed the special role of mankind. Yet, every religion has a different interpretation of it. Some Muslim scholars have explored the affinity between Islam and ecology in the context of postcolonialism.

Contemporary Muslim Environmentalist Debates

In March 1967, Lynn White made one of the most original contributions to the debate about the deeper causes of environmental degradation. In his article 'The Historical Roots of Our Ecological Crisis', he blamed Western Christianity for humanity's problematic relationship with nature. In his opinion, 'especially in its Western form, Christianity is the most anthropocentric religion the world has seen . . . [It] not only established a dualism of man and nature but also insisted that it is God's will that man exploit nature for his proper ends.'[9] Although his thesis has been, partly or wholly, rejected by several Western scholars, White's critique provoked a wider debate on religion and the environment.[10] Several Muslim scholars have risen to this intellectual challenge by offering the Islamic perspective on environmental protection.

Seyyed Hossein Nasr was the first Muslim thinker to respond to White. He was born in 1933 in Tehran and obtained a PhD in the history of science from Harvard University. From his point of view, Christian theology cannot be held responsible for the current environmental crisis. In *Man and Nature*, published in 1968, he blamed

> the gradual de-sacralization of the cosmos which took place in the West and especially the rationalism and humanism of the Renaissance which made possible the Scientific Revolution and the creation of a science whose function . . . was to gain power over nature, dominate her and force her to reveal her secrets not for the glory of God but for the sake of gaining worldly power and wealth.[11]

In other words, Nasr has blamed the secularisation of knowledge for the environmental degradation that the world has experienced in the last two centuries. Therefore, the solution to the environmental crisis can come only from religion, which has offered a spiritual rather than a materialistic understanding of nature.[12] Indeed, Nasr is a representative of the traditionalist school, which claims that modernity has led to the demise of metaphysics. At first sight, he embraces a growing trend of religious naturalism which claims that nature has sacred dimensions.[13] However, Nasr does not only provide a philosophical understanding of the relationship between God, humanity and nature. He wants to explain how Islam and other religions could help restore environmental harmony. Nasr adheres to perennialism, the belief that major religions share a single truth.[14]

Nature satisfies basic human needs (for example, food, drinking, clothing) but also nurtures spiritual growth and inner peace. Such a view is confirmed by a *hadith* narrated by Sahih Muslim, according to which the Prophet said, 'The whole earth has been made a mosque for us, and its dust has been made a purifier for us in case water is not available.'[15] Nasr has observed that the Arabic word for 'sign' is *ayah*, which is also used to describe a verse in the Qur'an. Since the creation of nature is a manifestation of God's greatness, nature is full of divine signs that mankind must discover for itself.[16] For instance, the Qur'an dictates, 'And of His signs are the night and the day and the sun and the moon. Adore not the sun nor the moon, but adore Allah Who created them, if He it is that you serve' (41:37). The effort to discover the deeper meaning of those signs can only be an esoteric process for every believer who seeks to discover God's will and serve Him dearly.

Without doubt, Nasr is a scholar who has inspired many Muslims. His contribution is reflective of a greater debate about the decay of Islamic civilisation. Western norms and practices of governance had been adopted by the former colonies or protectorates that imposed their own secular subjectivity.[17] In the context of postcolonial independence, Islam was only acknowledged as an essentialised, reformed religion.[18] Therefore, secularism came to be perceived by some Muslim thinkers as the legacy of colonialism, deeply entrenched in the new Muslim-majority states.

In the early 1960s, the Iranian novelist Jalal Al-e Ahmad had used the pejorative term *Gharbzadegi* ('Westoxification') to describe the loss of Iranian cultural identity through the adoption of Western economic theory and practice.[19] He was particularly critical of Western technology whose use undermined traditional Iranian industries (for example, carpet-weaving). Several years later, in 1970, the Algerian thinker Malek Bennabi elaborated on Western hegemony. He claimed that Muslims suffered from an inferiority complex vis-à-vis the West due to the colonisation of their minds. Thus, he dismissed the importance of material resources and stressed the role of ideas.[20] At the same time, the Iranian sociologist Ali Shariati viewed religion as an agent of liberation. He criticised the West for its anti-religious agenda. According to Shariati, colonial powers under the pretext of 'attacking fanaticism' fought religion and launched assaults against tradition to produce a people without history, without roots, without culture, without religion and without any other form of identity.[21] In this way, the public role of Islam came back to the forefront, albeit mainly in intellectual circles.

In the context of anti-Western critique, some scholars engaged in a public dialogue about Islam and the environment. In 1981, the Pakistani geographer Iqtidar Zaidi published an article titled 'On the Ethics of Man's Interaction with the Environment: An Islamic Approach', where he claimed that the ecological crisis is rooted in moral deprivation. Hence, he called for an Islamic environmental approach based on justice and *taqwa* (God-consciousness).[22] Zaidi had presented his work at the First Islamic Geographical Conference in Riyadh in January 1979.

Following the seizure of the Grand Mosque by insurgents in the November of the same year, Saudi Arabia enforced a rigid and doctrinal version of Islam.[23] The House of Saud felt pressured to 'Islamise' policies by recruiting experts in the early 1980s. One of them was the young Iraqi legal scholar Mawil Izzi Dien, who helped formulate a response to environmental issues from an Islamic point of view. Born in Baghdad in 1948, he studied Islamic law at the universities of Baghdad and Manchester. While in the Faculty of Law at King Abdulaziz University in Jeddah, he acted as an advisor to the Saudi government.[24]

Izzi Dien has shared Nasr's view on the negative influence of Western materialistic culture. In his opinion, 'the schism between the spiritual and the "scientific" was imported into the Muslim mind and land when the material, industrial culture was introduced, effectively separating the political system from the traditions of the community. This had a devastating effect on the indigenous culture and the environment and its biota.'[25] Izzi Dien has also offered suggestions about how Shari'a can help Muslims protect the environment, claiming that 'the conservation of the natural environment in Islam is both an ethical and a religious imperative which should be backed with legislation and effective enforcement of an environmental law'.[26] Hence, he has advocated rigid adherence to Islamic legal rules.

Additionally, he has observed that protected areas (*harim*) existed for centuries in the Muslim world because they produced public goods; for example, both wells and rivers can have a *harim*, namely an area that cannot be violated.[27] More importantly, Izzi Dien has elaborated on the *maslaha* (benefit)–*mafsada* (harm) dichotomy in Islam. From his point of view, the two concepts are not cost-free. It is a fact that decisions to address environmental issues often entail economic costs. However, the long-term benefits could outweigh the short-term consequences.[28] There is neither absolute benefit (*maslaha mutlaqa*) nor absolute harm (*mafsada mutlaqa*).

Mawil Izzi Dien has not been the only scholar insisting on a legalistic approach to environmental protection. The Palestinian scholar Mustafa Abu-Sway has shared the same understanding of environmentalism. Born in Amman in 1958, he is a professor of philosophy and Islamic studies at al-Quds University. Abu-Sway has pointed out that man's relationship with the environment falls within the scope of Islamic jurisprudence (*fiqh*) and is compatible with the objectives (*maqasid*) of Shari'a.

While Izzi Dien and Abu-Sway have embraced a Shari'a-based approach, others have focused more on Islamic metaphysics. In this regard, the Malaysian Islamic philosopher Osman Bakar has made an important contribution to the debate. He was born in 1946 and was educated in the UK and the USA. His PhD thesis was supervised by Seyyed Hossein Nasr. Bakar has argued that *ihsan* (perfection or excellence) is the first step towards *fitra* (a state of purity and innocence).[29] The achievement of *fitra* could lead to a harmonious connection with the environment because the latter is a mirror of human beings.[30] Moreover, he has claimed that *wasatiyya* (middleness) could help to achieve balance and justice. The concept applies not only to Muslim communities, but to global society.[31]

During the 1990s, the environmentalist debate reached Europe's diasporic Muslim communities. Faced with bigotry and discrimination, Europe's Muslims have shown growing interest in ecology which tends to be inclusive. In his effort to create a European Islam, for instance, Tariq Ramadan has supported the promotion of environmentalism. Born in Geneva in 1962, he is the grandson of Hassan al-Banna, who founded the Muslim Brotherhood in Egypt in 1928. His family history is perhaps a burden, but it also gives him an aura of authenticity and legitimacy that many other Islamic scholars lack. Ramadan calls himself a Salafi reformist because he advocates the use of reason for understanding the Qur'an.[32] He has argued that respect for nature is a step to 'spiritual elevation, an "ultimate goal" in the search for the Creator'.[33] Ramadan has criticised the consumerism of modern Muslims who have uncritically adopted Western lifestyles. Accordingly, he has called for a return to the guidance of the Qur'an. Ramadan has supported the development of a true spiritual ecology which would create an awareness of limitations based on ethical principles.[34] This new ecology would focus on the management of resources at global and individual levels. It would replace the ecology of protection that currently dominates the public debate and concentrates on excesses and their consequences without discussing individual responsibilities.

While these environmentalist thinkers emphasise different aspects of the Islamic approach to the environment, they do share a common platform of ideas and beliefs. From their point of view, the Qur'an and the *Sunna* offer divine wisdom for life's challenges. Therefore, they understand Islam as a religion that can provide solutions to the environmental challenges facing contemporary Muslim communities. Most of them criticise, implicitly or explicitly, Western capitalism for its reckless and senseless exploitation of the environment that undermines the future of humanity. They support the resacralisation of nature by rediscovering Islam's unique reconciliation of spirituality and science. These thinkers have grounded their arguments on canonical sources of the Muslim faith. As a result, they have paid little attention to cultural contributions from individual Muslim communities.[35]

The Muslim World and Environmentalism

In the postcolonial period, the expansion of national industry was perceived as a factor strengthening economic independence and state sovereignty in the Muslim world. Under the influence of socialist ideas, regimes in Algeria, Tunisia, Egypt, Syria and Iraq prioritised the economy over the environment. Even where socialism did not triumph, the dominant economic paradigm aimed at rapid industrial growth.[36] The results have often been catastrophic for regional and local eco-systems. Domestic migration and unplanned urbanisation have threatened the balance between humans and nature. Important river systems have been polluted, affecting the livelihood of communities. The management of the Nile, the Tigris and Euphrates and the Indus has been insufficient and ineffective. Deforestation has occurred within the boundaries of large Muslim-majority countries like Indonesia. The endangerment of animal species has become an urgent problem.

Environmentalism as a set of discourses and practices was mainly spread to the Muslim world during the first decade of the twenty-first century. It is a dynamic phenomenon, although its content is not always clear. The relatively recent emergence of environmentalism is the result of external and internal factors. To begin with, interest in political Islam skyrocketed following the 9/11 terrorist attacks in New York and Washington, DC.[37] The subsequent climate of tensions between the West and Islam has prompted religious leaders to engage more with seemingly apolitical issues. The protection of the environment is a truly global issue that can positively shape the image of Islam in the West and elsewhere, while promoting Muslim unity. In this way, Islam could regain its past glory as a universal religion of knowledge and reason.

Additionally, political elites cannot afford to ignore the ongoing ecological crises in their home countries. Environmental degradation has affected the lives of millions of people and is bound to affect many more in the future. The extensive use of the Internet and social media means that the speed of information can quickly change public perceptions about accountability and responsibility. Due to fast transmission of information and knowledge, Muslims can learn and exchange ideas about environmental issues. The growth of university education has also produced a new class of graduates with scientific degrees who are familiar with sustainability. International tourism and travel have increased cross-cultural contact and communication. Consequently, there is more awareness, engagement and participation. Care for the environment has become an integral part of the political agenda in many Muslim-majority countries. This development has not been reflected in the academic literature.

Since environmental politics are largely understood as a secular interdisciplinary field of research, the Islamic approach has been clearly neglected. It is hardly a coincidence that the flagship journal of the field, *Environmental Politics*, has not, at the time of writing, published a single article on Islam and the environment in its 31-year history. Apart from a few articles on Iran and Turkey, all other relevant articles have focused on Western and non-Muslim countries. The absence of academic attention reflects not only a deep-rooted reluctance to engage with the Muslim faith, but also the limits of secular rationality. Gary Haq and Alistair Paul have argued that environmentalism has had a strong scientific basis from the start.[38] It has mainly offered evidence-based solutions to environmental problems. Dialogue with religion does not seem desirable. It is perhaps beyond the intellectual borders of Western environmentalism to comprehend non-Western religious ideas and practices.

Nevertheless, a growing body of literature has addressed different aspects of the Islamic perspective on the environment.[39] The academic interest has been enhanced by the growing activism of environmentally conscious Muslims. In the last 15–20 years, Muslims around the world have shown strong interest in organising themselves for the protection of the environment. Many environmentalist groups have been established in Muslim-majority countries, as well as in the Muslim communities of North America and Western Europe. Even Islamic feminists have critically examined gender relations in relation to the environment.[40] The role of this emerging civil society has been the subject of some scholarly attention in recent years.[41] Notably missing from the existing literature is an exploratory study of the environmentalism of Islamist groups. In fact, we know very little about how Islamists view the environment and its components.

Unpacking Islamist Environmentalism

Some scholars have argued that Islamists have ignored environmental issues because they perceive ecology as a form of Westernisation and do not antici-pate political gains.[42] But in fact Islamist groups have increasingly addressed environmental problems and offered solutions. More and more Islamists talk about protecting water supplies, planting trees and reducing pollution. This book proposes that there is an Islamist environmentalism, defined as *the system-atic engagement of Islamist actors with environmental and environment-related issues*. The book investigates the emergence of Islamist environmentalism by examining five case studies. It seeks to answer the following two questions:

1. What is the environmental policy or approach of Islamist groups?
2. What role does religion play in Islamist environmentalism?

The first question requires a descriptive analysis, simply because the story of Islamist environmentalism has not yet been told. It takes a broad view of what constitutes the 'environment' and the 'environmental'. Therefore, it examines notions of territoriality and land governance, water management and water-related issues, trees and tree-planting, animal rights and related issues, and pollution and energy. The book distinguishes environmental policy from environmental approach. The former indicates the existence of a strategic plan of action, whereas the latter is more a viewpoint than a system-atic effort to deal with problems and issues. The Muslim Brotherhood, Hizb ut-Tahrir, Hizbullah and Hamas have formulated environmental policies, while al-Qaeda and ISIS have developed environmental approaches.

The second and more challenging question entails a qualitative analy-sis that examines the relationship between the Muslim faith and Islamist environmentalism. Hence, the book tries to assess the degree of influence that Islamic texts, rulings and principles have on the green policies and approaches of Islamists. In other words, it examines whether religion is the source of guidance or the means of legitimisation for Islamist environmentalists.

The book treats religion as a multifaceted phenomenon that has been part of human life since time immemorial. Peter Byrne has defined religion as a complex that has four dimensions: the theoretical (for example beliefs and doctrines), the practical (for example rites), the sociological (for example churches and leaders) and the experiential (for example emotions and visions).[43] Yet Islam lacks a church structure and does not fit Western-centric definitions of religion. For, according to the former pope Joseph Ratzinger, Islam 'does not have the separation between the political and the religious sphere that Christianity has had from the beginning'.[44] Islam is a distinct civilisation at least as much as it is a religion. It has produced its own legal system, philosophy and political theory. Thus, this volume adheres to Talal Asad's view that 'there cannot be a universal definition of religion, not only because its constituent elements and relationships are historically specific, but because the definition is itself the historical product of discursive processes'.[45] As Hamid el-Zein has argued, there is no single true Islam with a 'positive content which can be reduced to universal and unchanging characteristics'; as a result, there are many Islams.[46]

This book will not address questions of the historicity of the Qur'an raised by the revisionist school of Islamic studies. John Wansbrough has proposed a radical interpretation of early Islamic history based on form and source criticism, arguing that the Qur'an emerged more than 150 years after the death of the Prophet Muhammad.[47] In their famous book *Hagarism*, Patricia Crone and Michael Cook question the reliability of Islamic sources and portray Islam as a Jewish messianic movement.[48] The revisionist school has used a method of analysis that incorporates evidence from archaeology, history and linguistics. In contrast to these scholars' views, this book accepts the Qur'an as an authentic document of early Islamic history. This faith-sensitive approach has been advocated by many scholars who seek to understand collective expressions and manifestations of religious identity and piety.[49]

Still, it is necessary to describe the conceptual boundaries of terms critical to the topic of this book. The Iranian philosopher Abd el-Karim Soroush has argued that there is a distinction between religion per se and religious knowledge.[50] In his opinion, religion is beyond human reach because it is divine. Therefore, human beings can only pursue religious knowledge, which represents understandings of religions.[51] Hereafter, the adjective 'religious' incorporates interpretations of beliefs and practices based on Islam's authoritative sources. While some of these beliefs and practices (for example, the concept of *shura*) have political relevance, for reasons of clarity 'religious' refers to matters and attitudes of faith. The adjective 'political' is defined as the meanings and practices associated with the pursuit of power within a society. The two terms are not mutually exclusive as sometimes they overlap in the Muslim world.

Since it is difficult to ignore the subjectivity of certain categories, such as 'political' and 'religious', an interdisciplinary approach is necessary. Consequently, this volume seeks to expand the academic inquiry into Islamist environmentalism through the combined lens of political science and Islamic studies, to the degree possible. The parent discipline of political science can examine Islamist groups as political actors seeking influence and power. Islamic studies can take a closer look at meanings of Islamic terms and concepts. The ambition of this research is not only to explore an understudied area of Islamist engagement, but also to expand the interdisciplinary study of political Islam that has long been dominated by political science.

Methodology

This book has employed three research tools: interviews, documents and audio-visual materials. All interviews were conducted face to face, except one telephone and two email interviews. Face-to-face interviews lasted between forty-five minutes and one hour and were open-ended, focusing on key themes (for example, the Islamic understanding of the environment). They took place outside the Middle East and do not serve any quantitative purpose. Respondents were encouraged to share their thoughts and experiences. These interviews were not recorded because it was believed that this would help build trust between the interviewer and the interviewee. Instead, I made detailed notes.

While the use of interviews can enable the researcher to collect data, it has limited value due to time constraints and concerns about respondents' accuracy. Therefore, the preferred method of collecting data has been net-nography, which is a form of qualitative research in an online context. Since Islamist groups have a strong electronic presence, it is possible to download relevant data directly from their websites. Netnography was first used in the area of marketing and consumer research, but social scientists too have increasingly relied on the Internet to conduct research.[52] The Islamist groups under study do not constitute what Howard Rheingold called 'virtual communities', namely 'social aggregations that emerge from the net when enough people carry on . . . public discussions long enough, with sufficient human feeling, to form webs of personal relationships in cyberspace'.[53] On the contrary, the Muslim Brotherhood, Hizb ut-Tahrir, Hizbullah, Hamas and al-Qaeda/ISIS are vibrant organisations with a 'real' presence. They can mobilise human and tangible resources to pursue political goals; cyberspace is only a venue for propaganda and sometimes recruitment of members.

Hence it can be argued that documents produced by these groups reflect their position on the environment and other related areas. Since electoral programmes and press statements are crafted to persuade an audience, they can be treated as reliable sources of information. Moreover, transcripts of speeches by Islamist leaders can offer important insights regarding perceptions and positions on environmental issues. Those that were not available in English were translated with the help of a professional translator. The book also uses audio-visual material, such as YouTube videos, to collect data about Islamist environmentalism.

The use of the Internet for data collection has certain advantages and disadvantages. On the one hand, netnography can eliminate the physical distance between the researcher and the research object. This is particularly useful when fieldwork is not possible or suitable as a method. At the same time, online research can help the researcher to maintain a detached approach to data analysis; her/his judgement would not be influenced by interactions with others. On the other hand, netnography cannot substitute for personal contact with members of a group. Not to mention that observation through fieldwork could reveal valuable information that is not available online. For example, agricultural practices could indicate socio-cultural interpretations of the environment. Moreover, the reliability of digital sources is not always clear and cannot be measured exactly. In any case this research does not aim to build a theory of Islamist environmentalism. Rather, it seeks to understand the relevance of religion on green politics by focusing on five case studies that are sufficiently similar in design to allow a comparison.

Data selection can be a challenging undertaking. It refers to the process of determining the appropriate data type and source. In this book, data selection has been limited by disciplinary parameters and driven by the nature of the investigation. It certainly builds on my previous political science work, which has a strong qualitative component. The data selection procedure is based on three inclusion criteria: the content of the research questions; the scope of the investigation; and the digital accessibility of the sources. To begin with, the research questions dictate the appropriate type of data that can be extracted from online documents, namely, positions and policies on environmental issues. Secondly, the investigation has a limited focus on five Islamist groups and movements. Finally, all the Islamist actors under study have their own official and unofficial web sites that function as open-source platforms.

The collected data provides enough evidence regarding the essence and content of Islamist environmentalism, for three reasons. First, the data derives from important documents reflecting the deepening understanding of the environment. Although data from interviews is too small to rely upon, it offers a unique insight into opinions and views of knowledgeable individuals from a wide variety of backgrounds and affiliations. There is additional data from audio-visual materials that contributes to the research. The diversity of data sources could improve validity and reliability in research. Second, the collected data is sufficient because the scope of the research is limited. Data collection is centred on the study of political Islam and the environment, which precludes any gross error of interpretation. Third, the data gathered from various sources is not independent of the larger time context. The Islamists' interest in environmental issues is a relatively new development that has not produced too much data to process for the time being.

Notes

1. Hank Johnston, 'New Social Movements and Old Regional Nationalisms', in Enrique Laraña, Hank Johnston and Joseph R. Gusfield (eds), *New Social Movements: From Ideology to Identity* (Philadelphia: Temple University Press, 1994), p. 282.

2. See Mark Dowie, *Losing Ground: American Environmentalism at the Close of the Twentieth Century* (Cambridge, MA: MIT Press, 1995); Kenneth A. Gould, Allan Schnaiberg and Adam S. Weinberg, *Local Environmental Struggles: Citizen Activism in the Treadmill of Production* (Cambridge: Cambridge University Press, 1996).

3. See Russell J. Dalton, *The Green Rainbow: Environmental Groups in Western Europe* (New Haven, CT: Yale University Press, 1994); Elizabeth Bomberg, *Green Parties and Politics in the European Union* (London: Routledge, 1998).

4. John McCormick, *The Global Environmental Movement*, 2nd ed. (Chichester: Wiley, 1995), p. 15.

5. See Katherine V. Kortenkamp and Colleen F. Moore, 'Ecocentrism and Anthropocentrism: Moral Reasoning about Ecological Commons Dilemmas', *Journal of Environmental Psychology*, vol. 21, no. 3, 2001, pp. 261–72.

6. See Gordon Walker, *Environmental Justice: Concepts, Evidence and Politics* (Abingdon: Routledge, 2012).

7. See Stephen Fox, *The American Conservation Movement: John Muir and His Legacy* (Madison: University of Wisconsin Press, 1986).

8. See James M. Jasper and Dorothy Nelkin, *The Animal Rights Crusade: The Growth of a Moral Protest* (New York: Free Press, 1991).

9. Lynn White Jr, 'The Historical Roots of Our Ecologic Crisis', *Science*, 10 March 1967, pp. 1203–7.

10. Francis Schaeffer rejected White's thesis and argued that Christianity cannot be blamed for the environmental crisis; see his *Pollution and the Death of Man: The Christian View of Ecology* (Wheaton, IL: Tyndale House, 1970), pp. 59–60. For a more balanced critique see Michael S. Northcott, *The Environment and Christian Ethics* (Cambridge: Cambridge University Press, 1996), pp. 84–5.

11. Seyyed Hossein Nasr, *Man and Nature: The Spiritual Crisis of Modern Man*, new ed. (London: Unwin Paperbacks, 1990), p. 96.

12. See Seyyed Hossein Nasr, *Religion and the Order of Nature* (New York: Oxford University Press, 1996).

13. James W. Jones, *Can Science Explain Religion? The Cognitive Science Debate* (New York: Oxford University Press, 2016), p. 167.

14. See John Holman, *The Return of the Perennial Philosophy: The Supreme Vision of Western Esotericism* (London: Watkins, 2008).

15. Sahih Muslim, *The Book of Mosques and Places of Prayer*, Hadith 5, https://sunnah.com/muslim:522a (accessed 14 June 2022).

16. Seyyed Hossein Nasr, 'Sacred Science and the Environmental Crisis: An Islamic

Perspective', in Harifyah Abdel Haleem (ed.), *Islam and the Environment* (London: Ta-Ha, 1998), p. 120.

17. Wael B. Hallaq, *The Impossible State: Islam, Politics, and Modernity's Moral Predicament* (New York: Columbia University Press, 2013), p. 12.

18. Armando Salvatore, 'Modernity', in Gerhard Bowering (ed.), *Islamic Political Thought: An Introduction* (Princeton, NJ: Princeton University Press, 2015), p. 141.

19. See Jalal Al-e Ahmad, *Occidentosis: A Plague from the West* (Berkeley, CA: Mizan Press, 1983).

20. See Malik Bennabi, *The Question of Ideas in the Muslim World* (Petaling Jaya, Malaysia: Islamic Book Trust, 2003).

21. Ali Shari'ati, *What Is to Be Done? The Enlightened Thinkers and an Islamic Renaissance* (North Haledon, NJ: Islamic Publications International, 1986), p. 31.

22. Iqtidar H. Zaidi, 'On the Ethics of Man's Interaction with the Environment: An Islamic Approach', *Environmental Ethics*, vol. 3, no. 1, 1981, pp. 35–47.

23. Ali A. Allawi, *The Crisis of Islamic Civilization* (New Haven, CT: Yale University Press, 2009), pp. 86–7.

24. Richard C. Foltz, 'Mawil Izzi Dien', in Bron R. Taylor (ed.), *Encyclopedia of Religion and Nature* (London: Thoemmes, 2005), p. 890.

25. Mawil Izzi Dien, 'Islam and the Environment: Theory and Practice', *Journal of Beliefs and Values*, vol. 18, no. 1, 1997, p. 50.

26. Mawil Izzi Dien, *The Environmental Dimensions of Islam* (Cambridge: Lutterworth Press, 2000), p. 165.

27. Ibid., p. 184.

28. Ibid., p. 136.

29. Interview with Professor Osman Bakar, Bandar Seri Begawan, Brunei, 31 July 2018.

30. Ibid.

31. On the concepts of *ihsan, fitra* and *wasatiyya* see Chapter 1.

32. Matthew A. MacDonald, 'What is a Salafi Reformist? Tariq Ramadan and Sayyid Qutb in Conversation', *Political Theology*, vol. 15, no. 5, 2014, pp. 385–405.

33. Tariq Ramadan, *Introduction to Islam* (New York: Oxford University Press, 2017), p. 153.

34. Tariq Ramadan, *Western Muslims and the Future of Islam* (New York: Oxford University Press, 2004), pp. 18–19.

35. Richard C. Foltz, 'Islam', in Roger S. Gottlieb (ed.), *The Oxford Handbook of Religion and Ecology* (New York: Oxford University Press, 2006), pp. 208–9.

36. Arthur Saniotis, 'Muslims and Ecology: Fostering Islamic Environmental Ethics', *Contemporary Islam*, vol. 6, no. 2, 2012, p. 160.

37. Gilles Kepel, *Jihad: The Trail of Political Islam* (Cambridge, MA: Harvard University Press, 2002); Bernard Lewis, *The Political Language of Islam* (Oxford: Oxford University Press, 2002); Barry Rubin (ed.), *Revolutionaries and Reformers: Contemporary Islamist Movements in the Middle East* (Albany: State University of New York Press, 2003).

38. Gary Haq and Alistair Paul, *Environmentalism since 1945* (London: Routledge, 2011), p. 41.

39. See, for example, S. Waqar Ahmad Husaini, *Islamic Environmental Systems Engineering* (London: Macmillan, 1980); Ziauddin Sardar (ed.), *The Touch of Midas: Science, Values and Environment in Islam and the West* (Manchester: Manchester University Press, 1984); Fazlun M. Khalid and Joanne O'Brien, *Islam and Ecology* (London: Cassell, 1992); Harfiyah Abdel Haleem (ed.), *Islam and the Environment* (London: Ta-Ha, 1998); Richard C. Foltz, Frederick M. Denny and Azizan Baharuddin (eds), *Islam and Ecology: A Bestowed Trust* (Cambridge, MA: Harvard University Press, 2003).

40. Tahera Aftab, 'Text and Practice: Women and Nature in Islam', in Alaine Low and Soraya Tremayne (eds), *Sacred Custodians of the Earth? Women, Spirituality and the Environment* (New York and Oxford: Berghahn, 2001).

41. See, for instance, Rosemary Hancock, *Islamic Environmental Activism in the United States and Great Britain* (Abingdon: Routledge, 2017); Anna M. Gade, *Muslim Environmentalisms: Religious and Social Foundations* (New York: Columbia University Press, 2019).

42. A. Kadir Yildirim, 'Between Anti-Westernism and Development: Political Islam and Environmentalism', *Middle Eastern Studies*, vol. 52, no. 2, 2016, p. 228.

43. Peter Byrne, 'Religion and the Religions', in Stewart Sutherland and Peter Clarke (eds), *The Study of Religion, Traditional and New Religion* (London: Routledge, 1988), p. 7.

44. Joseph Ratzinger, *Salt of the Earth: The Church at the End of the Millennium – An Interview with Peter Seewald* (San Francisco: Ignatius Press, 1997), pp. 244–6.

45. S. Sayyid, *Fundamental Fear: Eurocentrism and the Emergence of Islamism* (London: Zed, 2003), p. 15.

46. Abdul Hamid el-Zein, 'Beyond Ideology and Theology: The Search for Anthropology of Islam', *Annual Review of Anthropology*, vol. 6, 1977, p. 254.

47. See John Wansbrough, *Quranic Studies: Sources and Methods of Scriptural Interpretation* (New York: Prometheus, 2004).

48. See Patricia Crone and Michael Cook, *Hagarism: The Making of the Islamic World* (Cambridge: Cambridge University Press, 1977).

49. Clinton Bennett, *Studying Islam: The Critical Issues* (London: Continuum, 2010), pp. 56–8.

50. See Mahmoud Sadri and Ahmad Sadri (eds), *Reason, Freedom, and Democracy in Islam: Essential Writings of Abdolkarim Soroush* (New York: Oxford University Press, 2000).

51. Allawi, *The Crisis of Islamic Civilization*, p. 125.

52. Robert Kozinets, *Netnography: Doing Ethnographic Research Online* (London: Sage, 2009), p. 2.

53. Howard Rheingold, *The Virtual Community: Homesteading on the Electronic Frontier* (Reading, MA: Addison-Wesley: 1993), p. 3.

1

ISLAM AND THE ENVIRONMENT

I slam was founded in a region with harsh climatic conditions and scarce resources. As a result, the Muslim faith is oriented towards conservation and protection of the environment. Like the rest of the planet, the Muslim world has greatly suffered from many environmental problems due to massive urbanisation, rapid economic growth and overexploitation of natural resources.

This chapter aims at providing an overview of the relationship between Islam and the environment (*al-bi'a*). It examines Islamic eco-theology as a distinct sub-category of theology dictating environmental ethics. It covers four distinct and interrelated thematic areas: land and water, trees, animals, and pollution and energy. The selection of these thematic areas is based on the availability of information, as well as their practical significance for the well-being of Muslim communities. While the list of topics is not exhaustive, the goal is to demonstrate how the Muslim faith views the relationship between humanity and nature.[1]

Moreover, the chapter describes the role of Shari'a in environmental matters, including the use of land, water management and animal rights. The increased environmental awareness has also compelled religious leaders to offer relevant fatwas.

The Content and Context of Islamic Eco-theology

Eco-theology is a sub-category of theology that examines the connection between religion and nature.[2] The term 'Islamic eco-theology' refers to the study of Muslim creed (*aqida*) in relation to environmental issues. It also focuses on the essence of religious ideas about man's relationship with nature. Islam was not established in isolation from other religions, however. In fact, it came to integrate pre-Islamic norms, values and beliefs. The Muslim faith was certainly influenced by the religions that existed in the Middle East before the seventh century.[3] For many centuries, the inhabitants of the Arabian Peninsula were polytheists or followed Judaism and Christianity. Nevertheless, Islam has a unique understanding of the environment that is centred on theosophy (the nature of divinity), cosmology (the origin of the universe) and ontology (the nature of humanity).

Islam teaches that God has ninety-nine names or attributes. Among other things, He is the First (*Al-Awwal*) who existed before the creation and is the Last (*Al-Akhir*) after the end of the world. God is also the Creator (*Al-Khaaliq*) and the Giver of Life (*Al-Muhyi*). In a deeper sense, it could be argued that God Himself is the ultimate environment which surrounds and encompasses all things.[4]

The Qur'an declares that God created the heavens and the earth in six days (32:4), but a day is defined as the equivalent of 1,000 earth years (32:5). The universe is divided into two domains (59:22). The first is the unseen (*alam-ul-ghaib*), which includes Allah, the Divine Throne (*al-arsh*), the seven heavens (*samawat*), the world of angels (*alam al-mala'ikah*) and the world of jinn (*alam al-jinn*). The second is the observable (*alam-ul-shahood*), which consists of the world of mankind (*alam al-ins*), the animal world (*alam al-hayawan*) the plant world (*alam al-nabat*) and the mineral world (*alam al-ma'adin*).[5]

Although mankind is one of the many creations of God, it has been at the centre of His divine plan. Human beings are the stewards of God on the planet. It is their responsibility to protect nature. According to Ismail al-Faruqi, 'nature in Islam is not an enemy. It is not a demonic force challenging and inciting humanity to conquer and subdue it . . . [N]ature is a perfectly fitted theatre where humanity is to do good deeds.'[6] Nature and its components (for example, trees, animals) are Muslim in essence because they worship God and submit to His will. In contrast, human beings and jinns (that is, supernatural creatures) have their own free will to decide how to live their lives. Still, submission to God is the only path to salvation.

As is the case with theology in general, Islamic theology is bound to time and space through language.[7] In particular, Islamic eco-theology is a contextualised form of theology through which Muslims can address new environmental challenges. This eco-theology is rooted in exoteric and esoteric exegesis of the Qur'an. Since most Muslims believe that the Qur'an is the word of God, the truth of its teachings is everlasting. Yet Islamic eco-theology is historically and culturally determined. It emerged as a reaction to postwar changes and crises, but also as a counter to the secular critique of religion.

The study of Islamic theology can explain the content of ethics as conceived by modern Muslim thinkers. Islamic ethics borrow principles and concepts from theology to offer moral guidelines to Muslims. Since they are inextricably bound, theology and ethics are historical and cultural enterprises within communities. Humanity's relationship with nature links theology and ethics into a triangle that forms the foundation of a new environmentalism. Tongjin Yang argues that 'environmental ethics deals with the ethical problems surrounding environmental protection, and it aims to provide ethical justification and moral motivation for the issue of global environmental protection'.[8] In this context, several scholars have argued that Islamic sources have set up the basis of environmental ethics by providing three principles: *tawhid* (unity of God), *khalifa* (vicegerent) and *akhirah* (accountability).[9]

Tawhid is the most fundamental principle of the Muslim faith. Therefore it has been widely discussed within the Muslim world.[10] The unity of God means that He alone is responsible for the creation of nature and mankind. Two of God's names, the Maker of Perfect Harmony (*Al-Bari*) and the Shaper of Unique Beauty (*Al-Musawwir*), reflect His primordial role in the organisation of the universe. The principle of *khalifa* entails certain obligations because God has entrusted the earth to human beings. The Qur'an states that when God decided to create man, He told the angels that 'I am going to place a ruler in the earth, [and] they said: Wilt Thou place in it such as make mischief in it and shed blood?' (2:30). Ali Mohamed al-Damkhi has argued that every man and woman has inherited power and accountability regarding the protection of the earth.[11] It is a collective duty, irrespective of religious affiliation. The principle of *akhirah* refers to the afterlife, when each man and woman will be held accountable by God for his/her deeds. It follows that those who have performed more good deeds will end up in *jannah* (paradise) and those whose bad deeds outweigh the good will be sent to *jahannam* (hell).

Furthermore, the Islamic tradition provides a set of concepts that can help humanity in its mission, including *adl* (justice), *shura* (consultation), *mizan* (balance), *rahma* (compassion), *maslaha* (public interest), *ihsan* (perfection or excellence), *fitra* (state of purity and innocence), *wasatiyya* (middleness) and *tahara* (cleanliness).[12] While the list is far from complete, it provides a normative framework for the development of Islamic environmental ethics.

The concept of *adl* has been at the heart of Islamic tradition and thought. The main aim of Islamic revelation is to create an ethical and just social order.[13] Two of the ninety-nine names of God relate to justice: 'Upholder of Equity' (*Al-Muqsit*) (3:18) and the 'Just' (*Al-Adl*) (16:90). The concept itself can be found throughout the Qur'an; for example, a verse states that 'Certainly We sent Our messengers with clear arguments, and sent down with them the Book and the measure, that men may conduct themselves with equity. And We sent down iron, wherein is great violence and advantages to men' (57:25).

In addition, *shura* could also contribute to the formation of environmental ethics. Two verses in the Qur'an refer to consultation: 'And those who respond to their Lord and keep up prayer, and whose affairs are [decided] by counsel among themselves, and who spend out of what We have given them' (42:38) and 'So pardon them and ask protection for them, and consult them in [important] matters' (3:158). One of the most influential contemporary Sunni religious leaders, Sheikh Yusuf al-Qaradawi, has argued that '[Western] democracy . . . can make whatever it wants as lawful or prohibit anything it does not like. In comparison, the Shari'a as a political system has limits. Our democracy is different. It is well connected to the laws of Shari'a.'[14] Likewise, the Turkish Sufi leader Fethullah Gülen has claimed that *shura* 'is a method, a process of government, and way of life for Muslims'.[15] The opinion of these two Islamic scholars is very important because they have a large following in the Middle East. In essence, the concept inherently includes the belief that all humans are equal in rights and responsibilities.

The concept of *mizan* can provide the ethical basis for the development of a new model of sustainable development. Nature has been created by God with absolute perfection and beauty. Its very existence is based on harmony (*itidal*) and peace. God created the world with balance and humans have the obligation not to distort it. The Qur'an specifies, 'Surely We have created everything according to a measure' (54:49). Moreover, al-Qaradawi has analysed the significance of a *hadith* that states, 'Whoever cuts down a lute-tree, Allah would direct his head to the Hell-fire'; from his point of view, it commands the protection of basic elements of nature which provide a balance among creatures.[16] All elements submit to His will and exist according to His commandments. Human beings are obliged to serve God's plan by not disturbing the cosmic balance. The benefits of human interventions must be balanced against the significant risks of ecological harm.

The importance of *rahma* lies in God's ability to respect both humans and non-humans. God is the ultimate source of compassion and mercy, as indicated by two of His names, *Al-Rahman* and *Al-Rahim* (Compassionate and Merciful). The phrase *Bi Ism-i-Allah al-Rahman al-Rahim* ('In the name of Allah Who Is Compassionate and Merciful') is used by Muslims during daily prayer and other forms of worship (for example, fasting). The Prophet Muhammad is also known as *Rahmatan lil Alamin* (Mercy of the Worlds). Like the Prophet Muhammad, believers must treat animals with compassion and mercy as far as humanly possible.

The concept of *maslaha* has deep roots in the Islamic tradition. Historically speaking, Muslim jurists have advocated the establishment of conservation zones (*hima*) and wildlife sanctuaries (*harim*) where commercial use of the land is not permitted.[17] This tradition persisted until recently. According to Mawil Izzi Dien, three types of *maslaha* exist: *maslaha daruriyya* includes major public interests covering basic necessities of life such as food and drink; *maslaha hajiyya* concerns complementary public interests like the human need for shelter; and *maslaha tahsiniyya* refers to desirable public interests like cleanliness.[18]

In addition, the notion of *ihsan* (literally 'doing what is beautiful') could contribute to the development of Islamic environmental ethics. Historically, *ihsan* was manifested through activities such as geometry, calligraphy and gardening. Those who embrace *ihsan* seek to live in peace with the environment and its different components.[19] In fact, it has been claimed that *ihsan* 'constitutes the highest form of worship'.[20]

The concept of *fitra* often refers to the natural inclination of people to follow Islam.[21] The Qur'an calls Islam *din al-fitra*, which indicates that humans are born to submit God's will and follow His commands. Therefore, *fitra* is a state of equilibrium between the Creator and the created that must not be disturbed; yet it is disturbed.[22] The concept of *fitra* has also a metaphysical meaning. A famous *hadith* states that 'every child is born according to *fitra*; then his parents make him into a Jew, Christian or Zoroastrian'.[23] Some Sufis believe that people must return to the primordial nature of purity through achieving transcendence. In this way, the believer can better understand the perfection of the cosmos.[24] Therefore, Sufis tend to advocate eco-spirituality, namely seeking and serving God within the totality of nature.[25]

Wasatiyya (middleness) too has an environmental dimension. According to the Qur'an, 'And thus, We have made you a medium nation that you may be the bearers of witness to the people and the Messenger may be a bearer of witness to you' (2:143). Many Islamic scholars have interpreted the verse as a God-given request for moderation. For instance, Yusuf al-Qaradawi has claimed that '*wasatiyya* is the balance between mind and Revelation, matter and spirit, rights and duties, individualism and collectivism, inspiration and commitment, the Text [that is, the Qur'an] and personal interpretation (*ijtihad*)'.[26] Practically speaking, believers must avoid anything that is extreme and excessive in their conduct vis-à-vis the environment.

Finally, *tahara* (cleanliness) is highly relevant to the question of environmental protection. Several *ahadith* centre on cleanliness. For example, one *hadith* says, 'Surely God is clean and loves the clean, so clean your courtyard,' while another one says, 'Surely Islam is clean so be clean, because nobody can enter Paradise except he who is clean.'[27] It should be noted that two of the five pillars of Islam, the prayer (*solat*) and the pilgrimage (*hajj*), must be undertaken only in a state of physical cleanliness, using clean water. Therefore, physical cleanliness is an important prerequisite for performing Islamic duties. Cleanliness has also a spiritual meaning, though. The heart, mind and soul of the believer must be free of hypocrisy and vices. According to one *hadith*, 'cleanliness is half of belief'.[28] The opposite of cleanliness is impurity (*najasa*).

Islamic principles and concepts could provide a social-moral space for building a consensus regarding minimum standards of sustainable environmental responses. Such eco-ethics offer guidance about how Muslim communities can ensure their activities comply with Islamic tradition and jurisprudence. In effect, ethics could function as a bridge between a community seeking answers to new challenges and the faith striving to provide spiritual support and guidance to the *umma*. However, these principles and concepts are based on different interpretations of Islamic sources. Scholars of various backgrounds have offered their own understandings, subject to errors of omission regardless of intent.

There is a conscious contextualisation of Islamic principles and concepts within the patterns of modern environmentalist trends. For instance, the concept of *adl* fits well with discourses about environmental justice; the concept of *rahma* is relevant to animal rights; and the concept of *mizan* is obviously applicable to conservation and development. However, there are other equally important concepts that have received little attention from scholars, such as *hikma* (the highest possible wisdom that a Muslim can possess), *birr* (piety and obedience to God) and *falah* (salvation in the Hereafter). Therefore, Islamic environmental ethics are the product of particular conjunctures in political and social life.

The chapter now examines the depth of Islamic eco-theology by focusing on four important areas: land and water, trees, animals and energy. Also, the question of pollution is briefly addressed in the sub-sections on water and energy.

Land and Water

In Islamic cosmogony, the earth (*ard*) has a special place in the universe. The Qur'an mentions it a total of 485 times.[29] An interesting range of metaphors has been used by the Qur'an to describe our home planet: resting place (*mustaqarr*) (40:64), carpet (*bisat*) (71:19) and cradle (*mahd*) (43:10). Ibn Qayyim al-Jawziyya (1292–1350), an Islamic theologian and writer, portrayed the earth as a gift of God. In his book *Miftah Dar as-Sa'adah* ('The Key to the House of Happiness'), he observes:

The wisdom of God made Earth like a mother that carries inside its womb different kinds of children. It acts for them as a container. The more they need a thing, the more is made available by God . . . The air (*hawa*) is made available for every living creature, and without it the entire world could suffocate from smoke and steam . . . Earth was spread out and made large enough to give space for the habitations of humans and animals that includes cultivatable land, pasture land, orchards, and vegetable gardens.[30]

Al-Jawziyya's metaphor of the earth as a mother clearly preceded Islam. In Greek mythology, Gaia was a goddess personifying the earth. In ancient Roman religion, Tellus Mater was the equivalent goddess. In both cases, the deity was portrayed as a mother figure that nourishes both humans and non-humans. Although Islam is strictly a monotheistic religion, the earth is perceived as very generous and caring.

Since the Muslim faith was born in the Middle East, it has explicitly and implicitly acknowledged the intrinsic value of water as a resource. The Qur'an has many water-related verses; indeed, the Arabic word for 'water', *ma'*, appears sixty-six times. The frequent mention of water obviously relates to the environment in which Islam first came into being. In the Arabian Peninsula, water was and still is a precious resource due to the climate and geological conditions. Islam came to recognise this reality and help the believers understand what that means for them.[31]

According to the late Syrian Islamic scholar Sheikh Wahbah Mustafa al-Zuhayli, different categories of water exist. First, seawater must be available to every human being, as is sunlight and air. Second, water from large rivers (for example, the Tigris and Euphrates) can be freely used by individuals, but irrigation is possible only if it does not affect the rights of others. Third, shared water (that is, natural mineral water, presumably) must be accessible to everyone, but irrigation is restricted. Finally, water contained in vessels is regarded as property, although it may be seized in time of emergency.[32]

Water conservation is more than a practical issue, though; it is a path to salvation. For example, a *hadith* reported by Imam al-Bukhari states that on the Day of Resurrection, when each man and woman will be held accountable for his/her deeds, 'Allah will neither talk to, nor look at' three types of people, one of which is 'a man who withholds his superfluous water'.[33]

Moreover, the Muslim faith provides certain restrictions and guidelines regarding the sustainable and just use of natural resources. For instance, various Qur'anic verses and *ahadith* call for the avoidance of waste. One *hadith* reports that the Prophet Muhammad asked his companion Sa'ad one day not to waste too much water for his ablutions.[34] The importance of sharing water has also been frequently stressed by *ahadith*; one of them warns that 'no one can refuse surplus water without sinning against Allah and against man'.[35] Water rights extend beyond human beings, though. Animals have the right to drink (*haqq al-shurb*) as indicated by this Qur'anic verse: '[Leave alone] Allah's she-camel, and [give] her [to] drink' (91:13).

Due to its divine origin, water is used for purification and cleanness. The Qur'an commands believers to wash themselves before prayers. The believer must perform ablution (*wudu*) by washing the hands, the nostrils and the face three times; rinsing the mouth; washing the right and left hand and arm; wiping the head and the neck; and washing the right and left foot three times. The Muslim faith prohibits the pollution of water for any reason. A *hadith* narrated by Jabir specifies, 'The Messenger of Allah forbade urinating into standing water.'[36] In this way, the contamination of water with human waste is prohibited under any circumstances.

In summary, water has been featured in the canonical sources for different reasons. First, it is a divine source of life that mankind must protect. Second, it is a natural resource that belongs to humans and non-humans alike. Additionally, it plays a central role in some important Islamic rituals as a purifying element.

Trees

Islam has viewed trees as symbols of life and beauty. The Qur'an and *ahadith* contain many references to them in which they are perceived as a gift of God. For example, the Qur'an states, 'And in the earth are tracts side by side, and gardens of vines, and corn, and palm-trees growing from one root and distinct roots – they are watered with one water; and We make some of them to excel others in fruit. Surely there are signs in this for a people who understand' (13:4). Hence, Islam commands the believers to plant and protect trees. It is a religious duty for all Muslims. From the Islamic point of view, their protection is an important component of salvation. Indeed, the Prophet is reported to have said, 'If any Muslim plants any plant and a human being or an animal eats of it, he will be rewarded as if he had given that much in charity.'[37] In other words, tree-planting is akin to a ritual that every Muslim must experience during his or her life.

Trees also have allegorical meaning because they are a metaphysical bridge between worlds. The Qur'an describes three supernatural trees that the believer may discover for himself or herself. The tree *Zaqqum* (or the Cursed Tree – *al-shajara al-mal'una*) is rooted in hell (37:62–8) and has three characteristics: its fruits are the food of the sinful (44:44); when they are eaten, they cause burning in the stomach (44:45); and its stems bear a resemblance to the head of Satan (37:65).[38] Secondly, *sidrat al-muntaha* (53:10–18) is a lote-tree located at the end of the seventh heaven symbolising the bounds of knowledge. It is the Tree of Uttermost Boundary since no one knows, except God, what lies beyond it. Interestingly, it is the final destination of martyrs' souls. Finally, there is the Tree of Eternity (*shajarat al-kholoud*) in the Garden of Eden that Adam ate from when he disobeyed God. The Qur'an narrates, 'But the devil made an evil suggestion to him; he said: O Adam, shall I lead thee to the tree of immortality and a kingdom which decays not?' (20:120). Some scholars have identified the Tree of Eternity with the Tree of Bliss (*shajarat al-tuba*), mentioned only in one *hadith*.[39] The tree is depicted on the exterior and the interior of the Dome of the Rock in Jerusalem.

Moreover, trees serve as symbolic locales in early Islamic history. The Pledge of the Tree (*Bay'at al-shajara*) took place prior to the Treaty of al-Hudaybiyah in 628 when the 1,400 *Sahaba* pledged to fight until death to avenge the rumoured death of Uthman by the Quraysh. These *Sahaba* are known as the People of the Tree (*ashab al-shajara*) and are highly regarded by Muslims.

The trees are not always passive living things, however. According to one *hadith*:

There was a trunk of a date-palm tree upon which the Prophet used to recline while delivering Khutbah (sermon). When a pulpit was placed in the mosque, we heard the trunk crying out like a pregnant she-camel. The Prophet came down from the pulpit and put his hand on the trunk and it became quiet'.[40]

Trees can behave like humans, but not only peacefully. In fact, there is a famous *hadith* about the final battle between Muslims and Jews that claims:

> The last hour would come when the Muslims would fight against the Jews and the Muslims would kill them until the Jews would hide behind a stone or a tree and a stone or a tree would say: Muslim, or the servant of Allah, there is a Jew behind me; come and kill him; but the tree Gharqad would not say, for it is the tree of the Jews.[41]

In this case, trees (together with rocks) are willing allies of Muslims in the apocalyptic battle against Jews; they can communicate with humans and join a common cause.

Overall, the Muslim faith perceives trees as living things that bring harmony into the world and can function as spiritual resources. Apart from its obvious self-interest to sustain flora, humanity has a religious obligation to work actively for the protection of trees.

Animals

Islam has long been preoccupied with animal welfare issues.[42] The medieval Islamic scholar Ibn Sina argued that animals possess two important abilities which differentiate them from plants: sensation (*al-ihsas*) and locomotion (*al-harakah*).[43] With its fine senses, an animal can be aware of the environment, avoid dangers and find food to survive. Animals can also run or fly away, migrate to another place or pursue prey. According to the Qur'an, they worship God in their own way, not understood by humans (38:19). Animals have their own life cycles and are independent of human beings.

Three Qur'anic chapters are named after animals ('The Cow', 'Cattle' and 'The Elephant') and three after insects ('The Ant', 'The Bee' and 'The Spider'), while more than 200 verses mention non-humans. Their central role in the organisation of the text reflects the positive approach of Islam towards animals. More importantly, the Qur'an states that animals form communities as human beings do: 'And there is no animal in the earth, nor a bird that flies on its two wings, but [they are] communities like yourselves. We have not neglected anything in the Book. Then to their Lord will they be gathered' (6:38). This verse essentially differentiates Islam from Judaism and Christianity, clearly asserting that animals and other non-humans have their own social life. According to the Islamic tradition, the Prophet Muhammad had strong bonds with animals and insects. When he left Mecca to go to Medina a spider and two doves covered his hiding place; the former used its web and the latter placed their nests at the entrance of the cave where he rested.[44]

On various occasions, the Qur'an and *ahadith* have discussed animal rights. From the Islamic viewpoint, humans have obligations and responsibilities towards animals because they have been entrusted by God to protect every form of life. The Prophet Muhammad called repeatedly for the ethical treatment of other living creatures by mankind. Imam al-Bukhari narrated a famous *hadith* about the protection of animals:

> A man felt very thirsty while he was on the way, there he came across a well. He went down the well, quenched his thirst and came out. Meanwhile he saw a dog panting and licking mud because of excessive thirst . . . So, he went down the well again and filled his shoe with water and watered it . . . The people said, 'O Allah's Apostle! Is there a reward for us in serving the animals?' He replied: 'Yes, there is a reward for serving any animate (living being).'[45]

This *hadith* is essentially an affirmation of the human responsibility to sustain life on the planet. As with water conservation, the protection of animal life could lead to salvation. This is clearer in a *hadith* relating the Prophet Muhammad's proclamation, 'If someone kills a sparrow for sport, the sparrow will cry out on the Day of Judgment, "O Lord! That person killed me in vain! He did not kill me for any useful purpose."'[46] The *hadith* implies that animals have the capacity for moral judgement and are conscious of their existence. Humans are not allowed to kill for pleasure; for instance, fox-hunting and cock-fighting are banned as cruel sports.

Interestingly, the Qur'an claims that living creatures have their own language. Solomon had the ability to communicate with ants and birds; one Qur'anic verse asserts, 'And Solomon was David's heir, and he said: O men, we have been taught the speech of birds, and we have been granted of all things. Surely this is manifest grace' (27:16). The Prophet also occasionally communicated with non-humans. Once a camel approached him to complain about its owner, and the Prophet asked the owner, 'Don't you fear God? This animal you own has complained to me that it is hungry and tired because you use it continuously in your work.'[47] These stories, again, emphasise the autonomous existence of non-humans which form their own communities. Indeed, the Prophet's mission was accepted by animals and birds that have their own spirituality and praise God in their own language.[48]

It is not a coincidence that the Qur'an mentions many animals, but each one of them enjoys different status. For instance, horses are viewed as worthy of human respect. Asserts one *hadith*, 'Good will remain in the foreheads of horses till the Day of Resurrection.'[49] This implies that horses are inherently good animals. The Prophet's empathy for horses is confirmed by a *hadith* narrated by Anas bin Malik, which says, 'There was nothing dearer to the Messenger of Allah after women than horses.'[50]

Similarly, cats are animals of high status because the Prophet was fond of them. He was kind and tender with cats; his favourite was one called Muezza. There is a legend about Abu Hurairah (a Companion and a major narrator of *ahadith*) who had a cat that saved the Prophet's life from an obnoxious snake.[51] Abu Hurairah also reported one *hadith* about a woman who was sent to hell because of a cat which she had kept caged until it died of hunger. For that reason, Allah's Messenger said, 'You neither fed it nor watered when you locked it up, nor did you set it free to eat the insects of the earth.'[52] However, the validity of this *hadith* was disputed by Aisha, the Prophet's youngest wife, who implicitly accused Abu Harairah of being misogynistic.[53]

In contrast, the place of dogs in the Muslim world is rather ambiguous. Several Qur'anic verses declare dogs as loyal and intelligent animals who can serve humans; for example, 'The good things are allowed to you, and what you have taught the beasts and birds of prey, training them to hunt – you teach them of what Allah has taught you; so eat of that which they catch for you and mention the name of Allah over it; and keep your duty to Allah' (5:4). Although the Qur'an tends to have a favourable view of dogs, there are *ahadith* that consider them to be ritually impure (*najis*).[54]

The animal kingdom has been featured in the writings of several Islamic scholars. For example, the eighth-century Arab scholar Al-Jahiz wrote the *Book of Animals* (*Kitab al-Hayawan*), describing 350 different creatures. More importantly, he offered a proto-theory of natural selection that grasped

the essence of evolution. He argued, 'Animals engage in a struggle for existence, and for resources, to avoid being eaten, and to breed . . . Environmental
factors influence organisms to develop new characteristics to ensure survival,
thus transforming them into new species. Animals that survive to breed can
pass on their successful characteristics to their offspring.'[55]

In summary, animals in Islam are not servants of humans. The Qur'an
states that animals speak their own language and form communities. While
humanity is commanded to act as steward, non-humans are autonomous
beings whose rights must be protected. Yet, the Qur'an shows a preference
for certain species. This preference reflects practical wisdom and cultural
heritage, rather than indicating hierarchical ordering of animals in relation
to divine causality.

Pollution and Energy

Apart from mentioning the sun and winds, the Qur'an does not discuss energy
issues. However, a famous *hadith* reported by Abu Dawud states, 'Muslims
have common share in three (things): grass, water and fire.'[56] Although this
hadith has been variously interpreted, some Islamic scholars have interpreted
the word 'fire' (*al-nar*) as any resource that can generate energy, principally
hydrocarbons.

Within Sunni Islam, different schools of jurisprudence (*madhahib*) have
different views on the ownership of energy resources. The Maliki school
dictates that minerals, including oil, cannot be privately owned, even if the
state licenses someone to search for and extract them.[57] The Hanbali school
also claims that minerals cannot be owned by individuals under any circumstances.[58] In contrast, the Hanafi school claims that minerals can be owned
by individuals as long as they pay royalties to the state.[59] The Shafi'i school
states that if minerals are found on private land, then the owner has the
exclusive right to exploit them and the revenue is subject to taxation. In case
of minerals found in state-owned land, the community owns them but the
state could grant concessions to investors.[60] According to Yusuf al-Qaradawi,
who favours inter-*madhahib* rapprochement, individuals and corporations
exploiting oil and gas are obliged to pay *zakat* (alms-giving) of one-fifth
because these mineral resources are *rikaz*; that is, they were buried in the
earth at the time of *jahiliyya* (the pre-Islamic period).[61]

The question of energy also relates to sustainability and environmental protection because some sources are polluting. Indeed, the hydrocarbon-centric analysis of Islamic scholars has not gone unchallenged. Ibrahim Abdul-Matin, an Afro-American intellectual who converted to Islam, has differentiated 'energy from heaven' (that is solar and wind), which is environmentally friendly, from 'energy from hell' (that is coal, oil and gas), which is hazardous to the environment.[62] From his point of view, Islam commands an environmentally friendly use of energy. While his opinion is not based on Islamic teachings and principles, it has created a debate regarding the use of renewable forms of energy and the transition to a new, low-carbon economy.

The chapter now proceeds to Shari'a's approach to the environment. Theology and Islamic law are interconnected since they are based on the reading of Islamic sources.[63]

Shari'a and the Environment

The relationship between humanity and nature is dictated by rules emanating from the Qur'an and the *Sunna*. The former offers general guidelines about the obligations of humans, the use of water, and the place of animals in the world. The latter reports the Prophet's concerns and suggestions about the protection of the environment and non-humans. Shari'a aspires to regulate every aspect of human life, including its connection with the environment.[64] The higher objectives of Islamic law (*maqasid*) have an environmental dimension, albeit not overtly. According to the medieval Islamic scholar Al-Shatibi, the five objectives are the following: the preservation of religion, the preservation of human life, the preservation of human reason, the preservation of progeny and the preservation of material wealth.[65] For different reasons, none of them can be fulfilled if the environment is not protected. For instance, the preservation of human life can only be achieved within an eco-system functioning at its optimum level.

Seyyed Hossein Nasr argues that Shari'a-based rules could greatly contribute to the protection of the environment because Muslims 'would see them as God's laws, rather than simply governmental regulations to be circumvented whenever possible'.[66] According to Fazlun Khalid, Shari'a dictates the following:

- The elements that compose the natural world are common property.
- The right to benefit from natural resources is a right held in common.
- There shall be no damage or infliction of damage to the environment because there will be future users.[67]

More specifically, the use of resources such as land, water and air is determined by three main principles: first, vital needs take precedence over non-vital ones; second, the needs of the poor are more important than the needs of the rich; and third, one may not cause harm for the purpose of obtaining a benefit.[68]

Nurdeng Deuraseh has argued that one of the higher objectives of Shari'a is the creation of a healthy environment which constitutes both a collective and an individual responsibility. He has utilised the concept of *insan adab* to emphasise the need for an inner struggle for self-awareness and self-improvement.[69] The Malaysian scholar Al-Attas has defined *insan adab* as 'the one who is sincerely conscious of his responsibilities towards the true God who understands and fulfils his obligations to himself and others in his society with justice and who constantly strives to improve every aspect of himself towards perfection'.[70] Living under Shari'a is the ultimate goal for a believer who wants to worship God.

Islamic law has formulated rules to protect the environment from mismanagement. Land is a key resource for the economic and social well-being of Muslims. It can be either *amir* (developed) or *mawat* (undeveloped).[71] To begin with, *amir* includes both settlements and agricultural land. The *iqta* system was introduced in the Caliphate during the mid-tenth century to increase tax revenue. There were two types of *iqta*. The first was *iqta* of private ownership (*iqta al-tamlik*), whereby owners of land paid a property tax (*kharaj*) or tithe (*'ushr*).[72] It should be noted that the land of the Caliphate was classified into land owned by non-Muslims, who had to pay *kharaj*, and land belonging to Muslims, who were obliged to pay *'ushr*.[73] The second is *iqta* of usufruct (*iqta al-istighlal*), which assigns tax revenue to a holder (*muqta*) relating to the use of a particular piece of land.[74] The *muqta* was sometimes a senior officer who provided military service to the Caliph and in return he had the authority to levy taxes on tenant farmers (*fallahun*).

Additionally, Islamic law has allowed the establishment of three public institutions for land management: *waqf* (charitable endowed land), *harim* and *hima*.[75] A *waqf* property is an inalienable endowment under Islamic law donated to the community for charitable purposes. It could include a piece of land, a building or other assets. The concept is derived from the *Sunna* of the Prophet. According to one *hadith*:

> Umar got some property in Khaybar and he came to the Prophet and informed him about it. The Prophet said to him, 'If you wish you can give it in charity.' So Umar gave it in charity the yield of which was to be used for the good of the poor, the needy, the kinsmen and the guests.[76]

Due to its social importance, *waqf* property is exempted from any taxation.

Harim zones were areas of significant cultural or historical importance that must be protected for the sake of the community. The Prophet Muhammad declared Medina a protected area a few years before he died.[77] As stated by one *hadith*:

> Medina is a sanctuary from that place to that. Its trees should not be cut and no heresy should be innovated nor any sin should be committed in it, and whoever innovates in it an heresy or commits sins then he will incur the curse of Allah, the angels, and all the people.[78]

Hence, one of the names given to Medina was *Harim Rasul Allah* (The Prophet's Sanctuary).

Additionally, the Prophet abolished private reserves of land and established public reserves (*hima*) for the benefit of the community. Indeed, one *hadith* proclaims, '[There is] no *hima* except for Allah and His Apostle.'[79] Consequently, he declared the area of al-Naqi, 100 kilometres from Medina, as a pasture for horses of war.[80] Historically, five types of *hima* have existed in the Arabian Peninsula: *hima* for trees in which woodcutting was prohibited or limited; *hima* in which grazing was prohibited; *hima* in which grazing was restricted at certain periods of time, such as the one for beekeeping during the flowering period; *hima* restricted to certain species and numbers of livestock; and *hima* for the welfare of a particular community which suffered from drought or another natural disaster.[81] During the 1960s, there were more than 3,000 *hima* in Saudi Arabia, varying in size from 10 to 1,000 hectares, but less than a dozen remain today.[82] The rationale for the maintenance of these protected zones was based on the concept of *maslaha*, discussed earlier in this chapter.

If an area of land was not used and was not considered to be *waqf*, *harim* or *hima*, then Shari'a declared it *mawat*. This category included dry land that had never been irrigated, flooded land that had not drained or land located far from settlements.[83] In this case, anyone had the right to cultivate it according to the *hadith* 'If anyone revives dead land, it belongs to him, and the unjust root has no right'.[84] In this context, *ihya' al-mawat* literally means 'the revival of the dead land'. Regarding the ownership of *mawat* land, opinions differ. According to the Shafi'i *madhhab*, any person who brings to life undeveloped land could become the lawful owner. In contrast, the Hanafi *madhhab* claims that the acquisition of *mawat* requires the consent of the ruler in order to avoid conflicting claims. Finally, the Maliki *madhhab* calls for a consent only if *mawat* is located near a settlement.[85]

Shari'a also dictates specific water rules and rights. The most important rule is the sharing of water since the Qur'an repeatedly mentions the principle of equity. For instance, the Qur'an states, 'And inform them that the water is shared between them; every share of the water shall be attended' (54:28). Additionally, Shari'a recognises the right to obtain drinking water for oneself and animals from a canal privately owned by someone else, known as *haqq al-shurb*; the right to fetch canal water from across land owned by someone else, known as *haqq al-majra*; the right to drain out wastewater over the property of someone else, known as *haqq al-masil*; the right of access to one's own property across the property of someone else, known as *haqq al-murur*; and the right of stopping one's neighbour from carrying out such modifications on his property that may cause harm to one, known as *haqq al-jiwar*.[86]

Contemporary scholars have also offered a description of animal rights in accordance with Islamic law and practice. Mohammad Yusuf Siddiq has argued that the animal world should be treated as a silent partner (*haywan ghayr natiq*) of mankind.[87] Moreover, the Shi'i jurist Hashem Najy Jazayery has offered the following imperatives stemming from animal rights:

1. Do not brand an animal on the face, and do not hit an animal on the face because animals pray and praise God Almighty.

2. Do not force an animal to carry a load greater than it is able to bear.
3. Do not force an animal to travel further than it is able to.
4. Do not stand on the back, waist or neck of an animal.
5. Do not use your animal's back as a pulpit.
6. Before filling your own stomach, think about filling the stomach of your animal and give it food.
7. Before slaking your own thirst, think of the thirst of your animal and take care of it.
8. When taming an animal, do not hit it unnecessarily.
9. When an animal is unruly, punish it only to the degree necessary.[88]

The implementation of Shariʻa rules has often been supervised by a specialised agency, which has the task of protecting the community through promoting the Islamic doctrine of *hizba*. It can be described as the obligation of the state to ensure that Muslims act in accordance with Shariʻa. It derives from this Qurʾanic verse: 'And from among you there should be a party who invite to good and enjoin the right and forbid the wrong. And these are they who are successful' (3:104). Traditionally, a senior administrator (*muhtasib*) headed such an agency and functioned as chief inspector of *hima* and *harim* zones.[89]

Moreover, religious leaders have issued fatwas to support environmental causes. A fatwa is a legal ruling issued by an Islamic jurist (*mufti*) on an issue of importance for the community. It can address subjects that jurisprudence (*fiqh*) has left untouched or underexamined. For many years, *ʻulama* almost completely ignored environmental issues.[90] However, many of them now understand that the evolution of Shariʻa is necessary if it is to remain relevant and applicable, regardless of time. Thus, they seek to address contemporary challenges that an increased number of Muslims find particularly worrying.

In September 2010, for instance, the Qatar Center for the Presentation of Islam issued a detailed fatwa on Islam and environmental conservation. It offered evidence from the Qurʾan and *ahadith* to assert, among other things, the following:

1. Muslims are instructed to cultivate barren lands and for such a task, a good reward is prepared for them in the Hereafter.

2. Islam urges its followers to keep the streets clean and free from any harm, and such work is considered as a part of faith.
3. All human beings are instructed to safeguard all animals, eatable or not, and those who hurt animals will be punished.
4. All human beings are ordered to maintain sources of water.
5. Islam forbids spoiling the seas with nuclear radiation, destroying surplus food fearing low prices, destroying trees and killing animals for amusement and safaris, wasting environmental resources, and committing hostile acts against others; all are condemnable acts.[91]

This fatwa summarises the main environmental duties of Muslims based on Islamic principles. While it includes duties that originate from the Qur'an (for example, cultivation of land, 32:27, 6:121), the fatwa also covers contemporary harmful practices such as the dumping of nuclear waste in the oceans and the destruction of food supplies to regulate market prices. Moreover, it implicitly underpins the Islamic method of slaughtering livestock, which minimises pain and suffering for the animal.

In March 2014, the Indonesian Council of 'Ulama (Majelis Ulama Indonesia) issued another fatwa requiring Muslims to protect endangered species like tigers, elephants, rhinos and orangutans. The fatwa stated that 'killing, harming, assaulting, hunting and/or engaging in other activities which threaten endangered species with extinction are forbidden, except for cases allowed under Shari'a, such as self-defence'.[92] Moreover, it made several recommendations to the Indonesian government, legislators, local authorities, businesses, religious leaders, and communities regarding the protection of endangered species in the country. The Indonesian fatwa is well-supported by Islamic evidence from the Qur'an and *ahadith*. It is difficult to measure its effectiveness, though, because fatwas are not legally binding.[93]

On 27 July 2016, the Indonesian Council of 'Ulama issued another fatwa forbidding the intentional lighting of fires in forests. According to Huzaemah Tahido Yanggo, head of the body's fatwa council, 'the Qur'an states that we are not allowed to harm the environment, and forest burning causes damage not only to the environment but also to people's health'.[94] During 2015, 125,000 fires broke out across Indonesia, emitting an estimated 1.75 billion tonnes of CO_2 into the atmosphere.[95] The fatwa stated that 'the burning of forests and land that can cause damage, pollution, harm to other persons, adverse health effects, and other harmful effects, is religiously forbidden (*haram*)'.[96] This fatwa not only bans the intentional burning of forests by farmers, but it also declares forests as a common good.

Conclusion

Islam perceives the relationship between humanity and nature as mutually complementary; human beings cannot exist without the natural world and vice versa. Certain concepts and principles deriving from the Qur'an and *ahadith* could offer a general framework of Islamic environmental ethics. The unity of God means that all His creation is interconnected and interrelated. Human beings are God's viceregents on earth and must always act accordingly. The accountability of mankind for its actions is the endpoint of human responsibility. Additionally, the concepts of *adl*, *shura*, *mizan*, *rahma*, *maslaha*, *ihsan*, *fitra*, *wasatiyya* and *tahara* could provide ethical guidelines and standards of conduct for an Islamic approach to environmental issues.

As part of this analysis, different thematic areas were covered. Islam is land-friendly and water-conscious due to its history, doctrine and tradition. The religion has also viewed trees as autonomous entities both practically and spiritually. Moreover, Islam has understood animals as creatures of God that humans must respect and protect. Non-humans are co-habitants of the planet that have their own rights. The Islamic perspective on energy is understandably centred on oil, due to the large reserves of hydrocarbons that can be found in the greater Middle East. Finally, the problem of pollution has preoccupied the Muslim faith, which advocates cleanliness and purity.

Shari'a dictates many rules that have an environmental dimension, directly or indirectly. While Shari'a is not fully applied in many Muslim-majority countries, it still provides a useful historical-legal framework for environmental protection and management. Its credibility derives from the historically successful regulation of environmental issues. Yet Shari'a is not as rigid as some may wish to believe. It is open to many interpretations since Muslims in different countries and communities constantly seek to reinterpret its rules. The remaining chapters examine the content of Islamist environmentalism and its relation to religion.

Notes

1. The chapter does not discuss issues that have received less attention, such as overfishing, toxic chemicals and population issues.

2. There is an extensive bibliography on eco-theology. See, for instance, Robert J. Jacobus, 'Understanding Environmental Theology: A Summary for Environmental Educator', *Journal of Environmental Education*, vol. 35, no. 3, 2004, pp. 35–42; Celia Deane-Drummond, *Eco-Theology* (London: Darton, Longman & Todd, 2008); Kyle S. Van Houtan and Michael S. Northcott (eds), *Diversity and Dominion: Dialogues in Ecology, Ethics, and Theology* (Eugene, OR: Cascade, 2010).

3. Daniel Brown, *A New Introduction to Islam*, 2nd ed. (Chichester: Wiley-Blackwell, 2009), p. 187.

4. Nurdeng Deuraseh, 'Earth in the Holy Qur'an: How to Protect and Maintain It?', *Jurnal Hadhari*, vol. 2, no. 2, 2010, p. 82.

5. Osman Bakar, *Qur'anic Pictures of the Universe* (Petaling Jaya, Malaysia: Islamic Book Trust, 2016), pp. 26–7.

6. See Ismail al-Faruqi, *Islam and Other Faiths* (Leicester: Islamic Foundation, 1998).

7. Andrew J. Spencer, 'Beyond Christian Environmentalism: Ecotheology as an Over-Contextualized Theology', *Themelios*, vol. 40, no. 3, 2015, https://theme lios.thegospelcoalition.org/article/beyond-christian-environmentalism (accessed 15 June 2022).

8. Tongjin Yang, 'Towards an Egalitarian Global Environmental Ethics', in Henk A. M. J. ten Have (ed.), *Environmental Ethics and International Policy* (Paris: UNESCO, 2006), p. 23.

9. See Iqtidar H Zaidi, 'On the Ethics of Man's Interaction with the Environment: An Islamic Approach', *Environmental Ethics*, vol. 3, no. 1, 1981, pp. 35–47; Mawil Y. Izzi Dien, 'Islamic Environmental Ethics: Law and Society', in J. Ronald Engel and Joan G. Engel (eds), *Ethics of Environment and Development: Global Challenge, International Response* (London: Belhaven, 1990); Lisa Wersal, 'Islam and Environmental Ethics: Tradition Responds to Contemporary Challenges', *Zygon*, vol. 30, no. 3, 1995, 451–9.

10. See Isma'il Raji al-Faruqi, *Al Tawhid: Its Implications on Thought and Life* (Herndon, VA: International Institute of Islamic Thought, 2000); Muhammad bin Abdul Wahhab, *Kitab At-Tawhid: The Book of Monotheism* (London: Darussalam, 2014).

11. Ali Mohamed al-Damkhi, 'Environmental Ethics in Islam: Principles, Violations, and Future Perspectives', *International Journal of Environmental Studies*, vol. 65, no. 1, 2008, p. 16.

12. Mohammad Muinul Islam, 'Towards a Green Earth: An Islamic Perspective', *Asian Affairs*, vol. 26, no. 4, 2004, p. 51.

13. Abdulaziz Abdulhussein Sachedina, *The Just Ruler (al-suktan al-adil) in Shi'ite Islam: The Comprehensive Authority of the Jurist in Imamite Jurisprudence* (New York: Oxford University Press, 1988), p. 120.

14. Idries de Vries, 'An open letter to Sheikh Yusuf Qaradawi – OpEd', *New Civilisation*, 4 January 2012, https://www.eurasiareview.com/04012012-an-open-letter-to-sheikh-yusuf-qaradawi-oped/

15. Leonid Sykiainen, 'Democracy and the Dialogue between Western and Islamic Legal Cultures: The Gülen Case', in Robert A. Hunt and Yüksel A. Aslandoğan (eds), *Muslim Citizens of the Globalized World: Contributions of the Gülen Movement* (Somerset, NJ: The Light, 2007), p. 126.

16. Yusuf al-Qaradawi, *Education and Economy in the Sunnah* (Cairo: Al-Falah Foundation, 2005), p. 23.

17. Arthur Saniotis, 'Muslims and Ecology: Fostering Islamic Environmental Ethics', *Contemporary Islam*, vol. 6, no. 2, 2012, p. 158.

18. Mawil Izzi Dien, *The Environmental Dimensions of Islam* (Cambridge: Lutterworth Press, 2000), p. 143.

19. Abdul Gafar Olawale Fahm, 'Factors Contending with Environmental Sustainability in Nigeria: An Islamic Approach', Proceedings of the Social Sciences Research, 9–10 June 2014, Kota Kinabalu, Malaysia.

20. Mahmoud M. Ayoub, *Islam: Faith and History* (London: Oneworld, 2004), p. 4.

21. On *fitra* see Yasien Mohamed, *Fitrah: The Islamic Concept of Human Nature* (London: Ta-Ha, 1996).

22. Oliver Leaman, *The Qur'an: An Encyclopedia* (Abingdon: Routledge, 2006), p. 211.

23. Zaizul Ab. Rahman, 'The Role of Fitrah as an Element in the Personality of a Da'i in Achieving the Identity of a True Da'i', *International Journal of Business and Social Science*, vol. 3, no. 4, 2012, p. 171.

24. Bill Whitehouse, *Reality without a Name: A Critique of 'Sufism: A Short Introduction'* (Bangor, ME: Interrogative Imperative Institute, 2009), p. 136.

25. On Sufis and environmentalism see Shireen Qudosi, 'Sufis Are Islam's Eco-Guardians', *Green Prophet*, 28 October 2009, http://

www.greenprophet.com/2009/10/sufis-are-islam%E2%80%99s-eco-guardians/ (accessed 16 June 2022).

26. Ana Belén Soage, 'Yusuf al-Qaradaqi: The Muslim Brothers' Favourite Ideological Guide', in Barry Rubin (ed.), *The Muslim Brotherhood: The Organization and Policies of a Global Islamist Movement* (New York: Palgrave Macmillan, 2010), p. 30.

27. Mohammad Shomali, 'Aspects of Environmental Ethics: An Islamic Perspective', *Thinking Faith*, 11 November 2008, http://www.thinkingfaith.org/articles/200 81111_1.htm (accessed 16 June 2022).

28. Sahih Muslim, *The Book of Purification*, Hadith 1, https://sunnah.com/mus lim/2 (accessed 16 June 2022).

29. Izzi Dien, *The Environmental Dimensions of Islam*, p. 51.

30. Ibid., pp. 25–6.

31. See John C. Wilkinson, 'Muslim Land and Water Law', *Journal of Islamic Studies*, vol. 1, no. 1, 1990, pp. 54–72; Ali Ahmad, 'Islamic Water Law as an Antidote for Maintaining Water Quality', *University of Denver Water Law Review*, vol. 2, no. 2, 1999, pp. 170–88; Naser I. Faruqui, Asit K. Biswas and Murad J. Bino (eds), *Water Management in Islam* (Tokyo: United Nations University Press, 2001).

32. Izzi Dien, *The Environmental Dimensions of Islam*, p. 31.

33. Hussein A. Amery, 'Islamic Water Management', *Water International*, vol. 26, no. 4, 2001, p. 487.

34. Roger Boase, 'Ecumenical Islam: A Muslim Response to Religious Pluralism', in Roger Boase (ed.), *Islam and Global Dialogue: Religious Pluralism and the Pursuit of Peace* (Farnham: Ashgate, 2010), p. 258.

35. Francesca De Chatel, 'Prophet Mohammed: A Pioneer of the Environment', Ummah.com, 25 February 2003, http://www.ummah.com/forum/showthread .php?88582-Prophet-Mohammed-A-Pioneer-of-the-Environment (accessed 16 June 2022).

36. Sunan Ibn Majah, *The Book of Purification and its Sunnah*, Hadith 343, https:// sunnah.com/ibnmajah:343 (accessed 16 June 2022).

37. Sahih al-Bukhari, *Good Manners and Form*, Hadith 43, https://sunnah.com/buk hari/78/43 (accessed 16 June 2022).

38. Noble Ross Reat, 'The Tree Symbol in Islam', *Studies in Comparative Religion*, vol. 9, no. 3, 1975, p. 8.

39. Ibid, p. 11.

40. Riyad as-Salihin, *The Book of Miscellaneous Ahadith of Significant Values*, Hadith 24, https://sunnah.com/riyadussalihin:1831 (accessed 16 June 2022).

41. Sahih Muslim, *The Book of Tribulations and Portents of the Last Hour*, Hadith 103, https://sunnah.com/muslim:2922 (accessed 16 June 2022).

42. See B. A. Masri, *Islamic Concern for Animals* (Petersfield, England: Athene Trust, 1987); Mustafa Mahmud Helmy, *Islam and Environment 2: Animal Life* (Kuwait: Environment Protection Council, 1989); James L. Wescoat Jr, 'The "Right of Thirst" for Animals in Islamic Law: A Comparative Approach', *Environment and Planning D: Society and Space*, vol. 13, no. 6, 1995, pp. 637–54.

43. Mulyadhi Kartanegara, *Essentials of Islamic Epistemology* (Bandar Seri Begawan: Universiti Brunei Darussalam, 2014), p. 48.

44. Coeli Fitzpatrick and Adam Hani Walker, *Muhammad in History, Thought, and Culture: An Encyclopedia of the Prophet of God* (Santa Barbara, CA: ABC-CLIO, 2014), p. 29.

45. Sahih al-Bukhari, *Oppressions*, Hadith 27, https://sunnah.com/bukhari/46/27 (accessed 16 June 2022).

46. Al-Damkhi, 'Environmental Ethics in Islam', p. 16.

47. Richard Foltz, *Animals in Islamic Traditions and Muslim Cultures* (London: Oneworld, 2014), p. 55.

48. Ibid.

49. Sahih al-Bukhari, *Fighting for the Cause of Allah*, Hadith 65, https://sunnah.com/bukhari/56/65 (accessed 16 June 2022).

50. Sunan an-Nasa'i, *The Book of the Kind Treatment of Women*, Hadith 3, https://sunnah.com/nasai:3941 (accessed 16 June 2022).

51. Annemarie Schimmel, *Deciphering the Signs of God: A Phenomenological Approach to Islam* (Albany: State University of New York Press, 1994), p. 32.

52. Sahih al-Bukhari, *Distribution of Water*, Hadith 13, http://sunnah.com/bukhari/42/13 (accessed 16 June 2022).

53. Fatima Mernissi, 'A Feminist Interpretation of Women's Rights in Islam', in Charles Kurzman (ed.), *Liberal Islam: A Sourcebook* (New York: Oxford University Press, 1998), p. 121.

54. Foltz, *Animals in Islamic Traditions and Muslim Cultures*, p. 130.

55. Jim al-Khalili, 'Science: Islam's Forgotten Geniuses', *The Telegraph*, 29 January 2008, http://www.telegraph.co.uk/news/science/science-news/3323462/Science-Islams-forgotten-geniuses.html (accessed 16 June 2022).

56. Sunan Abi Dawud, *Wages*, Hadith 62, https://sunnah.com/abudawud:3477 (accessed 18 July 2022).

57. Khaled Mohammed Al-Jumah, 'Arab State Contract Disputes: Lessons from the Past', *Arab Law Quarterly*, vol. 17, no. 3, 2002, p. 235.

58. Ibid., p. 236.

59. Khalid Bin Sayeed, *Western Dominance and Political Islam: Challenge and Response* (Albany: State University of New York Press, 1995), pp. 148–9.

60. Al-Jumah, 'Arab State Contract Disputes', p. 235.

61. Yusuf al-Qaradawi, *Fiqh al-Zakah: A Comparative Study of Zakah, Regulations and Philosophy in the Light of the Qur'an and Sunnah* (Jeddah: Scientific Publishing Centre, n.d.), p. 269.

62. See Ibrahim Abdul-Matin, *Green Deen: What Islam Teaches about Protecting the Planet* (San Francisco: Berrett-Koehler, 2010).

63. See Rumee Ahmed, 'Islamic Law and Theology', in Anver M. Emon and Rumee Ahmed (eds), *The Oxford Handbook of Islamic Law* (Oxford: Oxford University Press, 2018).

64. Safei El-Deen Hamed, 'Seeing the Environment through Islamic Eyes: Application of *Shariah* to Natural Resources Planning and Management', *Journal of Agricultural and Environmental Ethics*, vol. 6, no. 2, 1993, pp. 145–64.

65. Ahmad al-Raysuni, *Imam al-Shatibi's Theory of the Higher Objectives and Intents of Islamic Law* (Herndon, VA: International Institute of Islamic Thought, 2013), p. 12.

66. Seyyed Hossein Nasr, 'Islam, the Contemporary Islamic World, and the Environmental Crisis', in Richard C. Foltz, Frederick M. Denny and Azizan Baharuddin (eds), *Islam and Ecology: A Bestowed Trust* (Cambridge, MA: Harvard University Press, 2003), p. 99.

67. Fazlun Khalid, 'Islamic Basis for Environmental Protection', in Bron R. Taylor (ed.), *Encyclopaedia of Religion and Nature* (London: Thoemmes, 2005), p. 883.

68. Richard C. Foltz, 'Islam', in Roger S. Gottlieb (ed.), *The Oxford Handbook of Religion and Ecology* (New York: Oxford University Press), p. 211.

69. Interview with Professor Nurdeng Deuraseh, Sultan Sharif Ali Islamic University, Brunei, 1 August 2018.

70. Nurdeng Deuraseh, *Islam: Faith, Shari'ah and Civilization – An Interpretation for Better Civilization* (Kuala Lumpur: Attin Press, 2015), p. 598.

71. Rosemary Hancock, *Islamic Environmentalism: Activism in the United States and Great Britain* (Abingdon: Routledge, 2017), p. 60.

72. Tsugitaka Sato, *State and Rural Society in Medieval Islam: Sultans, Muqta's, and Fallahun* (Leiden: Brill, 1997), pp. 1–2.

73. More specifically, there were two types of *'ushr*: a 5 per cent tax on the value of harvests of irrigated land and 10 per cent on rain-watered land. See Seyyed Vali

Reza Nasr, *Islamic Leviathan: Islam and the Making of State Power* (New York: Oxford University Press, 2001), p. 144.

74. Sato, *State and Rural Society in Medieval Islam*, pp. 1–2.

75. Hamed, 'Seeing the Environment through Islamic Eyes', p. 154.

76. Sahih Bukhari, *Wills and Testaments*, Hadith 37, https://ahadith.co.uk/perma link-hadith-6127 (accessed 16 June 2022).

77. Hamed, 'Seeing the Environment through Islamic Eyes', p. 154.

78. Sahih al-Bukhari, *Virtues of Madinah*, Hadith 1, https://sunnah.com/bukhari: 1867 (accessed 16 June 2022).

79. Sahih al-Bukhari, *Distribution of Water*, Hadith 18, https://sunnah.com/bukha ri/42/18 (accessed 16 June 2022).

80. Hashim Y. Al-Mallah, *The Governmental System of the Prophet Muhammad: A Comparative Study in Constitutional Law* (Beirut: Dar al-Kotob al-Ilmiyah, 2011), p. 142.

81. Hamed, 'Seeing the Environment through Islamic Eyes', p. 156.

82. David L. Johnston, 'Intra-Muslim Debates on Ecology: Is Shari'a Still Relevant?', *Worldviews*, vol. 16, no. 2, 2012, p. 233.

83. Nurdeng Deuraseh, 'The Revival of the Dead Earth (Ihya' al-Mawat)', Alukah in English, 22 June 2013, http://en.alukah.net/Thoughts_Knowledge/0/2142/ (accessed 16 June 2022).

84. Muwatta Malik, *Judgements*, Hadith 26, https://sunnah.com/urn/414770 (accessed 16 June 2022).

85. Deuraseh, 'The Revival of The Dead Earth (Ihya' Al-Mawat)'.

86. Muhammad Akram Khan, *Islamic Economics and Finance: A Glossary*, 2nd ed. (London: Routledge, 2003), p. 72.

87. Mohammad Yusuf Siddiq, 'An Ecological Journey in Muslim Bengal', in Richard C. Foltz, Frederick M. Denny and Azizan Baharuddin (eds), *Islam and Ecology: A Bestowed Trust* (Cambridge, MA: Harvard University Press, 2003), p. 455.

88. Foltz, *Animals in Islamic Tradition and Muslim Cultures*, pp. 34–5.

89. Khalid, 'Islamic Basis for Environmental Protection', p. 883.

90. There were a few notable exceptions. In May 1992, the Grand Mufti of Yemen issued a fatwa that 'Islam prohibits the killing of animals except for those slaugh-tered for their meat (that is goats, cows and camels) or predatory animals for protection of mankind'. See Lucy Vigne and Esmond Martin, 'Price for Rhino Horn Increases in Yemen', *Pachyderm*, no. 28, 2000, p. 98.

91. 'Islam and Environmental Conservation', Fatwa no. 84117, 29 September

2010, http://www.islamweb.net/en/article/155585/islam-and-environmental -conservation (accessed 16 June 2022)

92. 'Indonesian clerics issue fatwa to protection endangered species', Alliance of Religions and Conservation, 5 March 2014, http://www.arcworld.org/newseb 86.html?pageID=689 (accessed 16 June 2022).

93. Interview with Dr Fachruddin Manguanjaya, Center for Islamic Studies, Universitas Nasional, Jakarta, 2 August 2018.

94. 'Indonesia Issues Fatwa against Forest Fires', *DW*, 14 September 2016, http:// www.dw.com/en/indonesia-issues-fatwa-against-forest-fires/a-19550725 (accessed 16 June 2022).

95. Ibid.

96. 'Law on the Burning of Forests and Land and the Control Thereof', Ulama Council of Indonesia, Fatwa 30, 27 July 2016, http://web.archive.org/web/202 10420070620/https://mui-lplhsda.org/wp-content/uploads/2016/08/FATWA -KARHUTLA-versi-English.pdf (accessed 28 June 2022).

2

THE MUSLIM BROTHERHOOD AND
THE ENVIRONMENT

The Egyptian Muslim Brotherhood (Al-Ikhwan al-Muslimun) was established by Hassan al-Banna in 1928. He was a primary school teacher
and preacher in the town of Ismailiya, near the Suez Canal. Although he
lacked formal religious education, al-Banna was a charismatic leader with
organisational skills. The Brotherhood grew rapidly in the 1930s and 1940s,
building cadres in towns and rural areas. Al-Banna denounced the British
involvement in Egyptian domestic affairs and mocked the country's nominal
independence.

From the beginning, the Brotherhood's relationship with the Egyptian
authorities was confrontational and antagonistic. Following the end of the
Second World War, it challenged the Egyptian political establishment and
its foreign patrons. The Arab–Israeli War of 1948 led to civil disturbances in
Egypt. As a result, thousands of Muslim Brothers were imprisoned and tor-
tured. The founder of the Brotherhood himself was assassinated by unknown
gunmen in February 1949.

The army coup of 1952 was initially welcomed by the Brotherhood
because the Free Officers, under Gamal Abdel Nasser, overthrew the pro-
British King Farouk.[1] Yet the new leader suppressed the Brotherhood because
it was viewed as a threat to his regime. In 1966, the intellectual leader of the
organisation, Sayyid Qutb, was executed for plotting to assassinate Nasser.[2]
Nasser's successors, Anwar Sadat and Hosni Mubarak, followed a less aggres-

sive and more engaging policy towards the Brotherhood in spite of its illegal status.

The ideology of the Brotherhood has not been static and unchanging over time. Indeed, it has proven dynamic and adaptive in response to political developments and societal changes. Al-Banna professed an ideology combining anti-colonialism, pan-Islamism and social justice, but he was a political entrepreneur rather than a theorist. It was Qutb who truly influenced the ideological identity of the Brotherhood. He claimed that many Muslims still lived in the age of *jahiliyya* (pre-Islamic ignorance) because they did not practise their religion.[3] More importantly, he proposed the collective condemnation of unbelief (*takfir*).[4] After his execution, the then leader of the Brotherhood, Hasan al-Hudaybi, attempted to moderate the ideology of the movement. In his book *Du'at la Qudat* ('Preachers, not Judges'), al-Hudaybi argued that the concept of *jahiliyya* does not apply to modern conditions and that only God can judge who has committed a major sin.[5]

The organisational structure of the Brotherhood is simultaneously vertical and horizontal. The Shura Council (*Majlis al-Shura*) consists of 100 senior members who set the political priorities and decide on strategic direction. The Guidance Office (*Maktab al-Irshad*) is composed of fifteen senior members and is chaired by the supreme guide (*murshid*), who represents the organisation at the top level. Additionally, the Ikhwan have established branches in several Arab countries at least since the 1940s. In Syria, Jordan and Qatar, the Brotherhood has been an influential political actor.[6] These branches have functioned independently from the mother organisation.

During the first decade of the twenty-first century, the Muslim Brotherhood went through a phase of pragmatisation by gradually integrating into Egypt's political system. In the 2005 parliamentary elections, it received 20 per cent of the vote and won 88 seats.[7] Although its candidates were forced to run as independents, the Mubarak regime implicitly recognised the Brotherhood as an opposition force. The Brotherhood also participated in the 2007 elections for the Shura Council, the upper house of the Egyptian parliament, and came close to participating in the 2008 municipal elections. However, it decided to boycott these elections because the Mubarak regime did not allow the organisation to compete for most seats.[8] This increased political exposure allowed the Ikhwan to develop a more sophisticated political platform covering different areas of public policy. Due to its endurance, the Brotherhood has managed to build extensive social networks that can support political action.

The Ikhwan did not officially participate in the Egyptian Revolution of 2011, mainly for two reasons. First, the organisation did not fully comprehend the new socio-economic dynamics in Egyptian society, the frustrations of the youth, and the role of social media. The Brotherhood did not believe that the revolution was a genuine popular revolt against the Mubarak regime. Second, it strongly feared the potential repercussions of its participation in the events. If the uprising had failed, the Brotherhood would have paid a heavy price for its involvement.[9] It chose to keep a low profile, although individual members did participate in the events.

Following the revolution and the overthrow of Mubarak, the Muslim Brotherhood was legalised. In April 2011, the Ikhwan established the Freedom and Justice Party (Hizb al-Hurriya wa al-Adala – hereafter FJP) to participate in the 2011–12 parliamentary elections. Indeed, the new party won 235 of 498 seats.[10] Although the supreme guide of the Brotherhood, Mohamed Badie, had declared that the organisation would not have a candidate for presidency, a senior member, Mohamed Morsi, did run in the presidential election of 2012. In June 2012, after two rounds of elections, Morsi was elected president of Egypt. His presidency soon proved to be autocratic, causing widespread unrest. On 3 July 2013, following massive protests against Morsi, the Egyptian military staged a coup d'état and overthrew him. The new regime of General Abdel Fattah el-Sisi outlawed the organisation and arrested thousands of members. Morsi himself and other senior figures were put on trial. He was later sentenced to twenty-five years in prison.[11] El-Sisi was elected president of Egypt in May 2014.

Most studies have examined either the Brotherhood's history or its contemporary political transformation.[12] This chapter first describes the Muslim Brotherhood's general perspective on the environment before and during Morsi's presidency. Therefore, it examines the writings and statements of Hassan al-Banna, Sayyid Qutb, Yusuf al-Qaradawi, Mohamed Badie and Morsi himself, as well as the 2005, 2007, 2008 and 2011 electoral programmes of the Brotherhood. It then turns to three areas of environmental activity, namely water management, animals, and pollution and energy.

Finally, the chapter examines the role of religion in the emergence of the Brotherhood's environmentalism.

The Brotherhood's General Perspective on the Environment

Despite its ideological flexibility and adaptability, some of the Brotherhood's environmental thinking is still based on the writings of Hassan al-Banna and Sayyid Qutb. Both examined mankind's relationship with God and nature. Al-Banna famously declared:

> Islam is an all embracing concept which regulates every aspect of life . . . It does not stand helpless before life's problems . . . Some people mistakenly understand by Islam something restricted to certain types of religious observances or spiritual exercises . . . [W]e understand Islam broadly and comprehensively as regulating the affairs of men, in this world and the next.[13]

From his point of view, Islam is more than a religion with its rituals and practices. It is a holistic system with codes of conduct and guidance to govern every aspect of human life, implicitly including environmental issues.

Indeed, the founder of the Brotherhood understood the environment as a domain of science. In an open letter to Egyptian leaders, he argued, 'God commands mankind to study nature.'[14] Thus, Muslims have a religious obligation to understand nature because it is a creation of God. He also used nature metaphorically to demonstrate the divine origin of his mission in Egypt. In his memoirs, al-Banna states, 'Allah has compared [his] message to a seed which bears fruit wherever it is planted.'[15]

Sayyid Qutb acknowledged the environment as part of human existence. His autobiography, *A Child from the Village*, published in 1946, offers insights into his relationship with animals. As a young boy, he developed an affection for the family's cow. When his father sold some of the family's land, Sayyid recalled how he worried about what would happen to the cow. Apart from providing milk and cream, he valued 'the firm friendship that bound him to her as it also did his sisters and mother. She had been there almost the whole time he and his sisters were growing up and had become a "personality" dear to him and to all in the house'.[16] His words reflect not only a child's innocent view of animals, but also a deeper appreciation of the villagers' closeness to nature and its creatures. Life in the village was more balanced and harmonious. This nostalgia for the life he left behind has underpinned the soul of the organisation that does not wish to look like an urban-only movement.[17] The Islam of Qutb's rural childhood was authentic and holistic.

Later, Qutb came to understand nature as a place of spiritual inspiration and religious experience. He blended Islamic cosmology and the metaphysics of human nature. In his famous book *Milestones* (*Ma'alim fi'l-Tariq*), Qutb observes, 'Man is part of the universe; the laws which govern human nature are no different from the laws governing the universe . . . Man's body is made of earthly material, yet God has bestowed upon him certain character-istics which made him more than the earth from which he is made.'[18] Qutb examined the essence of human existence only to emphasise the divine role of Shari'a . From his point of view, Shari'a is 'part of that universal law which governs the entire universe, including the physical and biological aspects of man'.[19] In his opinion, the application of Shari'a is the ultimate goal for Muslims because it will bring justice.

Nevertheless, the environment was clearly not a priority for the Brotherhood's early leaders. Although al-Banna and Qutb touched upon the relationship between humans and nature, they did not offer a blueprint of solutions other than Islamic revivalism. The application of Shari'a as the law of the land would solve any environmental problems. During its long period of clandestine existence, the Ikhwan concentrated more on education, social services and family support. Environmental issues were almost absent from their political agenda. This absence is hardly a surprise given the then lack of environmental awareness among the public and policymakers alike.

It is the second generation of Ikhwan scholars who examined in detail the Islamic perspective on the environment. Yusuf al-Qaradawi has proposed many rulings regarding environmental issues that have preoccupied Muslims in Egypt and elsewhere. He has argued:

> The environment was created in a balanced and better order than what humans caused it to be. The remedy for the environmental crisis could only be achieved by first reforming the humans from within and second by resorting to legal implementation of sanction to prevent the environmental corrupters from damaging the environment.[20]

In effect, al-Qaradawi has suggested a twofold response to the environmental crisis: a change of attitudes and a change of practices.

Moreover, he has encouraged believers to feel the true love of nature because in this way they can see the face of God.[21] This encouragement clearly belies a Sufi belief, but al-Qaradawi is not a Sufi. Indeed, he has proposed a merger between Sufism and Salafism since each can benefit from the other's strengths: the Sufi can learn from Salafism not to follow 'the fabricated *hadith*, polytheist rites and tomb-side rites', and the Salafi can embrace 'the Sufi tenderness, spirituality, and piousness'.[22] As a result, al-Qaradawi has attempted to offer a spiritual understanding of the environment which combines Sufi mysticism, Salafi doctrine and Islamic philosophy.

His preoccupation with the environment coincided with the Brotherhood's newly found commitment to environmentalism from the mid-2000s. Its programme for the 2005 legislative elections promised 'coordination between the Health and Agriculture Ministries for putting a plan into action to get rid of the different types of pollution'.[23] It was probably the first time that an official Brotherhood document mentioned the problem of pollution, although there was no apparent follow-up.

The deterioration in Egypt's environmental problems and the organisation's growing popularity continued to push the issue higher on the agenda. As a result, the Ikhwan's 2007 programme for the Egyptian Shura Council had a special section on the environment:

> One of the vital issues is preserving the environment through avoiding pollution because environment is the medium where man constructs the earth [*sic*] also it is the natural resource for all coming generations . . . This can be carried out through a cooperative work between the government, NGOs and private sector as well as the co-ordination with international organizations in order to set at the end a system for dealing with all residuals in all kinds and to protect the natural and water resources.[24]

Hence, the organisation suggested environmental solutions based on co-operation between different stakeholders to increase effectiveness. It also welcomed the involvement of international organisations. Next, the document outlined the proposed environmental policy, comprising these ten steps:

1. To establish the supreme council for health and environment by bringing together different institutions and initiatives.
2. To protect the Nile River, which is a gift from Allah Almighty, through establishing a national council for protecting it.
3. To solve the problem of water in the countryside and cities through using purification technologies rather than traditional ones.
4. To control industrial pollution through devising and offering financial incentives for clean industries.
5. To solve the problem of air pollution by encouraging people to use gas as a substitute for fuel and carry on a monthly check on such engines and fine all violators.
6. To find innovative solutions for solid residuals and use them as fertilisers.
7. To reduce the pollution of agricultural land and water reservoirs from pesticides.
8. To prevent pollution of the coasts from shipping and oil spills.
9. To solve the problem of noise pollution through preparing and implementing policies and legislation.
10. To adopt a set of educational policies and procedures for Egyptian citizens in the field of the environment through educational curricula, mass media and places of worship.[25]

This list of measures reveals important information about the Brotherhood's conception of environmental issues. First, it attempted to combine religious rhetoric with environmental science. It viewed the Nile as a 'gift from God' but called for the establishment of a new institution to monitor the river's pollution problem. It also favoured the use of the more environmentally friendly gas as fuel for cars. The Brotherhood proposed education and media as major means for increasing environmental awareness, although it also foresaw a role for mosques in this effort.

In January 2010, Mohamed Badie became the new supreme guide of the Muslim Brotherhood. His first statement declared, 'Our concern includes that of all Egyptians, Arabs and Muslims; the whole humanity shares the same concern over the future of the world, which is threatened by conflicts, epidemics, and diseases . . . because of the global warming, desertification and drought'.[26] In this way, he demonstrated awareness and commitment to environmental protection, while projecting the image of a leader who had a global vision. He did not ignore the problem of global warming but stressed the problems of desertification and drought that have plagued Egypt.

Three months later, Badie issued a message titled 'Do no mischief on the earth' to elaborate on the Ikhwan's position:

> It is a reality and a frightening consequence that man's greed and care-lessness cause environmental pollution caused by industrial dumping and man's lust for more produce. Pollution will affect all aspects necessary for man to flourish. Pollution from the use of pesticides also affects air, water, plant and animal life. Man must return to his roots and sow through organic farming and biological control methods . . . The message of Islam advocates respect and regard to all of the world's resources and most importantly to man himself. It is imperative that we remember that the world is fragile and we must handle it with care.[27]

Remarkably, his statement consisted of four distinct parts. First, it implicitly blamed capitalism and its drive for economic growth caused by human imperfection. Second, he described the extent of the problem of pollution; it is massive in scale. This reality points to the urgency of responding to environmental challenges. Third, Badie proposed new methods of farming and environmental management. Finally, he briefly offered the Islamic view about the protection of nature. This carefully crafted message indicated preparation and deep thought to offer a response that acknowledged social and environmental realities.

As mentioned earlier, the Brotherhood did not participate in the January 2011 revolution. However, it followed developments closely and grasped the feeling of the protesters. Many of them demanded better living conditions and improved quality of life. One environmental researcher even claimed 'environmental and resource-related issues were at the very core of the Egyptian Revolution' because protesters frequently raised the issue of pollution.[28] For example, two of the key slogans of the revolution were 'The cancer is everywhere, and the gas is sold for free' and 'Husni Mubarak, you agent, you sold the gas and [only] the Nile is left [to be sold].'[29] Both slogans acknowledged the problem of pollution, while accusing the Mubarak regime of corruption. The slogans also referred to the controversial export of Egyptian gas to Israel that will be discussed later.

It was in this period of political upheaval that the Brotherhood decided to promote the Renaissance Project for the reform of Egypt's government, economy and civil society.[30] The first of the three phases of the proposed project included, among others, sanitation issues.[31] The Brotherhood-sponsored FJP was the government in waiting and had to indicate visionary leadership. In January 2012, six months before becoming president of Egypt, Mohamed Morsi outlined his vision for a new environmental policy:

> The FJP believes that the ecological balance between man and what he builds in his urban environment on the one side and between God's creation in the natural environment on the other, is the basic framework that should govern and control the process of populating the world. Hence, the party has set priorities and policies to deal with all types of environmental pollution, from reducing the impact of pollution, to treatment mechanisms, and safeguard policies to prevent recurrence.[32]

Here, Morsi attempted to provide assurance on the Brotherhood's ability to govern. At the same time, he described the proper relationship between God, man and nature to indicate his Islamic credentials.

Nonetheless, the Morsi government did not attempt to 'Islamise' environmental policy. The new prime minister, Hesham Qandil, appointed Mostafa Hussein Kamel as the minister of environmental affairs. Kamel was an academic who had been selected for this position first by Kamal el-Ganzouri's post-Mubarak interim government in December 2011. The position was offered to the Salafi al-Nour party, but it was rejected as an insult.[33] Khaled Abdel Aal took over the ministry following a cabinet reshuffle in January 2013, but he resigned five months later due to massive anti-government protests. Neither Kamel nor Aal were members of the Ikhwan. On the contrary, they were known as secular technocrats who had worked with previous governments. Independents were also appointed to the Qandil cabinet in other environment-related ministries. For example, Mohamed Bahaa Eldin served as minister of water and irrigation, Salah Abdel Moamen as minister of agriculture and land reclamation, and Abdel Qawi Khalifa as minister of utilities, drinking water and sewage. Members of the FJP and other Islamists were appointed to head ministries that carry more influence, such as the Ministry of Industry and Trade, the Ministry for Youth, the Ministry of Media, the Ministry of Housing and Urban Development and the Ministry of Higher Education.

In summary, the Brotherhood has relatively recently begun to take significant notice of environmental problems. Its founder only generally addressed issues related to nature. Since the mid-2000s, the organisation has made a systematic effort to propose a policy agenda in response to the country's ecological crisis. The chapter now turns to examine how the Brotherhood has viewed water management, animals, and pollution and energy.

Water Management

Egypt's livelihood depends on the River Nile for drinking water and irrigation. Hassan al-Banna once declared, 'We want to secure our southern borders by preserving our rights in Eritrea . . . and Upper Nile . . . those areas where the blood of the Egyptian conqueror mingled with its soil, and was built by the Egyptian hand.'[34] Moreover, he held the opinion that 'if Egypt needs Sudan to be reassured about the water of the Nile, which is its life, then Sudan is more in need of Egypt in all aspects of life as well, and they are both part of complementing the other'.[35] Thus, the founder of the Brotherhood acknowledged the threat of losing the Nile waters and recommended some form of unity between Egypt and Sudan.[36] His approach was apparently nationalist and pan-Islamist at the same time. Nevertheless, the Ikhwan apparently ignored water issues for many years. For example, they neither supported nor opposed the construction of the Aswan Dam during the 1960s.

The Ikhwan have showed a strong interest in water management only since entering parliament. In May 2008, a Muslim Brotherhood MP, Abbas Abdul-Aziz, submitted a parliamentary question regarding the pollution of the Nile. He asked, 'When will the government feel responsible for entering laws into force and punish the corrupt who affects the people's health, and when will the ruling NDP [National Democratic Party] nightmare be eliminated?'[37] Thus, water pollution became a political weapon in the hands of the Ikhwan to undermine the legitimacy of the Mubarak regime.

Two months earlier, the Brotherhood had published its 2008 municipal election platform. Water management proposals were included in the electoral programme: bringing drinking water to all deprived regions; reno-vating and consolidating networks in overpopulated regions; continuously monitoring water distillation plants; curbing repeated water outages, follow-ing up regular maintenance and seeking solutions for permanent problems; digging deep wells on the delta to contribute to solving the drinking water problem; establishing sewerage projects in every big village; and continuously campaigning for saving water.[38] The proposals were pragmatic and aimed at offering a modern water management system.

The Arab Spring revolution created an opportunity for the Brotherhood to draw attention to water management and efficiency. In November 2011, Ali el-Salmi, the deputy prime minister of the interim government during the second half of that year, presented the Declaration of the Fundamental Principles of the New Egyptian State. The document had a provision about the Nile which states, 'It is the lifeline to the land of Egypt. The State is com-mitted to good management and protection of the Nile from pollution and abuse, and to maximise the use of its waters and maintain the historic rights of Egypt in this regard.'[39] Not surprisingly, under conditions of political competition, the Ikhwan decided to address water issues more thoroughly. The 2011 electoral programme of the FJP placed emphasis on irrigation and water management. It proposed the following measures:

1. Developing surface irrigation systems and increasing the efficient use of irrigation water to save 20–25 per cent of irrigation water currently used. Water saved in this way can be directed to the irrigation of new areas in reclamation zones.
2. Training water advisors to accompany and assist agricultural advisors.
3. Making use of modern irrigation systems in most of the new reclamation areas, as well as banning use of surface irrigation systems, except for prac-tical necessities in these areas.[40]

The proposed policy clearly focused on the building of an effective water management system, especially for the new reclamation areas in the Nile Delta that largely depend on groundwater.

Prime Minister Qandil took a personal interest on this matter because he had previously served as a minister of water resources and irrigation. Consequently, the FJP-led government promoted the recycling of water for irrigation in reclaimed land and the desalination of water in coastal areas.[41] However, the political timing did not allow the immediate implementation of its water management proposals. As soon as Morsi became president, a diplomatic crisis broke out with Ethiopia regarding the sharing of the Blue Nile, one of the two main tributaries of the river Nile. Addis Ababa had decided to build a dam on the river that could have affected the supply of water on the Egyptian side, which depends almost entirely on the Nile. The new president leveraged aggressive rhetoric against Ethiopia because water security has always been a challenge for Egypt. During a speech, he declared, 'If a single drop of the Nile is lost, our blood will be the alternative,' and warned the Ethiopian leadership that 'all options are open'.[42] Despite his belligerent tone, Morsi avoided any religious talk against the Christian-majority country and even called Ethiopia 'a friend'.[43] Indeed, he chose diplomacy to manage the crisis, as did previous Egyptian leaders before him.

However, Morsi's moderate stance was not fully shared by the Ikhwan as a whole. In May 2013, Muslim Brotherhood media spokesman Ahmed Aref claimed that 'Zionists attempted to lure some African countries to sell Nile water, in order to turn water into a commodity and a tool to put an economic stranglehold on Egypt. The construction of dams and other river facilities . . . is only a manifestation of that policy.'[44] His words implied that the root cause of Egypt's dispute with upstream countries was the commercialisation of water that served the 'Zionist interests' in the region. Aref concluded his statement by declaring, 'May God protect Egypt, its people and River Nile from all evil.'[45] The conflation of anti-capitalism and anti-Semitism perfectly fitted the narrative of an organisation defending the fundamental principle of equal access to public goods like water, while fighting the 'archenemy' of Egypt and Islam: the Jews.

The Nile waters issue has been raised by the Brotherhood more than once since the overthrow of Morsi. In December 2015, the signing of an agreement between Egypt, Sudan and Ethiopia on the Grand Ethiopian Renaissance Dam provoked an angry response from the Ikhwan. The organisation issued a statement that claimed:

> Junta-controlled media has misled the Egyptian people, as it celebrated the Ethiopian Renaissance Dam agreement signed by Sisi, and pictured it as a

great achievement! Now, it has been revealed that with this agreement Sisi and his gang forfeit the Egyptian people's right to Nile water. Evidently, the traitorous Sisi is implementing a Zionist plot to eliminate Egypt's historical achievements [see appendix].[46]

In July 2020, the organisation reaffirmed its opposition to 'any agreement, whether it was signed in 2015 or will be signed later, affecting the Egyptian people's historical right to the internationally agreed waters of the Nile'.[47]

Therefore, the Brotherhood has accused President el-Sisi of treason because he supposedly abandoned the country's rights over the river. Moreover, it has promoted again the conspiracy theory about Jewish aspirations to destroy Egypt by stealing its water. Since there is no known involvement of Israel in the negotiation process over the sharing of Nile waters, it is possible that the Brotherhood is implicitly criticising Ethiopia's strong connection to Israel and Judaism. For the Ikhwan, water is both a scarce natural resource and a politically contested issue. The organisation has promoted the securitisation of the Nile by adopting a polemical approach against both political adversaries and foreign governments.[48]

Animals

The Ikhwan have maintained an ambiguous position towards animal rights. As discussed above, Sayyid Qutb's recollection of his childhood in the Egyptian countryside revealed a deep affection for the family's cow. The young Sayyid felt responsible for the fate of the animal. It was part of his family, not just a source of milk, but more like a loyal companion. This view derives from the Islamic notion of *khilafa* (stewardship). Qutb romanticised animals in the context of rural Islam.

Yusuf al-Qaradawi has offered a more explicit Islamic perspective on animal rights. In *The Lawful and Prohibited in Islam*, published in 1960, he states:

> Thirteen hundred years before any societies for the prevention of cruelty to animals were established, Islam had made kindness to animals a part of its faith and cruelty to them a sufficient reason for a person to be thrown into the Fire . . . Never, prior to Islam, had the world witnessed such concern for animals, a concern which was beyond its imagination'.[49]

At first sight, his view can be easily described as animal-friendly. However, what al-Qaradawi really wants is to defend the moral superiority of Islam over other religions.

Nevertheless, the Brotherhood has paid little attention to animal issues. In April 2009, a Muslim Brotherhood MP, Hamdy Hasan, made a statement concerning the swine flu that had spread around Cairo. He posited, 'The issue must be taken with full seriousness as it is a first-degree national security issue and can't be delayed as was the case the past three years.'[50] The securitisation of swine flu enraged many Egyptian Copts because pork is part of their diet. The anti-pig prejudice of the Brotherhood seems to derive from the Islamic ban on pork and pork-related products.

In addition, senior leaders of the organisation have used animals to insult perceived enemies. In 2010, for example, Mohamed Morsi gave an interview to Lebanon's Al-Quds TV where he declared that 'either [you accept] the Zionists and everything they want, or else it is war ... This is what these occupiers of the land of Palestine know – these blood-suckers, who attack the Palestinians, these warmongers, the descendants of apes and pigs.'[51] This anti-Semitic statement was based on a Qur'anic verse, 'Say: Shall I inform you of those worse than this in retribution from Allah? They are those whom Allah has cursed and upon whom He brought His wrath and of whom He made apes and swine, and who serve the devil' (5:60). Morsi later retracted his statement.

The constitution of 2012, which was drafted by the Ikhwan and Salafis, included a general provision about environmental protection. More specifically, Article 63 declared that

> every person has the right to a healthy, undamaged environment. The state commits itself to the inviolability of the environment and its protection against pollution. It also commits itself to using natural resources in a way that will not harm the environment and to preserving the rights of all generations to it.[52]

The constitution did not mention animal rights; yet activists approached the Brotherhood and the al-Nour Party during the drafting period and proposed the following constitutional provision protecting animals that was largely based on Shari'a:

The state confirms that animals are creatures with rights as living beings; they are not things. To preserve animal resources of different kinds, the state through its legislation ensures the availability of basic rights to animals. This is done in a way that will fulfil human benefits from them while also providing protection, care and kindness (al-rifq) in dealing with them, according to what the relevant laws provide and according to the Islamic Shariʿa and international treaties and agreements.[53]

Surprisingly, both parties ignored pleas for protection of animal rights for unknown reasons.

In contrast, Article 45 of the 2014 constitution, supported by the military, states that 'the State shall protect and develop the green space in the urban areas; preserve plant, animal and fish resources and protect those under the threat of extinction or danger; guarantee humane treatment of animals [al-rifq bi-l-hayawan], all according to the law'.[54] Thus, the el-Sisi regime took a progressive stance on the issue by infusing Islamic values into the new constitution.

Pollution and Energy

Egypt has suffered from high levels of pollution and poor air quality.[55] It is a problem that has long been neglected by policymakers but affects the life of millions of people. As shown earlier, the 2007 programme proposed certain measures to tackle the problem of pollution, including the use of water purification technologies, offering financial incentives for clean industries, the use of gas as a substitute for other fuels, the banning of pesticides, and the prevention of pollution from shipping and oil spills.

The 2008 municipal election platform included many proposals for the control and prevention of pollution at the local level. More specifically, the Brotherhood suggested the following measures: increasing rubbish collections in villages and urban districts; increasing supervision of cleaning companies working in cities; preventing the burning of rubbish inside or near residential blocks; following up the implementation of waste recycling projects; co-ordinating with schools, mosques, churches, charities and health units to carry out education campaigns to get citizens on board with the cleaning issue and ensure all people know that 'cleanliness is next to godliness', offering a prize for the cleanest street or unit; hanging posters campaigning for cleanliness and preservation of the environment; planting trees on roadsides and in entrances to homes and increasing the size of green areas in cities and villages; preventing the discharge of sewage in open waterways, especially irrigation canals.[56]

Moreover, the Ikhwan examined the environmental problems of the Red Sea where the country's new tourism industry is concentrated. Consequently, the Morsi campaign organised a conference days before the runoff of the presidential election where proposals for the environment were put forward, including measures to prevent the loss of Egypt's coral reefs.[57] Such efforts allowed the Brotherhood to rebrand itself as a modern organisation concerned about the ecological health of the country.

According to former minister of planning and international co-operation Amr Darrag, the management of pollution was a priority for the Morsi government.[58] The new authorities promoted recycling to discourage the burning of rice straw, which adds to air pollution. Additionally, the government invited private investors to establish a system of industrial waste management in Cairo and elsewhere.[59]

In July 2012, the newly elected President Morsi launched the Clean Homeland Campaign with the help of social and youth groups.[60] The Ministry for Environmental Affairs, under the independent Dr Mostafa Hussein Kamel, took charge of the campaign. The minister declared that 'work will take place using three methods of hygiene and public cleanliness in parallel, by removing piles of accumulated garbage, improving sidewalks and pavements, planting street trees and increasing environmental awareness'.[61]

Having said that, the Brotherhood has almost ignored the challenges of global warming and climate change. The rationale was aptly described by the former spokesman Gehad el-Haddad, who contributed to the formation of Brotherhood's environmental policy. In his words:

> To allocate part of the budget for something like this, you really have to have met the basic needs of the citizens, otherwise the outcome will be negative either way. If you talk about people dying in the next 200 years, there are people dying this year and this will always be more pressing. But we will make sure that what we do now, doesn't affect what will come later.[62]

Thus, the Brotherhood prioritised local over global issues because it needed to address the concerns and problems of its constituency. Despite its narrow-mindedness, it is a political strategy that acknowledged the realities of modern Egypt.

The Brotherhood has understood pollution as the outcome of the existing energy policy. The 2011 electoral programme of the FJP suggested 'increasing use of alternative energy, especially renewable types, focusing on solar energy projects, and working on nationalising and developing technologies relevant to those projects'.[63] Furthermore, the party advocated 'the establishment of a Higher Council for Industry and Energy and Mining that works for the integration of efforts in these three sectors'.[64] More importantly, it claimed that electricity production can reach a maximum capacity of 30–35 gigawatts (GW) if the following steps are taken:

- Substituting diesel with natural gas in power stations.
- Increasing the pace of building power plants based on renewable water, wind and solar energies.
- Developing electrical energy joint projects with the Nile Basin countries.[65]

Indeed, the Muslim Brotherhood is probably the first Islamist group openly discussing the need for a policy on renewable energy that could improve the energy security of Egypt. In addition to a massive nationalisation program, the Ikhwan favoured institutional reform to face energy challenges.

The Brotherhood also criticised the Mubarak regime for exporting Egyptian gas to Israel. Yet it opposed sabotage actions against the 90-kilometre Arish–Askeron gas pipeline and called for peaceful protests.[66] In the summer of 2010, the Brotherhood intensified its criticism, claiming that electricity blackouts were the result of Egyptian gas exports to the neighbouring country.[67] The 2011 electoral programme included certain recommendations regarding the gas trade with Israel. For example, it recommended a review of 'the contracts to export Egyptian natural gas, especially to Israel. This should provide additional revenue of up to US$18 billion.'[68] In April 2012, Kamal el-Ganzouri's interim government cancelled a twenty-year contract to supply Israel with gas. When the Brotherhood came to power, Morsi did not freeze economic relations with Israel; the new government was very keen to prove to the United States and Europe that it did not plan to change Cairo's foreign policy towards Tel Aviv.[69] Nonetheless, Morsi did not resume gas exports to Israel, probably as a gesture of solidarity with the embattled Hamas.

Furthermore, the Egyptian government utilised gas exports as a foreign policy tool against Amman. The Jordanian economy depended on Egyptian gas supplied under a bilateral agreement signed in 2001. Following the outbreak of protests by the Jordanian branch of the Muslim Brotherhood in winter 2011, the Morsi government reduced gas exports to its neighbour to keep the pressure on Amman. Consequently, the Jordanian national electricity company came close to bankruptcy when it resorted to costlier heavy fuel oil.[70]

Finally, the use of nuclear power became a controversial issue for the Brotherhood. Gehad el-Haddad once argued:

> [The FJP] is an anti-nuclear party and our energy program has a substantial portion of renewable energy. It ties into the Renaissance Project of the Muslim Brotherhood in Egypt. For us, renewable energy is the energy source for the globe within the next fifty years, whether that's wind, solar or water'.[71]

However, this view probably reflected only his own background and experience.[72] The Morsi government tried to revive the nuclear programme that Hosni Mubarak had started in 1996. In July 2012, the Ministry of Energy and Electricity conduced a feasibility study for the construction of a nuclear energy plant at the Mediterranean city of El-Dabaa.[73] In April 2013, during a visit by Morsi to Moscow, the Russian energy minister Aleksandr Novak announced that Egypt proposed 'to resume cooperation in peaceful nuclear projects' to jointly construct new nuclear power plants.[74] More specifically, the Egyptian government planned to build 4GW of nuclear power facilities by 2025. For this purpose, Cairo invited Moscow to step into the joint development of uranium mines in Egypt.

One can only speculate about the real intentions behind Morsi's apparent enthusiasm for a nuclear programme. While Egypt has growing energy needs, it is possible that the Morsi government viewed nuclear energy as a national project that could foster patriotism. Moreover, some analysts have claimed that that the Ikhwan have supported the acquisition of nuclear weapons, although this suggestion hardly seems a realistic possibility.[75] In the past, however, some senior figures like deputy supreme guide Mohammed Habib supported the Iranian nuclear programme for both peaceful and military purposes because 'it will create a sort of balance between the two sides, the Arab and Islamic side and the Israeli side'.[76] These nuclear ambitions could have been the result of the influence that Yusuf al-Qaradawi wields as the intellectual leader of the Muslim Brotherhood. He has not objected to the use of nuclear power for peaceful purposes and has even supported the acquisition of nuclear weapons.[77]

The Role of Religion

The Muslim Brotherhood is one of the oldest Islamist organisations in the world, enduring repression and persecution. Hence, it has maintained a strong claim to Islamic authenticity. In fact, it was the Brotherhood that developed Islamism as an ideology. Hassan al-Banna defined Islam as 'a comprehensive system which deals with all spheres of life'.[78] Islamism offers a rigid understanding of the Muslim faith, but not necessarily extremist. The founder of the Brotherhood called for 'Islamic solutions to the contemporary problems of the society'.[79] Thus, the Ikhwan claim that Shari'a can dictate every aspect of public and private life.

Although the Brotherhood has portrayed itself as an organisation guided by Islam, its environmental proposals are not based on Shari'a. This mismatch presents a puzzle in view of the fact that actually most Egyptians support the introduction of Islamic law. A May 2012 public opinion survey, for example, showed that 66 per cent of Egyptians supported making Shari'a the basis of Egyptian law.[80] While 83 per cent of interviewees wanted a modernised version of Shari'a, some 17 per cent supported a literal application of it.[81] There has even been a provision in every Egyptian constitution since 1971 that the principles of Shari'a are the main source of legislation, although the Napoleonic Code is equally applicable.[82]

Instead of Shari'a rules, the Brotherhood has proposed technocratic measures for the protection of the environment. The presence of many scientists within the organisation is one possible explanation for this development. Since the late 1980s, the Ikhwan have had a strong following among the country's engineers.[83] Regardless of its self-identification as a faith-based organisation, most of the Brotherhood's leading figures do not have a theological background. Mohamed Morsi was the head of the Engineering Department at Zagazig University, while the supreme guide, Mohamed Badie, is a professor of veterinary medicine. Thus, its secularly trained cadres are not inclined to search for Shari'a-compliant environmental solutions.

However, the Brotherhood cannot afford to ignore the religious environment in which it operates. Yusuf al-Qaradawi has written about the environment and non-humans in the form of religious rulings and teachings. For his point of view, the environment is a space where religious obligations must be fulfilled. It is the viewpoint of a theologian which has limited applicability. Al-Qaradawi is an influential and respected Islamic scholar offering legal advice to Sunni Muslims in the Middle East and elsewhere, but he has not been involved in policy formulation in Egypt.

Nevertheless, Badie and Morsi popularised the Brotherhood's environmental approach by using religious rhetoric. In one of his pre-coup statements, Badie stated that 'the message of Islam advocates respect and regard to all of the world's resources and most importantly to man himself'.[84] It was one of the few times that the supreme guide of the Brotherhood referred to the environmental message of the Muslim faith. Before his presidency, Morsi also occasionally used religious rhetoric to emphasise environmental responsibility. Both instrumentalised religion to champion the protection of the environment, but they did not elaborate further.

The former spokesman Gehad el-Haddad explained the convergence of religious commitment and policy formulation by acknowledging the role of Islam in environmental care:

> There are close to fifty sayings of the Prophet Muhammad that we relate to the environment issue in various [ways]. One is especially well known to Egyptians: if the day of judgement is called for, and you have a seed or a small tree in your hand do not drop it and go on to do something else, but plant it and you will be rewarded for it. That's the kind of considerations that feed into the environmental protection of the Islamic movement in general. Also, when you understand Egyptian people and the weight of religion in governing their daily life choices and decisions, you can really capitalise on that being such a deep motivation for them. They might respect it more than any law.[85]

Thus, El-Haddad suggested the use of religious beliefs and rules to accelerate policies and measures that can protect the environment.

As evidenced by its electoral programmes, the Brotherhood does not view adherence to Shariʿa as a prerequisite for a better environment. The issue of water has been understood both as a technical issue and as one of national security. The organisation has called the Nile a 'gift from God' to stress the river's importance, but the proposed measures for its protection do not have a religious justification or purpose. Indeed, Shariʿa water rules and rights are overlooked. The same applies to animal life. The organisation has not considered Islamic rules regarding non-humans. Only its position on swine flu and pork can be traced to Islamic tradition. Regarding pollution prevention and energy, the Brotherhood has generally taken a non-religious stance. From time to time, however, it has used religious arguments to support its position. In February 2010, for instance, the Brotherhood issued a statement arguing that 'the cleanliness of the environment in Islam has been linked directly to purity'.[86]

In conclusion, the Muslim Brotherhood does not really follow a faith-based approach to environmental issues. In fact, it is fair to argue that the Brotherhood's environmental policy relies more on science, despite the occasional religious rhetoric. Most policy proposals were well articulated and well planned, with the possible exception of nuclear energy. The absence of Shariʿa-compliant solutions is somewhat paradoxical and suggests other factors that could have influenced the Brotherhood's environmental policy.

Notes

1. Carrie Rosefsky Wickham, *The Muslim Brotherhood: Evolution of an Islamist Movement* (Princeton, NJ: Princeton University Press, 2013), p. 27.
2. See John Calvert, *Sayyid Qutb and the Origins of Radical Islamism* (London: Hurst, 2009).
3. Barbara H. E. Zollner, *The Muslim Brotherhood: Hasan al-Hudaybi and Ideology* (Abingdon: Routledge, 2009), p. 57.
4. Ibid., p. 149.
5. Emmanuel Sivan, *Radical Islam: Medieval Theology and Modern Politics* (New Haven, CT: Yale University Press, 1985), p. 109.
6. See, for instance, Raphaël Lefèvre, *Ashes of Hama: The Muslim Brotherhood in*

Syria (New York: Oxford University Press, 2013); Shmuel Bar, *The Muslim Brotherhood in Jordan* (Tel Aviv: Moshe Dayan Center, 2000).

7. Jeremy M. Sharp, 'Egypt: 2005 Presidential and Parliamentary Elections', CRS Report for Congress, 15 January 2006, p. 5.

8. 'Egypt opposition boycotts polls', BBC News, 7 April 2008, http://news.bbc.co .uk/2/hi/middle_east/7334191.stm (accessed 16 June 2022).

9. Mariz Tadros, *The Muslim Brotherhood in Contemporary Egypt: Democracy Redefined or Confined?* (Abingdon: Routledge, 2012), p. 31.

10. 'Egypt's Islamist parties win elections to parliament', BBC News, 21 January 2012, http://www.bbc.co.uk/news/world-middle-east-16665748 (accessed 16 June 2022).

11. Haithem Ahmed, 'Egyptian court sentences ex-President Morsi to 25 years for spy case', *Jerusalem Post*, 16 September 2017, http://www.jpost.com/Middle -East/Egyptian-court-sentences-ex-President-Morsi-to-25-years-for-spy-case-50 5237 (accessed 16 June 2022).

12. There is an extensive bibliography on the Muslim Brotherhood. See, for example, Barry Rubin (ed.), *The Muslim Brotherhood: The Organization and Policies of a Global Islamist Movement* (New York: Palgrave Macmillan, 2010); Tarek Osman, *Egypt on the Brink: From Nasser to the Muslim Brotherhood* (New Haven, CT, and London: Yale University Press, 2013); Eric Trager, *Arab Fall: How the Muslim Brotherhood Won and Lost Egypt in 891 Days* (Washington, DC: Georgetown University Press, 2016); Martyn Frampton, *The Muslim Brotherhood and the West: A History of Enmity and Engagement* (Cambridge, MA: Belknap Press, 2018).

13. Hassan al-Banna, 'Our Mission', in International Islamic Federation of Student Organizations, *Majmu'at Rasa'il al-Imam al-Shahid Hasan al-Banna* ('Collection of Messages of the Martyr Imam Hassan al-Banna') (Kuwait City: International Islamic Federation of Student Organizations, 1996), p. 83.

14. Hassan al-Banna, 'Toward the Light', in Roxanne L. Euben and Muhammad Qasim Zaman (eds), *Princeton Readings in Islamist Thought: Texts and Contexts from al-Banna to Bin Laden* (Princeton, NJ: Princeton University Press, 2009), p. 66.

15. Hasan al-Banna, *Memoirs of Hasan al-Banna Shaheed* (Karachi: International Islamic Publishers, 1982), p. 180.

16. Sayyid Qutb, *A Child from the Village* (Syracuse, NY: Syracuse University Press, 2004), p. 127.

17. Magdi Abdelhadi, 'The Muslim Brotherhood connects with Egypt's

rural majority', *The Guardian*, 25 June 2012, https://www.theguard
ian.com/commentisfree/2012/jun/25/muslim-brotherhood-egypt (accessed
16 June 2022).

18. Sayyid Qutb, *Milestones*, rev. ed. (Chicago: American Trust, 2005), p. 66.
19. Ibid., p. 67.
20. Mawil Izzi Dien, 'Islam and the Environment: Towards an "Islamic" Ecumenical
    View', *Quranica*, vol. 5, no. 2, 2013, 39–40.
21. Yusuf al-Qaradawi, *Faith and Life* (Cairo: Al-Falah Foundation, 2004),
    p. 73.
22. 'A conversation with Sheikh Yusuf al-Qaradawi', IkhwanWeb, 27 December
    2010, http://www.ikhwanweb.com/article.php?id=27682 (accessed 16 June
    2022).
23. 'The Muslim Brotherhood's program 2005', IkhwanWeb, 13 June 2007, http://
    www.ikhwanweb.com/article.php?id=811 (accessed 17 June 2022).
24. 'The electoral programme of the Muslim Brotherhood for Shura Council in
    2007', IkhwanWeb, 14 June 2007, http://www.ikhwanweb.com/article.php?id
    =822 (accessed 17 June 2022).
25. Ibid.
26. 'Letter from the MB new chairman Mohammed Badie', IkhwanWeb, 16
    January 2010, http://www.ikhwanweb.com/article.php?id=22665 (accessed 17
    June 2022).
27. 'MB chairman: Do no mischief on the earth, after it has been set in order',
    IkhwanWeb, 6 May 2010, http://www.ikhwanweb.com/article.php?id=24637
    (accessed 17 June 2022).
28. Mohamed Abdel Raouf Abdel Hamid, 'Middle East Revolutions: An
    Environmental Perspective', Middle East Institute, 1 June 2011, https://www
    .mei.edu/content/middle-east-revolutions-environmental-perspective (accessed
    17 June 2022).
29. Ibid.
30. 'Muslim Brotherhood works to implement "renaissance project"', *Egypt
    Independent*, 24 December 2011, http://www.egyptindependent.com/mus
    lim-brotherhood-works-implement-renaissance-project/; 'Al-Shater outlines
    Egyptian renaissance project at first press conference', IkhwanWeb, 9 April
    2012, http://www.ikhwanweb.com/article.php?id=29859 (both accessed 17
    June 2022).
31. Nadine Marroushi, 'Renaissance man: Gehad El Haddad works as the Islamist
    project's pragmatist', *Egypt Independent*, 31 July 2012, http://www.egyptinde

pendent.com/renaissance-man-gehad-el-haddad-works-islamist-project-s-prag matist/ (accessed 17 June 2022).

32. 'FJP chair: FJP visions for Egypt's future', IkhwanWeb, 6 January 2012, http:// www.ikhwanweb.com/article.php?id=29518 (accessed 17 June 2022).

33. Steven Viney, 'Environmentalists disappointed with holdover minister', *Egypt Independent*, 9 August 2012, http://www.egyptindependent.com/environment alists-disappointed-holdover-minister/ (accessed 17 June 2022).

34. والحماية الوفاء من تاريخ ..النيل ونهر الإخوان ('The Brotherhood and the river Nile: a history of loyalty and protection'), Ikhwan Online, 22 October 2019, https:// www.ikhwanonline.com/article/237266 (accessed 17 June 2022).

35. Ibid.

36. In fact, al-Banna had called for the unification of Egypt and Sudan, which would have presumably solved the water dispute between the two countries. See والسودان سيناء :عن يكتب البنا حسن الشهيد الإمام ('Imam Hassan al-Banna writes about Sinai and Sudan'), Ikhwan Online, 28 April 2012, https://www.ikhwanonline. com/article/107234/ (accessed 17 June 2022).

37. 'Muslim Brotherhood MP warns against pollution of Nile River', IkhwanWeb, 20 May 2008, http://www.ikhwanweb.com/article.php?id=17137 (accessed 17 June 2022).

38. 'Muslim Brotherhood 2008 municipal election platform', IkhwanWeb, 9 March 2008, https://www.ikhwanweb.com/article.php?id=16257 (accessed 17 June 2022).

39. 'Text of Selmi's controversial supra-constitutional principles', IkhwanWeb, 4 November 2011, http://www.ikhwanweb.com/article.php?id=29360 (accessed 17 June 2022).

40. Freedom and Justice Party, 'Election Program 2011', p. 33, https://www.scribd .com/document/73955131/FJP-Program-En (accessed 17 June 2022).

41. Interview with former minister of planning and international co-operation Amr Darrag, 3 June 2019 (email correspondence).

42. 'Egypt warns Ethiopia over Nile dam', Al Jazeera, 11 June 2013, http://www .aljazeera.com/news/africa/2013/06/201361144413214749.html (accessed 17 June 2022).

43. Ibid.

44. 'Muslim Brotherhood: Official and popular diplomacy will resolve any water crisis', IkhwanWeb, 29 May 2013, http://www.ikhwanweb.com/article.php?id =30983&ref=search.php (accessed 17 June 2022).

45. Ibid.

46. 'Egyptians paying for Sisi's selling out of Egypt historical Nile water share', IkhwanWeb, 27 December 2015, http://www.ikhwanweb.com/article.php?id= 3238 (accessed 17 June 2022).

47. مصر نيل ('Egypt's Nile is a red line'), Ikhwan Online, 6 July 2020, www.ikhwanonline.com/article/240362 (accessed 17 June 2022).

48. Securitisation is the process of transforming an issue into a security threat. See Barry Buzan, Ole Wæver and Jaap de Wilde, *Security: A New Framework for Analysis* (Boulder, CO: Lynne Rienner, 1998).

49. Yusuf al-Qaradawi, *The Lawful and Prohibited in Islam*, Wisdom International School for Higher Education Studies (WISHES), n.d., p. 172, https://web.ar chive.org/web/20191101111748/http://www.usislam.org/pdf/Lawful&Prohibi ted.pdf (accessed 28 June 2022).

50. 'MP: 400,000 pigs in Cairo threaten spread of human epidemic', IkhwanWeb, 27 April 2009, http://www.ikhwanweb.com/article.php?id=20015 (accessed 17 June 2022).

51. 'Morsi called Israelis "descendants of apes and pigs" in 2010 video', *Haaretz*, 4 January 2013, https://www.haaretz.com/2013-01-04/ty-article/morsi-cal led-israelis-apes-and-pigs-in-2010/0000017f-dc67-db22-a17f-fcf7a27f0000 (accessed 17 June 2022).

52. See Constitution of the Arab Republic of Egypt 2012, available at http://www .wipo.int/edocs/lexdocs/laws/en/eg/eg047en.pdf (accessed 17 June 2022).

53. See Kristen A. Stilt, 'Constitutional Innovation and Animal Protection in Egypt', *Law and Social Inquiry*, vol. 43, no. 4, 2018, p. 1375.

54. See 'Constitution of the Arab Republic of Egypt 2014', 18 January 2014, available at http://www.sis.gov.eg/Newvr/Dustor-en001.pdf (accessed 17 June 2022).

55. Mariam Rizk, 'Air pollution: new attempts to tackle Cairo's black cloud', BBC News, 7 March 2017, http://www.bbc.co.uk/news/world-middle-east-3910 8213 (accessed 17 June 2022).

56. 'Muslim Brotherhood 2008 municipal election platform'.

57. Wickham, *The Muslim Brotherhood*, p. 273.

58. Interview with former minister of planning and international co-operation Amr Darrag, 3 June 2019 (email correspondence).

59. Ibid.

60. '"Clean Homeland" campaign launched today in Cairo and other governorates', IkhwanWeb, 27 July 2012, http://www.ikhwanweb.com/article.php?id=30212 (accessed 17 June 2022).

61. Ibid.

62. Does Vandousselaere, 'Greenwashing the Brotherhood', *Green Prophet*, 18 April 2012, https://www.greenprophet.com/2012/04/greenwashing-egypt-brotherh ood/ (accessed 17 June 2022).

63. Freedom and Justice Party, 'Election Program 2011', p. 34.

64. Ibid.

65. Ibid.

66. 'MB MP: Against sabotage even if to halt gas exports to Israel', IkhwanWeb, 12 January 2009, http://www.ikhwanweb.com/article.php?id=19026 (accessed 17 June 2022).

67. 'MB MP requests ending of gas exports to Israel to accommodate Egypt's demands', IkhwanWeb, 24 August 2010, http://www.ikhwanweb.com/article .php?id=26148 (accessed 17 June 2022).

68. Freedom and Justice Party, 'Election Program 2011', p. 28.

69. On Morsi's foreign policy vis-à-vis Israel see Zack Gold, 'Why Israel will miss Morsi', *Foreign Affairs*, 20 August 2012, http://www.foreignaffairs.com/articles /139835/zack-gold/why-israel-will-miss-morsi (accessed 17 June 2022).

70. 'Jordan seeks to reopen natural gas supply from Egypt', *Times of Israel*, 7 November 2012, http://www.timesofisrael.com/jordan-seeks-to-reopen-natural -gas-supply-from-egypt/ (accessed 17 June 2022).

71. Vandousselaere, 'Greenwashing the Brotherhood'.

72. El-Haddad was born in Alexandria in 1981 and studied architectural engineer- ing at the local university. He is the son of Essam El-Haddad, who is a member of the Brotherhood's Guidance Office. He was employed for some time by the Clinton Foundation's Climate Initiative. Gehad El-Haddad acted as a media spokesman for the Brotherhood from May 2013 until his arrest by the Egyptian military in September the same year.

73. 'Egypt: Electricity minister reports on Dabaa nuclear program to Morsi', AllAfrica, 9 July 2012, http://allafrica.com/stories/201207091559.html (accessed 17 June 2022).

74. 'Egypt invites Russia to mine uranium, build nuclear power plants', Russia Today, 20 April 2013, https://www.rt.com/news/putin-morsi-nuclear-uranium -132/

75. See Raymond Stock, 'Egypt: The Muslim Brotherhood Bomb?', Gatestone Institute, 7 September 2012, https://www.gatestoneinstitute.org/3333/egypt -muslim-brotherhood-bomb (accessed 17 June 2022).

76. Israel Elad Altman, 'Egypt', in Barry Rubin (ed.), *Guide to Islamist Movements* (Armonk, NY: M. E. Sharpe, 2010), vol. 1, p. 240.

77. Yusuf al-Qaradawi, *Fiqh al-Jihad* ('The Jurisprudence of Jihad') (Cairo: Wehbe Press, 2009), pp. 612–25.

78. Hassan Al-Banna, 'Message of the Teachings', in International Islamic Federation of Student Organizations, *Majmu'at Rasa'il al-Imam al-Shahid Hasan al-Banna* ('Collection of Messages of the Martyr Imam Hassan al-Banna') (Kuwait City: International Islamic Federation of Student Organizations, 1996), p. 7.

79. Ibid., p. 9.

80. Anwar Sadat Chair for Peace and Development, University of Maryland, 2012 Public Opinion Survey, p. 7, https://www.brookings.edu/wp-content/uploads/2016/06/Egypt_Poll_Results.pdf (accessed 17 June 2022).

81. Ibid., p. 8.

82. See Stilt, 'Constitutional Innovation and Animal Protection in Egypt', p. 1368.

83. Ninette S. Fahmy, 'The Performance of the Muslim Brotherhood in the Egyptian Syndicates: An Alternative Formula for Reform?', *Middle East Journal*, vol. 52, no. 4, 1998, pp. 551–62.

84. Badie, 'Do no mischief on the earth'.

85. Vandousselaere, 'Greenwashing the Brotherhood'.

86. 'الإسلامي التراث في البيئة نظافة' ('The cleanliness of the environment in Islamic heritage'), Ikhwan Online, 24 February 2010, http://www.ikhwanonline.com/Mobile/MArticle.asp?ArtID=60911&SecID=293.

3

HIZB UT-TAHRIR AND THE ENVIRONMENT

Hizb ut-Tahrir al-Islami (the Islamic Party of Liberation) has thousands of members in more than thirty-five countries across five continents.[1] It was established by Taqiuddin an-Nabhani, a Palestinian Islamic scholar, in East Jerusalem in 1953. In the early 1950s, he developed his political vision claiming that the restoration of the Caliphate was the only solution for the revival of the Muslim world.[2] An-Nabhani proposed three stages of action: recruitment of members and establishment of cells, spreading the group's propaganda to Islamise society, and the takeover of a Muslim-majority country to serve as the nucleus of the Caliphate.[3] From the beginning, the group declared its intention to follow the example of the Prophet Muhammad, who did not use violence before establishing the first Islamic state in Medina.

An-Nabhani's political vision was based on well-established principles of Islamic governance, such as *al-amr bi-l-ma'ruf wa l-nahy 'an il-munkar* (enjoining the right and forbidding the wrong), *shura* (consultation) and *al-muhasaba* (calling rulers to account).[4] He envisioned an omnipotent caliph who would rule with wisdom and benevolence. The Palestinian scholar implicitly embraced a Sunni-oriented understanding of the future Islamic state. The Sunni orientation of Hizb ut-Tahrir became more obvious in the 1970s, when Ayatollah Khomeini proposed the system of *vilayat-i faqih* (the guardianship of the jurist), based on 'the most sacred canonical sources of Shi'i Islam'.[5]

Following the Iranian Revolution of 1979, the group approached Khomeini and asked him to become caliph of all Muslims. He rejected the offer because Hizb ut-Tahrir's political programme did not resonate with Shi'a beliefs.[6]

An-Nabhani had failed to register Hizb ut-Tahrir as a legal party in Jordan. The official excuse was that the group rejected the institution of monarchy and promoted pan-Islamism.[7] Consequently, the Jordanian authorities issued a decree banning the party and arrested its leadership in March 1953.[8] Despite its clandestine status, Hizb ut-Tahrir managed to propagate its ideology in Jordan and expand to neighbouring countries. Its members endured arrests and torture by hostile authorities without resorting to political violence, although the group was implicated in army coups in Jordan and Iraq.[9] From the 1950s through to the 1970s, it remained active in certain Middle Eastern countries (for example, Lebanon and Syria).

Hizb ut-Tahrir has a pyramidal hierarchical structure that protects it from factionalism. At the lowest level, members and new recruits are organised in study circles (halaqah) of five people. The head of each study circle (mushrif) supervises junior members. At the district level, there is a local committee (naqib) which is responsible for the administration of group affairs in a certain city or town. At the provincial level, there is a committee headed by a provincial representative (mu'tamad) who oversees group activities. The mu'tamad is appointed by the central committee of the international party, headed by the supreme leader (amir) of Hizb ut-Tahrir.[10]

The group has proposed a constitution allegedly based on the Qur'an and the Sunna.[11] Thus, it has criticised countries like Sudan and Pakistan for claiming to be Islamic states, since they do not fulfil all criteria.[12] Additionally, Hizb ut-Tahrir has denounced the declaration of a caliphate by ISIS because it did not follow the proper methodology.[13] The group wants to re-establish the Islamic state that existed in the seventh century under the Prophet Muhammad and his first four successors, namely the Rightly Guided Caliphate (al-khulafa al-rashidun). The Islamic system of government must include the following principles:

- Sovereignty is for Shari'a and not for the umma.
- Authority is for the umma because the appointment of a caliph is its God-given right and the caliph governs the umma on its behalf.

- The appointment of a caliph is an obligation on all Muslims. There must be only one caliph in the Islamic State.
- The caliph alone has the right to adopt and enforce laws and legislation.[14]

An-Nabhani died in Beirut on 20 December 1977. He was replaced by Abdul Qadeem Zaloom, a founding member and a fellow Palestinian who was also trained as a teacher in Egypt. The new leader was credited with the expansion of the group outside the Middle East. When Zaloom died in April 2003, he was succeeded by Ata Abu al-Rashta, an Egyptian-educated civil engineer of Palestinian origin and former party spokesman in Jordan. The new leader probably resides in Beirut.

The group has a proactive recruitment strategy focusing on university students, professionals and businessmen to gain influence in certain segments of the society. Since the early 1980s, it has gradually expanded into the Muslim communities of Europe, sub-Saharan Africa and south-east Asia. As a result, Hizb ut-Tahrir must now address audiences with different social characteristics and needs. The group has increasingly used the Internet and the new media to spread its ideology.

The chapter first examines the group's general perspective on the environment, based on the writings of its founder and subsequent documents. Next, it describes Hizb ut-Tahrir's position on water management, which is an issue of contention in many regions. The question of animal rights is seen by Hizb ut-Tahrir as a battleground between Islam and other religions. Also, the group has addressed the implications of pollution in Muslim-majority countries and offered its own perspective on energy issues. Finally, the chapter examines the role of religion in the emergence of Hizb ut-Tahrir's environmentalism.

Hizb ut-Tahrir's General Perspective on the Environment

In the beginning, Hizb ut-Tahrir overlooked environmental issues, probably due to lack of awareness and knowledge about the scale of the problem. Another explanation is that there was no homegrown movement to campaign for ecology in Jordan at the time. During the early postwar period, an-Nabhani mostly focused on the ideological battle against Western colonialism. Even his later writings were silent on environmental problems.

Nonetheless, Hizb ut-Tahrir's constitution includes a brief description about how the future Islamic state would deal with the disposal of land. According to Article 129:

> Tithed land (*al-ushriyyah*) constitutes land within the Arabian Peninsula and land whose owners had embraced Islam whilst possessing the land [for example, Indonesia]. Tax land (*al-kharaajiyyah*) is all land, other than the Arabian Peninsula, which was opened by conquest. *Al-ushriyyah* land, together with its benefits, is owned by individuals. *Al-kharaajiyyah* land is owned by the State, and individuals own its benefits. Everyone has the right to exchange, through contracts, tithed land and the benefits from tax land.[15]

The division between tithed and tax land is an essential part of the group's land policy.

In *The Economic System of Islam*, an-Nabhani elaborated on the question of land management. He explained that even if the inhabitants of a tract of land embrace Islam or sell it to Muslims, it will remain *al-kharaajiyyah* until the Day of Judgment because it is war booty. In this case, the new Muslim landlords must pay both *kharaj* and *'ushr*.[16] For non-Muslims, *kharaj* is considered like *jizya* (a poll tax paid by non-Muslims). If the land is *al-ushriyyah*, the owners must pay *zakat* to the authorities; this is one-tenth of the actual production of the land if it is irrigated by rainwater and one-twentieth if it is irrigated artificially. For this rule, an-Nabhani used the *hadith* 'One tenth is put on what is irrigated by the rivers and rain and half of the tenth is put on what is irrigated by the waterwheel', as evidence.[17] The distinction between *al-kharaajiyyah* and *al-ushriyyah* land can be found in early Islamic history, but Article 131 clarifies that 'leasing land, whether *al-ushriyyah* land or *al-kharaajiyyah* land, for agriculture is forbidden. Sharecropping of land planted with trees is permitted and sharecropping on all other land is forbidden.'[18]

Additionally, an-Nabhani examined the concept of *ihya' al-mawat* (cultivation of barren land), expressing the opinion that both Muslim and non-Muslim citizens of the Caliphate could claim such land irrespective of whether it is *al-kharaajiyyah* or *al-ushriyyah*. The new owner must use the land, otherwise after three years he loses the right of ownership. For this rule, an-Nabhani mentioned the consensus (*ijma'*) of the Companions.[19] Despite their archaic meaning, the group still considers the terms *'ushr* and *kharaj* as relevant and applicable to the modern world; they define 'Islam's 'land policies'. Whether in terms of revenues or in terms of fencing unused land, this can have massive implications in 'feudal' lands like Pakistan.[20]

Progressively, the group came to adopt an agenda that combines environmental concerns and neo-caliphatist ambitions. Yet, the starting point is the instrumentalisation of history that asserts the superiority of Islamic civilisation. Thus, Hizb ut-Tahrir has provided a nostalgic account of Muslim Spain's environmental management and urban planning. From its point of view, the combination of architecture and nature illustrates the balanced approach of Islam to environmental responsibility and stewardship. The group has argued:

> The Arabs introduced irrigation and agricultural methods that transformed [Muslim Spain] into a garden. Cotton, rice, sugar cane, asparagus, oranges, lemons, and pomegranates were some of the plants and fruits brought from outside and cultivated in Spain . . . The famous gardens of Persia, Spain, and Morocco, with well-planned arrangements of trees, shrubs, and flowers, with their filled floors, their rivulets and fountains of water built with an aesthetic taste, establishing harmony between architecture and vegetation, throws lights on their interest in agriculture, gardening, and love for flowers.[21]

The idealisation of al-Andalus (Muslim Spain) serves as a valuable cultural resource that evokes collective memories of a distant glorious past. In effect, it is portrayed as an environmental utopia in which aesthetics and functionality meet. From Hizb ut-Tahrir's perspective, this historical example proves the compatibility of Islam and ecology.

This compatibility is in sharp contradiction with the current environmental crises in the Muslim world. The group is not against science, *per se*. On the contrary, it has argued that 'science flourished under Islam'.[22] For this purpose, it has provided a list of scientific achievements by Muslim scholars during the Middle Ages, including new irrigation and agricultural methods.[23] Nevertheless, only in the late 2000s did the group decide to offer a blueprint for its proposed environmental policy. In December 2009, during the climate change conference that took place in Copenhagen, the Danish branch published a pamphlet titled *The Environmental Problem: Its Causes and Islam's Solution*. The group declared:

> According to the capitalistic logic, priorities of profit size and maximization exceed protecting the environment and human dignity. Since the implementation of capitalism is the cause of the apparent destruction which man and the environment suffer from, the sensible person should wonder about the motives of the capitalists' concern about mankind's future life and the preservation and protection of the environment![24]

This analysis blamed Western governments and corporations for being greedy and overexploiting the planet. Such criticism clearly resembles that of secular environmental groups, which identified capitalism as the cause of ecological disasters. Now, however, the (secular) environmental discourse is increasingly controlled by pro-capitalist actors who argue that new technologies developed by the private sector could solve environmental problems.[25]

Yet, Hizb ut-Tahrir's understanding of environmental matters is permeated by an anti-capitalist discourse. In fact, the group has borrowed ideas and concepts from the environmental movement of the 1970s and 1980s.[26] More specifically, it has been influenced by the environmental justice sub-movement, which has focused on environmental racism, climate justice, food sovereignty, land-grabbing and water justice.[27] From Hizb ut-Tahrir's perspective, the pursuit of environmental justice is associated with confronting Western secularism and capitalism. The group has promoted a vision of environmental responsibility connected with the restoration of the Caliphate. The all-powerful state would enforce Shari'a rules and bring environmental justice. It is a state-centric understanding of environmental management that conflicts with the community-oriented position of secular environmentalists.

Thus, the group has described how the future Islamic state would tackle environmental challenges. While the caliph would be the supreme leader, Hizb ut-Tahrir has proposed a judicial system of monitoring the caliphate's environmental policy. It would consist of three judges. The first would be the supervisory judge (*qadi al-hizba*), who would check the compliance of factories, hospitals and markets with Shari'a environmental rules. Moreover, this judge would inspect and supervise the environmental activities of companies. The second would be the judge of disputes (*qadi al-khusamat*), who would deal with lawsuits of people who have been exposed to toxic waste and pollution. Finally, the judge of unjust acts (*qadi al-madhalim*) would resolve disputes that arise between the ruler and the citizens of the caliphate in the area of environmental protection.[28] In this way, Hizb ut-Tahrir's caliphate would have a strong judicial system to prevent abuses of power from occurring. It is described as a system of checks and balances that could increase accountability and transparency that Western societies supposedly lack.

Nevertheless, the group has adjusted environmentalism to its grandiose political ambitions. Like its nemesis, capitalism, the group has proposed not an ecocentric but an anthropocentric policy. From its point of view, humanity is entitled to control nature and its resources. The priority is not to secure ecological sustainable development, but to build an industrialised caliphate that could confront its adversaries and achieve world hegemony. In September 1990, the current leader of Hizb ut-Tahrir, Ata Abu al-Rashta, gave a lecture in Amman titled 'The Manufacturing Policy and Building an Industrial State from the Viewpoint of Islam', where he offered a vision for the caliphate's industrial policy. In his words:

> The industry must be established on the basis of warfare, so that military industry would be the basis of heavy manufacturing as well as other industrial sectors . . . In Islam, the heavy manufacturing is inseparable from the military industry since it is the basis because it is the requirement of Jihad, which is the pinnacle of Islam.[29]

This is a vision of a powerful state in which the economy serves an aggressive defence policy aiming at territorial expansion. Harm to the environment is a collateral damage Muslims must bear.

The establishment of a perfect Islamic state can take a significant amount of time. Therefore, Hizb ut-Tahrir has also focused on more urgent matters. For instance, it has examined the outbreaks of famine in African countries which have Muslim majorities or significant Muslim minorities. Unlike many environmental groups, Hizb ut-Tahrir has not viewed climate change as the prime cause. Instead, it has blamed international organisations and Western powers for the suffering of local Muslims. For instance, the group has maintained that 'deaths from famine are man-made and the causes are always linked back to wars, conflicts, corrupt governments, neglect by rulers'.[30] Hizb ut-Tahrir has claimed that the proposed caliphate would be more prepared to deal with famines because 'if any province of the Khilafah suffers a disaster such as a famine then funds will be collected from all other provinces to alleviate the problem. The Charities Department (*Diwan as-Sadaqat*) and the Public Properties department of the Treasury (*Bait ul-Mal*) will allocate funds to the famine.'[31] It is a simplistic suggestion for dealing with such a complex problem facing many communities, but again it serves the purpose of promoting the caliphate as an ideal state.

In summary, Hizb ut-Tahrir's general perspective on the environment is based on the instrumentalisation of Islamic history, an anti-capitalist discourse with Islamist political vocabulary, and the notion of Islamic superiority. The chapter now turns to three distinct areas of Hizb ut-Tahrir's environmentalist activity, namely water management, animals, and pollution and energy.

Water Management

Hizb ut-Tahrir has systematically focused on water resources, perhaps because most Muslim-majority countries have suffered from water scarcity or floods. The group has argued that water is a public property (*al-milkiyyah al-ammah*) due to the following *hadith*: 'Muslims are partners in three things, in water, green pastures and fire.' Yet, Hizb ut-Tahrir holds the opinion that

> if one scrutinised the issue [one] would find that the Prophet allowed the possession of water in At-Taif and Khaybar by individuals, and they actually possessed it for the purpose of irrigating their plants and farms ... [therefore] water could be possessed by individuals, but this is prohibited if the community cannot manage to live without it.[32]

In this way, the group has adopted a pragmatic position regarding the public-private balance in water management and ownership.

Hizb ut-Tahrir has also focused on the issue of water scarcity. According to Wasif Abu Yusuf, a member of the group, 'water scarcity can be a result of two mechanisms: physical (absolute) water scarcity and economic water scarcity — where physical water scarcity is a result of inadequate natural water resources to supply a region's demand, and economic water scarcity is a result of poor management of the sufficient available water resources'.[33] Basically, the group has attempted to conceptualise the causes of droughts in the Muslim world. The differentiation between physical and economic water scarcity is logical and useful.

Most secular environmental groups have blamed climate change for floods. In contrast, Hizb ut-Tahrir has promoted an alternative explanation. From its point of view, the cause is corruption, a social practice embedded in local context; floods are human-induced catastrophes that can trigger social upheaval. Following the 2017 torrential rain disaster in Mombasa, the Kenyan branch argued that 'corruption from top leaders to the masses is the cause of this disaster. People sell or buy plots to build places where they are not supposed to . . . [O]fficials from Nation Land Commission do not follow through these cases because they have been silenced in one way or another through bribery.'[34] In a similar fashion, the group has attributed the 2014 floods in Kashmir to the Indian government's decision to allow 'the commercialization of wetlands and waterways'.[35]

Like other Islamist groups, Hizb ut-Tahrir has viewed rivers as public property. More specifically, it has argued that 'the great rivers such as Tigris, Euphrates and the Nile are a public property that no one privately owns or uses it'.[36] This position certainly takes into account the geographical and economic realities in the greater Middle East. The group has also called for the 'religionisation' of river management. Since the question of river access has preoccupied many Muslim communities, Hizb ut-Tahrir has again instrumentalised Islamic history to offer a blueprint for action. It has argued that the Caliphate 'used to enable the people to attain the benefit from the major rivers for drinking, domestic utility, feeding the livestock, to water the agricultural lands and for travel and transportation'.[37] From its point of view, the original caliphate's management of major rivers indicates Islam's wisdom and fairness.

Furthermore, Hizb ut-Tahrir has described the future policy of the caliphate regarding international rivers. In this case, the new entity would sign an agreement with the neighbouring states about the joint management of those rivers. If diplomacy fails, the group has also considered the possibility of military action, as evidenced by the following quote:

If an act of aggression or hostility occurs from another state by preventing the flow of water of the major river from reaching the Islamic state or by its exploitation in a manner that harms the interests of the Muslims, then the state will take the political, economic and military measures that enable it to remove the harm brought about by the other state, even if the matter reaches the point of war against the aggressing state to take back the *haqq* (right).[38]

In this context, the concept of *haqq* means 'right' in the sense of something owed to others.[39] It is a morally robust claim implying a God-given mandate over such rivers.

Currently, the River Indus has become a source of tension between India and Pakistan. As a result, Hizb ut-Tahrir has accused the Pakistani leadership of submitting to the US government. It has claimed:

Pakistan abandoned claims over three rivers under the Indus water treaty. And following US dictates now is imperilling Pakistan's access to the remaining rivers and making them subservient to the whims of the belliger-ent Hindu State. The water problem was created because India occupied part of Kashmir and it will only be solved by liberating occupied Kashmir . . . as part of the efforts to return the Indian Subcontinent to the rule of Islam, as it was for centuries.[40]

Therefore, the group has advocated the 'liberation' of Kashmir as a possible solution to Pakistan's water problem because the source of the Indus lies in the Muslim-majority Indian province. This is a rather typical Islamist under-standing of the water dispute between the two countries.[41] The Pakistani branch goes one step further, however, advocating the Islamisation of the whole Indian subcontinent. Thus, water security is a means to achieve ter-ritorial expansion.

Additionally, the Sudanese branch of Hizb ut-Tahrir has closely moni-tored the series of negotiations between Egypt, Sudan and Ethiopia regarding the management of the Blue Nile. Like the Muslim Brotherhood in Egypt, Hizb ut-Tahrir has accused the Ethiopian leadership of supporting a hidden Israeli agenda to gain access to regional water resources. Moreover, the local branch condemned the regime of Omar al-Bashir for supporting the construction of Ethiopia's Grand Renaissance Dam on the Blue Nile, which is the main tributary of the River Nile.[42] For this reason, it called for solidarity between Sudan and Egypt and pan-Islamic unity.[43]

Other branches of Hizb ut-Tahrir have considered a diverse set of water-related challenges. Following the Fourth Water Conference in Kabul in March 2017, the Afghan branch criticised the government for promoting water management based solely on 'national interests' (see appendix). The group has argued that 'water resources that begin and end within the territory of Islamic lands – regardless of how many countries they pass through – are the common property of all Muslims. No single country or person can claim ownership'.[44] In other words, Hizb ut-Tahrir has advocated joint management of water resources as a source of Muslim unity.

The group has also addressed environmental justice issues in sub-Saharan Africa. In Kenya, the local branch has criticised the government for launching 'an operation to evict over 40,000 people from Mau Forest . . . [T]he Forest is the prime source of numerous rivers which feeds Lake Victoria the source of the Nile river . . . [P]oor management of resources alongside inhumane land policies by the secular government has brought all this mess'.[45] Hizb ut-Tahrir has raised the question of fair treatment of local communities, while expressing a concern over the future of the Nile river system. This seemingly non-religious environmentalism draws its legitimacy from perceptions of social injustices that often result from tribal discrimination.

Apart from being a precious resource, water has also a metaphorical meaning that Hizb ut-Tahrir has not ignored. In *Concepts of Hizb ut-Tahrir*, Taqiuddin an-Nabhani argued:

> The society is similar to water in a large kettle: if anything that causes the temperature to drop is placed beneath the kettle then the water freezes and transforms to ice. Similarly, if corrupted ideologies are introduced into the society then it would freeze in corruption and continue in deterioration and decline . . . However if flaming heat was put under the kettle, the water would warm and then boil and effuse an intense stirring vapour. Similarly, if the correct ideology was introduced into the society it would be a flame whose heat would transform the society to boiling point and then to a dynamic force.[46]

Thus, water could be a force of change leading to progress and salvation if it was used appropriately.

In summary, Hizb ut-Tahrir has paid increasing attention to water-related issues that have arisen in recent years. While branches have focused on different aspects of hydropolitics, the common denominator has always been the quest for the restoration of the caliphate, which would apply effective and sustainable management of water resources.

Animals

Hizb ut-Tahrir has stressed that 'Muslims are accountable to Allah for the way they treat animals'.[47] The group has declared that 'Islam prohibits hunting animals for sport, treating them cruelly, overburdening them, making them fight each other for entertainment, maiming them while alive and neglecting pets'.[48] For this purpose, it has used several *ahadith* as evidence that Muslims are required to respect animal rights.[49] It is fair to say that the group adheres to mainstream Islamic principles regarding relations with non-humans.

Against this background, Hizb ut-Tahrir has participated in a polarised debate about the selling of halal meat in Europe. In March 2014, Hizb ut-Tahrir Britain issued a detailed response to the president of the British Veterinary Association, which had called for an outright ban of halal slaughter in the United Kingdom. The group observed that 'animals continue to be used to test products before they are consumed by humans in the West, not only by the pharmaceutical industry for drugs, but also for cosmetics'.[50] According to Hizb ut-Tahrir, the problem lies in the profit-oriented treatment of animals as objects. It is hardly a coincidence that the group raised the issue of animal testing, which has provoked much controversy in the West.

Nevertheless, the debate over Islam and animal rights is not as simple as it may seem. From Hizb ut-Tahrir's perspective, '[Westerners] do not have a monopoly on animal welfare when in fact such topics were a normal part of Islamic teachings more than 1,000 years ago . . . [T]here is a trend to attack Muslims and try to convince them that their way of life is barbaric.'[51] Hizb ut-Tahrir has embraced the conflict-of-civilisations thesis to explain the tensions over halal meat.[52] Western governments have supposedly conspired against Islam out of fear and aggressiveness. Thus, the production and consumption of halal meat has become a contentious issue with serious political and social implications.

In India, the question of cattle slaughter has proved particularly heated. Hindu nationalists have long blamed Muslims and Christians for the slaughtering of cows, which are considered sacred in Hinduism. On the other hand, Hizb ut-Tahrir has insisted that Hindus themselves have consumed beef and have exported it abroad.[53] It has argued that 'it would be hypocritical to prevent an animal from being slaughtered on compassionate grounds only to let it meander about the streets malnourished, feeding on plastic, paper, and even human waste thus developing a disease called "Pica"'.[54] In this way, the group has been able to shift the debate from the slaughter of cattle to the protection of stray cows. This tactic allows Hizb ut-Tahrir to appear compassionate, but also firm in its determination to defend the large Muslim community in the country.

Animal rights have also become an issue of contention in eastern Africa where Hizb ut-Tahrir has established a presence. The group has come close to defending the government of Tanzania against British allegations of corruption regarding illegal wildlife trade. In February 2014, the deputy media representative of Hizb ut-Tahrir in east Africa, Masoud Msellem, remarked that while 'poaching and smuggling of wildlife is a chronic problem in Tanzania . . . America uses it to cement itself in Tanzania especially in military matters . . . Britain . . . criticizes Tanzania . . . because of jealousy and paranoia . . . [The country] used to be a British fortress which has been captured by America.'[55] Interestingly, the group has long supported a theory about US–British antagonism that can explain geopolitical dynamics in the Muslim world.[56] The group was not defending animal rights but the principle of non-intervention in the domestic affairs of a sovereign country. According to Hizb ut-Tahrir, Western powers have used animal rights violations and the endangerment of wildlife to promote and defend their national interests. It is a claim that fits well with the narrative of Western neo-colonialism in the region.

The group perceives animal rights as important only because they serve the overarching goal of confronting its adversaries. While Hizb ut-Tahrir subscribes to the Islamic treatment of animals, its attitude is reactive – not proactive. It will take a position on animal rights only if Muslims are involved.

Pollution and Energy

Pollution is one of the most urgent and important problems in the Muslim world. Hizb ut-Tahrir has framed it as the inevitable consequence of capitalist development, blaming both Western governments and pro-Western elites. In effect, it has capitalised on anti-colonial sentiments that are still strong in many Muslim-majority countries.

Hizb ut-Tahrir has dismissed the Kyoto Protocol as a Western conspiracy and has criticised the Clean Development Mechanism for being 'imperialist' because they prevent developing countries from increasing their production.[57] Similarly, it has taken a critical stance on the Paris Agreement of 2016, which was signed by 195 countries. The group has observed that for such agreements

> to hold any substantial value or actually have a real impact on tackling climate change, they must be binding rather than voluntary with real repercussions if a country was not to adhere to them. However, the nature of capitalism will not permit this, as it will go against a fundamental aspect of its nature, the need for continuous economic growth.[58]

Once again, Hizb ut-Tahrir displays a polemic view on capitalism that highlights its ideological constraints.

Yet the group has accepted the need to battle climate change by clarifying that the future Islamic state 'would . . . follow the science. This is because technical matters demand consulting those with technical expertise.'[59] Moreover, Hizb ut-Tahrir has not excluded the possibility of seeking global solutions to environmental crises. Therefore, it has been argued,

> the Caliphate would want to engage in a global discussion, presenting Islamic solutions to human problems, working via treaty with other states where needs be or exposing the plans of colonial states to manipulate debates for their own interests. But the UN cannot be seen as a credible forum for this, with its rigged structure and supposedly 'legally binding nature'.[60]

Even in this instance, while retaining its pragmatism, the group has maintained its highly critical stance against the West and the liberal world order.

In this context, Hizb ut-Tahrir has perceived pollution as a failure of capitalism, which is inherently exploitative. According to the Bangladeshi branch, 'today Capitalists rule the world and their focus is on making quick cash rather than thinking of future generations'.[61] Hizb ut-Tahrir has also challenged notions of apathy and passivity that exist in Muslim societies, claiming that

> as Muslims we know that Allah will account us and therefore we should treat the earth and its resources with due consideration . . . The collective resources of the Muslim lands are ample to provide the umma and the world with energy . . . that will not cost heavily in people's health and pollute the air.[62]

In this way, the group has assigned responsibilities to Muslims themselves because they have a religious obligation to protect the environment and exploit resources with regard to future needs. The anti-capitalism of Hizb ut-Tahrir is not the end but the means to a better life.

In any case, the Bangladeshi branch has also argued that the coastal areas of the country are increasingly polluted as 'no proper management of toxic industrial waste has ever been taken by any ruling democratic regimes of Bangladesh'.[63] More specifically, it has accused prime minister Sheikh Hasima of being 'a puppet of the West' because she allows Western powers to exploit the country's resources.[64] Moreover, Hizb ut-Tahrir Bangladesh has used environmental issues as a political weapon against India. It has claimed that

> a coward belligerent state like India could make Bangladesh a dumping zone for their experiment and chemical wastes . . . when India has abandoned establishing coal-based power plant at their side of [the] Sundarban [delta], the same Indian company has established the said plant at our side of Sundarban to bring mayhem in our country's ecology.[65]

The group has preached anti-Indian conspiracy theories because Bangladesh's relations with neighbouring India have been strained in recent years.

In Malaysia, Hizb ut-Tahrir has criticised the government for ignoring air pollution. In June 2013, smoke from forest fires on the Indonesian island of Sumatra spread over large parts of Malaysia. The group claimed that both small farmers and big corporations were responsible for the smoke; the former burned the forests for a 'bowl of rice', whereas the latter did it for 'profit without regard of the consequences'. Thus, the local branch avoided confronting those who have practised 'slash and burn' agriculture and instead condemned the economic elite for the pollution of the air. The group explained that 'Islam does not forbid man from enjoying Allah's blessings, nor does it forbid him to work, nor gain earnings and wealth . . . However, Islam does not accept that some people overconsume while others suffer.'[66] Here, Hizb ut-Tahrir used the language of social justice to portray overconsumption as immoral behaviour. In other words, the group implicitly evoked the Islamic ethical principles of *mizan* (balance), *maslaha* (public interest) and *wasatiyya* (middleness).

In 2015, the spokeswoman of Hizb ut-Tahrir Indonesia, Iffah Ainur Rochmah, offered suggestions for the prevention of forest fires. She argued that 'the management of forests as public property must be made by the state for the benefit of the people . . . If forest and land fires still happen . . . the government will be held accountable for it.'[67] Therefore, Hizb ut-Tahrir has advocated a state-centric view of the management of forest fires that includes state-imposed education and community awareness, as well as government accountability.

Additionally, the Sudanese branch has proposed certain measures for the reduction of pollution. In October 2014, the group organised a workshop in Khartoum titled 'The Three Wings of Death: Cancer, Waste and Pollution Circle Sudan's Skies'. The deputy spokesman of Hizb ut-Tahrir Sudan, Mohammad Hashim, described the main goals of the anti-pollution policy of the future Islamic state as follows: banning the use of fertilisers and plastics; reviewing all sewerage systems; prohibiting the use of all carcinogenic substances in drinking water purification; eliminating emissions from factories; funding the construction of water facilities from the Treasury of the Islamic State (*Bait ul-Mal*); building infrastructure in line with environmental and health standards; and empowering the *qadi al-hizba* to eliminate corruption.[68] The local branch has apparently supported measures favoured by many environmentalists in Sudan and elsewhere. In particular, the banning of plastics has been discussed by many international organisations, governments and NGOs. In October 2018, for instance, the

European Parliament voted for a complete ban on single-use plastics to stop pollution.[69]

Simultaneously, Hizb ut-Tahrir has maintained an understanding of energy centred on oil and gas. It has repeatedly called for public ownership of energy in accordance to Shari'a. For instance, the Pakistani branch has argued that 'in Islam, gas is a public property that cannot be handed over to private owners who then profiteer at public expense. The benefit of gas, whether from its use directly or from its price from sales, is for looking after the affairs of the population collectively.'[70] Therefore, the group has not favoured a total de-hydrocarbonisation of energy systems. The Pakistani branch has explained that

> the umma possesses over half of the world's proven oil reserves and over forty percent of the world's proven gas reserves . . . [R]egarding developing other forms of electricity generation to meet future short falls, such as solar, tidal and wind generation, the Islamic ummah possess [sic] brilliant sons and daughters who are more than capable to deliver results.'[71]

Hizb ut-Tahrir does not wish to abandon the use of oil and gas for electricity generation because industrial growth takes precedence over environmental protection.

During the 2021–22 energy crisis, the group took the opportunity to denounce capitalism because Western energy companies 'acquire ownership of most of the world's petroleum products through various agreements and contracts, and then sell them worldwide at high prices and then the agent regimes of the Capitalists impose taxes on top of that'.[72] In effect, Hizb ut-Tahrir has attempted to capitalise on growing public discontent about high gas prices by stressing that 'Islamic Shariah rules on energy and taxes provide a clear and effective solution which removes this inhumane burden on the people by preventing the high price of oil and gas'.[73]

The question of nuclear energy is indicative of the way that environmental issues are sometimes approached by Hizb ut-Tahrir. Most environmental groups view nuclear energy as an existential threat to the environment, but Hizb ut-Tahrir has favoured its use both for peaceful and for military purposes. For example, the Bangladeshi branch has called for the 'large supplies of . . . uranium [to] be used in the power sector to supplement or replace gas usage. Uranium can also, be used in the research and development of nuclear-based weapons.'[74] From its point of view, nuclear energy is an important instrument of state power. The obsession with power can also explain why the group has fervently defended Pakistan's nuclear arsenal.[75] And yet, the possession and use of nuclear weapons goes against the Muslim faith because the principle of proportionality is the cornerstone of the Islamic law of war.[76]

The group has also occasionally discussed the importance of technology for environmental purposes. The starting point is the differentiation between *hadhara* (civilisation) and *madaniyya* (civil in the sense of secular). Hizb ut-Tahrir claims that a civilisation can be either a spiritual divine one (for example, Islamic civilisation) or a man-made one (for example, Western civilisation).[77] The term *madaniyya* refers to material objects produced by Western or universal science. As long as they are neutral and value-free, Hizb ut-Tahrir is not against using any universal technologies that can protect the environment.[78]

Overall, Hizb ut-Tahrir has viewed pollution as a problem caused by human failings. The West and its allies have acted irresponsibly to the point of endangering the ecological balance of the planet, whereas Islam can bring harmony and stability. The use of this Manichean logic can mobilise those Muslims who harbour anti-Western sentiments and worry about the deterioration of environmental conditions. At the same time, the group has followed an oil- and gas-centric approach that undermines its anti-pollution stance.

The Role of Religion

From the beginning, Hizb ut-Tahrir has promoted itself as the most authentic Islamist group. There are two reasons for this claim. First, its founder, Taqiuddin an-Nabhani, was an Islamic scholar who had studied at the world-famous al-Azhar University in Cairo and worked as a Shari'a judge in Palestine. His family history was remarkable. Both of his parents were scholars of Islamic jurisprudence. His maternal grandfather was Yusuf an-Nabhani, a prominent Palestinian judge who had himself studied at al-Azhar University and influenced the young Taqiuddin. Second, Hizb ut-Tahrir was established at a time when the Muslim Brotherhood was a popular group. An-Nabhani criticised the Brotherhood for not being 'Islamic' enough. His writings offered strong theological evidence to prove authenticity and claim superiority.

This strong attachment to Islamic sources has been internalised by Hizb ut-Tahrir's leaders and members. Although the current leadership lacks proper religious education, its statements always offer a justification based on the Qur'an and the *Sunna*. Hizb ut-Tahrir has relied on its self-perceived intellectual-theological supremacy to offer proposals and solutions that are seemingly Islamic. Still, it perceives the environment less as a spiritual space and more as a physical one where the *umma* needs to defend its interests.

Consequently, Hizb ut-Tahrir has maintained a holistic conception of the Muslim world by condemning sectarianism. Nonetheless, it remains a Sunni organisation with apparently no Shi'i following. The group does not accept the main Shi'a beliefs, like the infallibility of the twelve imams and the concept of the imamate. Hizb ut-Tahrir has only utilised Sunni *ahadith* and Sunni interpretations of Shari'a. The Sunni orientation is a taboo issue that has not been discussed by members openly. In theory, Hizb ut-Tahrir is open to both Sunni and Shi'a Muslims.

This illusion of Muslim unity is essential to the establishment of a future Islamic state. The group has envisioned a system of checks and balances for the implementation of the Caliphate's environmental policy, which is broad and flexible. Hizb ut-Tahrir has stressed self-reliance as a major goal of environmental policy, although there are economic and security implications. Hence, it has been against free trade by advocating a policy of autarky. For example, the group has criticised the Egyptian authorities for importing large quantities of wheat. It has claimed that 'Egypt prior to separation from the Islamic state was the largest source and producer of wheat in the region, and Egypt was self-sufficient and also exported wheat to the world . . . The problem in Egypt is not tied to agriculture, water resources or cultivable land.'[79] Hizb ut-Tahrir has provided an idealised view of Egypt's Islamic past to reinforce its messages of Muslim isolationism and anti-capitalism.

Hizb ut-Tahrir has also focused on water scarcity and water justice, defined as a combination of environmental and social justice applied to water governance. It has extensively examined international river disputes, involving Muslims and non-Muslims. Water is more than anything else a source of conflict between the imagined *umma* and its perceived enemies. Hizb ut-Tahrir has viewed rivers as a public property owned by Muslims and managed by authorities.

Equally, Hizb ut-Tahrir has chosen confrontation over compromise in animal affairs. The group has defended animal rights when it serves its political goals. Religious knowledge is not as static as Hizb ut-Tahrir suggests. For instance, the group has overlooked Hashem Najy Jazayery's approach to animal rights, mentioned in Chapter 1. The group's understanding of animals is not compassionate but dispassionate to the extent that it is indifferent. As a result, it has not promoted vegetarianism as part of a pious life, although a growing number of Muslims have stopped eating meat.[80]

Hizb ut-Tahrir has examined pollution prevention and control in different parts of the Muslim world, but again this interest is politically determined. The group has identified global capitalism as the main cause of pollution. In this way, it has ignored contemporary efforts to provide an Islamic perspective on climate change, such as the Islamic Declaration on Global Climate Change.[81] In regard to oil and gas, Hizb ut-Tahrir has followed the mainstream Islamic approach dictating that minerals cannot be privately owned.

In fairness, the group has sometimes tried to be Shari'a-compliant. Hizb ut-Tahrir's position on land management is indicative of its insistence on justification by faith. The constitution of the future Islamic state has provisions on the use of tithed land (al-ushriyyah) and tax land (al-kharaajiyyah). The former is owned by individuals, while the latter is owned by the state. The difference between them derives from Islamic law and history. Hizb ut-Tahrir has endorsed a faith-based differentiation between land owned by non-Muslims, who had to pay kharaj, and the land of Muslims, who were obliged to pay 'ushr. This position coheres with the traditional Islamic view on land management described in Chapter 1.

Many of Hizb ut-Tahrir's environmental positions are seemingly based on Islamic texts, rulings and principles because the quest for authenticity is an inherent element of its modus operandi. For this purpose, the group has started promoting the concept of taqwa, which means God-fearing piety or God consciousness.[82] A new emphasis on spirituality is emerging. Abdul Wahid, chair of the Executive Committee of Hizb ut-Tahrir Britain, has argued that 'Islam balances owning and enjoying the good things of life, against not making the possession of these things a goal in life'.[83] In effect, Hizb ut-Tahrir's anti-consumerism turns into anti-materialism.

Yet the group has not really engaged in theological-legal debates about the various aspects of the environmental crisis. Although the group has called for the application of Shari'a, it has not discussed how the higher objectives of Islamic law (*maqasid* of Shari'a) could protect the environment. Shari'a aims at benefiting both the individual and the community, but Hizb ut-Tahrir has used it to promote its political goals only.

In conclusion, Hizb ut-Tahrir is more consistent than the Muslim Brotherhood in offering theological evidence and argumentation for policy proposals. Although religious conformity is embedded in the group's policies, religion does not always dictate its decisions and responses. The extensive use of Islamic sources does not change the fundamental character of the group. Hizb ut-Tahrir is a political organisation with a religious orientation.

Notes

1. There is an extensive literature on Hizb ut-Tahrir. See, for example, Suha Taji-Farouki, *A Fundamental Quest: Hizb al-Tahrir and the Search for the Islamic Caliphate* (London: Grey Seal, 1996); Reza Pankhurst, *Hizb ut-Tahrir: The Untold History of the Liberation Party* (London: Hurst, 2016); Mohamed Nawab Mohamed Osman, *Hizbut Tahrir Indonesia and Political Islam: Identity, Ideology and Religio-Political Mobilization* (Abingdon: Routledge, 2018).

2. See Taqiuddin an-Nabhani, *A Warm Call from Hizb ut-Tahrir to the Muslims* (London: Al-Khilafah, 1962); Hizb ut-Tahrir, *Khilafah Is the Answer* (London: Al-Khilafah, 1989).

3. Hizb ut-Tahrir, *The Methodology of Huzb ut-Tahrir for Change* (London: Al-Khilafah, 1999), pp. 32–3.

4. See Anke Iman Bouzenita, 'Early Contributions to the Theory of Islamic Governance: 'Abd al-Rahman al-Awza'i', *Journal of Islamic Studies*, vol. 23, no. 2, 2012, p. 138.

5. Hamid Dabashi, *Theology of Discontent: The Ideological Foundations of the Islamic Revolution in Iran* (New York: New York University Press, 2006), p. 447.

6. Mahan Abedin, 'Al-Muhajiroun in the UK: An Interview with Sheikh Omar Bakri Mohammed', *Spotlight on Terror*, vol. 2, no. 5, 25 May 2005, https://jamestown.org/interview/al-muhajiroun-in-the-uk-an-interview-with-sheikh-omar-bakri-mohammed/ (accessed 20 June 2022).

7. Taji-Farouki, *A Fundamental Quest*, p. 6.

8. Amnon Cohen, *Political Parties in the West Bank under the Jordanian Regime, 1949–1967* (Ithaca, NY: Cornell University Press, 1982), p. 210.

9. International Crisis Group, *Radical Islam in Central Asia: Responding to Hizb ut-Tahrir* (Brussels: ICG, 2003), p. 3.

10. Taji-Farouki, *A Fundamental Quest*, pp. 115–30.

11. Hizb ut-Tahrir, *The Ruling System in Islam*, 5th ed. (London: Al-Khilafah, 1996), p. 20.

12. 'The elections law for the year 2018 contradicts Islam and enshrines falsehood', Hizb ut Tahrir Central Media Office, 23 November 2018, http://www.hizb -ut-tahrir.info/en/index.php/leaflet/sudan/16491.html; 'Pakistan's constitution is anything but Islamic', Hizb ut-Tahrir Britain, 13 July 2018, http://www.hizb.org.uk/viewpoint/pakistans-constitution-is-anything-but-islamic/ (both accessed 20 June 2022).

13. 'Media statement regarding ISIS's declaration in Iraq', Hizb ut-Tahrir Britain, 2 July 2014, http://www.hizb.org.uk/current-affairs/media-statement-regarding -isiss-declaration-in-iraq (accessed 20 June 2022).

14. Hizb ut-Tahrir, *The Ruling System in Islam*, pp. 43–9.

15. Taqiuddin an-Nabhani, *The Islamic State* (London: Al-Khilafah, 1990), pp. 264–5.

16. Taqiuddin an-Nabhani, *The Economic System in Islam* (London: Al-Khilafah, 1990), p. 122.

17. Ibid., p. 120.

18. An-Nabhani, *The Islamic State*, p. 265.

19. An-Nabhani cited Umar ibn al-Khattab, who said, 'The one who circles a land has no right in it after three years.' He made this statement in the presence of the *Sahaba*, who made no objection, confirming their consensus. See an-Nabhani, *The Economic System in Islam*, p. 72.

20. Interview with three members of Hizb ut-Tahrir, London, 13 December 2018.

21. Hizb ut-Tahrir, *Science and Islam* (London: Al-Khilafah, 2002), pp. 34–35.

22. Ibid, p. 13.

23. Ibid.

24. Hizb ut-Tahrir Denmark, *The Environmental Problem: Its Causes and Islam's Solution* (Copenhagen: Hizb ut-Tahrir Denmark, 2009), p. 25.

25. Gordon Hak, *Locating the Left in Difficult Times: Framing a Political Discourse for the Present* (Cham: Palgrave Macmillan, 2017), pp. 152–3.

26. On the environmental movement see John Callaghan, 'Environmental Politics, the New Left and the New Social Democracy', *Political Quarterly*, vol. 71, no. 3, 2000, 300–8.

27. Joan Martinez-Alier et al., 'Is There a Global Environmental Justice Movement?', *Journal of Peasant Studies*, vol. 43, no. 3, 2016, p. 731.

28. Hizb ut-Tahrir Denmark, *The Environmental Problem*, pp. 42–4.

29. Ata Abu al-Rashta, 'The Manufacturing Policy and Building an Industrial State from the Viewpoint of Islam', Amman, 18 September 1990, http://www.hizb -ut-tahrir.org/PDF/EN/en_books_pdf/Siyasat_al-Tasnii_EN_26.05_.2015_1_ .pdf (accessed 20 June 2022).

30. 'Famines are man-made disasters', Hizb ut-Tahrir Britain, 22 March 2017, http://www.hizb.org.uk/viewpoint/famines-are-man-made-disasters/ (accessed 20 June 2022).

31. Ibid.

32. *After the Arab Spring: The Islamic Khilafah – A Manifesto for Change*, Hizb ut-Tahrir Britain, June 2012, pp. 30–2, https://www.hizb.org.uk/wp-content/up loads/2012/07/The-Islamic-Khilafah-A-Manifesto-for-Change.pdf (accessed 20 June 2022).

33. Wasif Abu Yusuf, 'Mars discovering water and covering other cracks in capitalism', Hizb ut-Tahrir Britain, 14 October 2015, http://www.hizb.org.uk/view point/part-2-mars-discovering-water-and-covering-over-cracks-in-capitalism/ (accessed 20 June 2022).

34. Mgeni J. Salim, 'Effects of rain is a result of corruption in the country', Hizb ut-Tahrir Kenya, 10 June 2017.

35. 'Democratic rulers and politicians neglect to safeguard Kashmir from floods', Hizb ut-Tahrir Central Media Office, 25 September 2014, https://hizb-ut-tah rir.info/en/index.php/radio-broadcast/radio-broadcast/5791.html (accessed 18 July 2022)

36. 'An-Nahdha (Grand Renaissance) Dam and the Threats of Water War; Negligence of the Rulers and the Duty of the Ummah', Hizb ut-Tahrir Wilayah of Sudan, September 2017, p. 53, http://www.khilafah.com/images/images /PDF/Books/Sudan_Booklet_22.09.2017_EN.pdf (accessed 20 June 2022).

37. 'The Shar'i principles for dealing with rivers', Hizb ut Tahrir Central Media Office, 12 November 2016, http://hizb-ut-tahrir.info/en/index.php/qestions/ju risprudence-questions/11800.html (accessed 20 June 2022).

38. Ibid.

39. On the concept of *haqq* see Paul L. Heck, 'Knowledge', in Gerhard Bowering

(ed.), *Islamic Political Thought: An Introduction* (Princeton, NJ: Princeton University Press, 2015), p. 119.

40. 'Through water talks, normalization picks up pace: the Khilafah will solve the water issue by destroying the "Greater India" plan', Hizb ut-Tahrir Pakistan, 22 March 2017, http://www.hizb-pakistan.com/home/press-releases/local-prs/water-talks-normalization-picks-pace/

41. Another Islamist group, Jamaat-e-Islami, has also emphasised the water dimension of the Indian–Pakistani dispute. In February 2012, its deputy general secretary, Dr Farid Ahmed Piracha, accused India of launching 'water terrorism' against Pakistan and called for a 'permanent water policy'. The party official pointed to the construction of sixty dams on the Indian side that 'steal [Pakistan's] share of water in clear violation of the Indus Water Treaty' and raised the issue of Kashmiri self-determination so that the water resources could be controlled only by Pakistan. See 'JI demands permanent water policy', Jamaat-e-Islami Pakistan, 29 February 2012, https://web.archive.org/web/20120312014116/http://jamaat.org/beta/site/general_detail/news/3480 (accessed 28 June 2022). In February 2018, Liaqat Baloch, the general secretary of Jamaat-e-Islami, claimed that India was blocking the water of Pakistani rivers to convert his country into a desert. See 'Kashmiri leaders thanks Pakistanis for support', 6 February 2018, http://jamaat.org/en/news_detail.php?article_id=1369

42. 'An-Nahdha (Grand Renaissance) Dam and the Threats of Water War', p. 22.

43. Ibid. p. 49.

44. 'Only Khilafah "Caliphat" Rashedah can solve the problems of water resources on a regional and international level', Hizb ut Tahrir Central Media Office, 9 March 2017, http://www.hizb-ut-tahrir.info/en/index.php/press-releases/afghanistan/12649.html (accessed 20 June 2022).

45. Shabani Mwalimu, 'Mau Forest crisis: poor management of natural resources by capitalist-secular governments', *The Khilafah*, 4 August 2018, http://www.khilafah.com/mau-forest-crisis-poor-management-of-natural-resources-by-capitalist-secular-governments/ (accessed 20 June 2022).

46. Taqiuddin an-Nabhani, *Concepts of Hizb ut-Tahrir* (London: Al-Khilafah, n.d.), p. 62.

47. 'Halal meat on the chopping block again!', Hizb ut-Tahrir Britain, 7 January 2019, http://www.hizb.org.uk/viewpoint/halal-meat-on-the-chopping-block-again/ (accessed 20 June 2022).

48. 'Cow slaughter ban in India – milking the democracy loophole', Ibn Ahmed blog, 14 April 2013, https://petraria.wixsite.com/ibnahmed/single-post/20

13/04/14/cow-slaughter-ban-in-india-milking-of-the-democracy-loophole (accessed 20 June 2022),

49. For instance, a *hadith* narrated by Abu Hurairah states, 'A prostitute was forgiven by Allah, because, passing by a panting dog near a well and seeing that the dog was thirsty, she took off her shoe, and tying it with her head-cover she drew out some water for it. So Allah forgave her because of that.' See 'Halal meat on the chopping block again!'.

50. 'Halal meat on the chopping block again!'.

51. Ibid.

52. See Samuel P. Huntington, *The Clash of Civilizations and the Remaking of World Order* (New York: Simon & Schuster, 1996).

53. 'Cow slaughter ban in India – milking the democracy loophole'.

54. Ibid.

55. Masoud Msellem, 'Crime by Britain and America is greater than poaching', no date, http://www.hizb-ut-tahrir.info/en/index.php/2017-01-28-14-59-33 /news-comment/download/1635_765c33067ee80d8d1fa1cce4205965f2.html (accessed 27 June 2022)

56. See 'Britain's disruption of American interests', in 'From the Question & Answer of the Ameer of Hizb ut Tahrir, Ata Bin Khalil Abu al-Rashtah, Part 8', Hizb ut Tahrir Central Media Office, 30 April 2017, http://www.hizb-ut-tahrir .info/en/index.php/archives/speeches/13008.html (accessed 20 June 2022).

57. Hizb ut-Tahrir Denmark, *The Environmental Problem*, pp. 15–20.

58. Tanish Choudrhy, 'Was the 21st Climate Change Conference really a "monumental triumph"?', *The Khilafah*, 23 December 2015, http://www.khilafah .com/was-the-21st-climate-change-conference-really-a-monumental-triumph/ (accessed 20 June 2022).

59. Abdul Wahid, 'Islam and the environmental challenge: part five – Islam's unique architecture and vision for humanity', Hizb ut-Tahrir Britain, 30 November 2021, https://www.hizb.org.uk/resources/in-depth/islam-the-environmental-ch allenge-part-five-islams-unique-architecture-and-vision-for-humanity (accessed 20 June 2022).

60. Interview with three members of Hizb ut-Tahrir in London, 13 December 2018.

61. Nazia Rehman, 'Polluted air health emergency', *The Khilafah*, 2 October 2016, http://www.khilafah.com/polluted-air-health-emergency/ (accessed 20 June 2022).

62. Ibid.

63. Fehmida Binte Wadud, 'Only under the leadership of a God-fearing Khaleefah will the future generation of Bangladesh be ready to tackle all kinds of environmental challenges', *The Khilafa*, 26 September 2015, http://www.khilafah.com /only-under-the-leadership-of-a-god-fearing-khaleefah-will-the-future-gener ation-of-bangladesh-be-ready-to-tackle-all-kinds-of-environmental-challenges/ (accessed 20 June 2022).

64. Ibid.

65. Imadul Amin, 'Havoc in Bangladeshi swamplands due to uranium-mixed flood water from India', *The Khilafa*, 8 May 2017, http://www.khilafah.com/havoc -in-bangladeshi-swamplands-due-to-uranium-mixed-flood-water-from-india/ (accessed 20 June 2022).

66. 'Haze chokes Singapore and Malaysia!', Hizb ut Tahrir Central Media Office, 28 June 2013, http://www.hizb-ut-tahrir.info/en/index.php/2017-01-28-14-59 -33/news-comment/2303.html (accessed 20 June 2022).

67. 'Indonesian democratic government fails to end suffering of millions children [*sic*] due to forest fire', Hizb ut Tahrir Central Media Office, 18 October 2015, http://hizb-ut-tahrir.info/en/index.php/2017-01-28-14-59-33/news-comment /8772.html (accessed 20 June 2022).

68. 'Report on the issues of the Ummah forum Hizb ut Tahrir stirs the Ummah's resolve to face the Three Wings of Death', 25 October 2014, http://www.hizb -ut-tahrir.info/en/index.php/multimedia/video/6151.html

69. 'Single-use plastics ban approved by European Parliament', BBC News, 24 October 2018, https://www.bbc.co.uk/news/world-europe-45965605 (accessed 20 June 2022).

70. 'Pakistan headlines 30/11/2018', Hizb ut Tahrir Central Media Office, 30 November 2018, http://www.hizb-ut-tahrir.info/en/index.php/2017-01-28-14 -59-33/headlines/16499.html## (accessed 20 June 2022).

71. 'Pakistan's Economy under the Khilafah', Hizb ut Tahrir / Wilaya Pakistan, 12 June 2013, p. 30, http://www.hizb-ut-tahrir.org/PDF/EN/en_books_pdf /PK_Revival_of_the_Economy_in_Pakistan_EN_22.06_.2013_.pdf (accessed 20 June 2022).

72. 'O people! The price-hike of diesel-kerosene is manifestation of the tyranni-cal policy of Hasina Regime, the agent of the capitalists', Hizb-ut-Tahrir, 12 November 2021, http://www.hizb-ut-tahrir.org/index.php/EN/wshow/4740 (accessed 20 June 2022).

73. Ibid.

74. 'How the Khilafat Will Solve Bangladesh's Economic Crisis', Hizb ut-Tahrir

Bangladesh, June 2003, p. 11, https://www.systemofislam.com/pdf/khilafah _solve_bangladesh_economic_crisis.pdf (accessed 18 July 2022).

75. 'Q&A: Pakistan's request to join the Nuclear Suppliers Group', *The Khilafah*, 12 June 2016, http://www.khilafah.com/qa-pakistans-request-to-join-the-nucle ar-suppliers-group/ (accessed 27 June 2022).

76. Rolf Mowatt-Larssen, *Islam and the Bomb: Religious Justification For and Against Nuclear Weapons*, Belfer Center for Science and International Affairs, January 2011, pp. 24–5, http://www.belfercenter.org/sites/default/files/legacy/files/uplo ads/Islam_and_the_Bomb-Final.pdf (accessed 20 June 2022)..

77. Hizb ut-Tahrir, *The Inevitability of the Clash of Civilisation* (London: Al-Khilafah, 2002), pp. 5–7.

78. Interview with three members of Hizb ut-Tahrir, London, 13 December 2018.

79. Mohammed Barrou, 'Egyptens hvedeproblem er politisk' ('Egypt's wheat problem is political'), Hizb-ut-Tahrir.dk, 17 August 2010, http://www.hizb-ut-tah rir.dk/content.php?contentid=26&caller=http://hizb-ut-tahrir.dk/category.php ?searchword=dyr&startrow=21 (accessed 20 June 2022).

80. Joseph Mayton, 'Eating less meat is more Islamic', *The Guardian*, 26 August 2010, https://www.theguardian.com/commentisfree/belief/2010/aug/26/meat -islam-vegetarianism-ramadan (accessed 20 June 2022).

81. In August 2015, Islamic Relief Worldwide and the Islamic Foundation for Ecology and Environmental Sciences (IFEES) organised the International Islamic Climate Change Symposium in Istanbul. The event was attended by Muslim scholars, non-governmental organisations and United Nations representatives to discuss the Islamic response to climate change. The symposium issued the Islamic Climate Change Declaration, stating, 'Our species, though selected to be a caretaker or steward (*khalifa*) on the earth, has been the cause of such corruption and devastation on it that we are in danger [of] ending life as we know it on our planet. This current rate of climate change cannot be sustained, and the earth's fine equilibrium (*mizan*) may soon be lost.' See Islamic Declaration on Global Climate Change, 18 August 2015, https://www.ifees.org .uk/wp-content/uploads/2020/01/climate_declarationmmwb.pdf (accessed 20 June 2022).

82. John L. Esposito (ed.), *The Oxford Dictionary of Islam* (New York: Oxford University Press, 2003), p. 314.

83. Wahid, 'Islam and the environmental challenge'.

4

HIZBULLAH AND THE ENVIRONMENT

For almost four decades, Hizbullah has played an important role in Lebanese political and military affairs. The group mainly represents Twelver Shiʿa Muslims (*Ithna ashariyyah*), who constitute the second-largest religious group in the country.[1] The very name Hizbullah derives from the Qurʾanic verse 5:56: 'And whosoever takes Allah and His messenger and those who believe for friend – surely *the party of Allah*, they shall triumph'.[2] According to Islamic theology, there are two parties: the Party of God (*Hizbullah*) and the Party of Satan (*Hizb ul-Shaytan*). Thus, Hizbullah is more than a party because it represents God on earth.

From its founding in the early 1980s, Hizbullah recognised Ayatollah Khomeini as the official *marjaʿal-taqlid* (highest-ranking religious-legal authority) of the Islamic Republic and the first *faqih* (Islamic jurist) after the Major Occultation.[3] The 1979 Iranian Revolution had led to the overthrow of the Shah and the return of Khomeini from France. The founder of the Islamic Republic posed as a champion of Islamic revival to appeal to the wider Muslim world.[4] However, his version of Islamism soon became a revolutionary force for the defence of Shiʿa rights in the Middle East.[5]

Khomeini claimed the world is divided into two groups: *mustakbirin* (the oppressors) and *mustadʿafin* (the oppressed).[6] The terms can be found in the Qurʾan, but Khomeini provided a political interpretation of them. He argued:

It is our duty to be helper to the oppressed and an enemy to the oppressor. This is nothing other than the duty that the Commander of the Faithful (*Amir al-Mu'minin*, namely Imam Ali) entrusted to his great offspring (that is Hassan and Hussein) in his celebrated testament 'Be an enemy to the oppressor and a helper to the oppressed'.[7]

Indeed, Khomeini viewed the Shi'a as the representatives of 'oppressed peoples' of all religions.[8]

Revolutionary Iran sought to export its ideology to Lebanon because the country had a large Shi'i community and because its clerics maintained strong links with their Iranian counterparts. In the early 1980s, Lebanon was in the middle of a bloody civil war and the Shi'a population largely relied on the Amal militia for protection.[9] Following the disappearance of its founder, Imam Musa al-Sadr, en route to Libya in August 1978, Amal broke up into a pro-Syrian and a pro-Iranian faction. Hizbullah draws its origins from the pro-Iranian faction of the Amal movement, the Lebanese branch of Iraq's Islamic Da'wa Party and other radical Shi'a groups.[10] With the help of Iran's Revolutionary Guards, Hizbullah was established in the early to mid-1980s.[11] Yet Hizbullah had only minimal participation in the Lebanese civil war of 1975–90, something in which it takes pride.

The organisation was established to be run by Shi'a clerics, who form the majority in the primary decision-making body of the Shura Council. Hizbullah has promoted a culture of martyrdom that is inspired by the death of the Prophet Muhammad's grandson Imam Hussein during the Battle of Karbala in 680.[12] In the words of its deputy secretary general, Sheikh Naim Qassem, 'we have learned through Imam Hussein that the love of martyrdom is part of the love of God'.[13] While the annual commemoration of Imam Hussein's martyrdom and the ritualised mourning constitute a fundamental part of Shi'i identity, Hizbullah has assigned political meaning to these religious practices. Hence, Qassem has claimed that 'martyrdom is . . . the supreme manifestation of self-giving, a form of confrontation with the enemy within clear, legitimate Shari'a guidelines'.[14] In this way, the Lebanese group has instrumentalised Islamic history and Shi'i theology to mobilise supporters and to confront its enemies.

The 1989 Taif Agreement signalled the end of the Lebanese civil war in calling for 'the disbanding of all Lebanese and non-Lebanese militias'.[15] Hizbullah refused to disarm and continued its guerrilla campaign against the Israeli army throughout the 1990s. Nonetheless, under the new leadership of Sayyed Hassan Nasrallah, the group joined the Lebanese political system and initiated a rapprochement with non-Islamist parties. It even participated in the 1992 parliamentary election, the country's first election since 1972. This development prompted some analysts to claim that Hizbullah was going through a process of 'Lebanonisation'.[16]

The unilateral Israeli withdrawal from southern Lebanon in May 2000 was hailed as a victory for Hizbullah that achieved its primary goal of unifying the country. However, the group did not disarm. On 12 July 2006, it launched Operation Truthful Promise by ambushing an Israeli patrol, kidnapping two soldiers and killing several others. The Olmert government approved a ground invasion of southern Lebanon to save the soldiers and punish the group. During the 33-day war, Hizbullah kept bombing Israel with rockets despite Israeli retaliation.

The group came out of the war with a sense of confidence in its resilience and capabilities. Hizbullah subsequently attempted to play a greater role in the country's political system. The assassination of Lebanese prime minister Rafik Hariri had led to the outbreak of the Cedar Revolution in 2005, which called for the withdrawal of Syrian troops from Lebanon. In early November 2006, the Shi'a members of the cabinet resigned in protest at the establishment of the Special Tribunal for Lebanon, which investigated Hariri's assassination. One month later, massive Hizbullah-led demonstrations shook the country's political system. The situation remained tense throughout 2007.

Finally, the deadlock between the ruling March 14 Alliance and the Hizbullah-led March 8 Alliance was resolved by the Doha Agreement in May 2008. The group has continued to prosper politically. Following the May 2018 elections, Hizbullah now holds fifteen seats in the 128-member Lebanese parliament. It also still provides an assortment of social services for Lebanon's Shi'i community, including hospitals, schools, orphanages and youth centres.

There is an extensive literature regarding the history, ideology and strategy of Hizbullah.[17] Many analysts have, perhaps understandably, viewed the group as the long arm of the Iranian regime in Lebanon. Nevertheless,

Hizbullah is not a typical non-state armed group. Contrary to Western perceptions, it has developed a sophisticated political platform drawing attention to economic, social and environmental issues. This chapter first describes the group's general approach to the environment, including its understanding of territoriality, by exploring party documents. It then turns to three areas of environmental activity, namely water management, tree-planting, and pollution and energy. Finally, the chapter examines the role of religion in the emergence of Hizbullah's environmentalism.

Hizbullah's General Perspective on the Environment

To preface Hizbullah's general perspective on the environment, it is useful to consider its ideological component. The group remains committed to Ayatollah Khomeini's political theology, which has cosmological and ontological parameters. The starting point is the Twelver Shi'a doctrine of the imamate, which calls for a divinely guided, infallible leader who would lead the *umma*. According to mainstream Shi'i theology, the twelve imams were male descendants of the Prophet Muhammad and were infallible (*ma'sum*), that is free from sin and error. Therefore, the imam is God's proof (*hujja*), the pillar of the universe, the 'gate' through whom the believer can approach God.[18] Most Shi'a believe that the Mahdi, the twelfth imam or the so-called hidden imam, disappeared and will one day return to bring justice. The guardianship of the believers has been delegated from God to the Prophet and from him to the twelve imams. In the absence of the twelfth imam, Khomeini argued, his power is delegated to a just and capable scholar (*faqih e-adil*).[19]

Moreover, the Iranian cleric expanded the concept of the guardian of the believers (*wali amir al-mu'minin*). The Qur'an states that 'Only Allah is your friend (*wali*) and His Messenger and those who believe, those who keep up prayers and pay the poor-rate while they bow down' (5:55). The word *wali* means 'friend', 'supporter' or 'protector', and gives rise to the word *wilayat* (*vilayat* in Farsi). The latter can be interpreted as 'guardianship', which can be absolute (*wilayat al-mutlaqa*) or discretionary (*wilayat al-tasarruf*).[20] Hence, Khomeini introduced the system of *vilayat-i faqih* (the guardianship of the jurist).[21]

Against this theo-ideological background, Hizbullah has approached the environment from an angle that combines pan-Islamism and nationalism, but also sectarianism. To begin with, the Lebanese group has offered different interpretations of the concept of territoriality. During the 1980s, it challenged the existing understanding of Lebanese sovereignty and statehood. In the famous Open Letter, published on 16 February 1985, the group declared that 'we are a community connected to Muslims from every corner of the world . . . [W]hatever assails the Muslims in Afghanistan, in Iraq, in the Philippines, or anywhere else assaults the body of the Muslim nation, of which we are an indivisible part.'[22] Therefore, Hizbullah initially presented itself as a pan-Islamic organisation with a universal mission. Its yellow flag incorporates an image of the globe because the group seeks international influence. At that time, the unit of identification was not the Lebanese state but the imagined *umma* of oppressed Muslims. This form of pan-Islamic extra-territoriality derived from the Islamism of Ayatollah Khomeini in that it was not tied to nationalist exclusivity.

Following its gradual Lebanonisation, Hizbullah proclaimed as its *raison d'être* the liberation of all Lebanese territory. Its programme for the 1992 parliamentary elections stated that 'the protection of Lebanon, of its unity and cultural affinity with its Islamic and Arab vicinity, requires of us to adopt the path of resistance against the Zionist occupation until all occupied soil is liberated'.[23] In this way, Hizbullah embraced a narrower territorial identity which was bound by space and time. It advocated a version of nationalism based on common religion and language because it perceives the Arab and Islamic worlds as homogeneous and static entities.

Yet Hizbullah's concept of territoriality has not remained unchanged. The group has shifted between extra-territoriality, territoriality and hydro-territoriality. The programme for the 2000 parliamentary elections offered a broader definition of territoriality:

> to ensure the full preservation of our national rights and interests in order to achieve the full liberation of our Lebanese territory, to take full sovereignty over our land and water . . . rights, and not to neglect any part of it, especially the disputed areas . . . and refusal to coexist with the Zionist invaders . . . in order to affirm the right of the Palestinian people to return to their entire land in Palestine.[24]

In other words, the group has redefined the meaning of territoriality to include disputed areas, natural resources and the land of the historical Palestine. Hizbullah has not explicitly provided an Islamic justification for the different understandings of territoriality. However, its self-perception as the Party of God with a holistic mission could explain the ease of politico-ideological change. The religious foundation of Hizbullah serves as a useful normative framework for action.

The 2009 electoral programme clarified the question of Lebanon's occupied areas and hinted again at a hydrological dimension to the dispute with Israel. It declared that the group

> is determined to complete the liberation of the remaining occupied territories, especially in the Shebaa Farms and the hills of Kafrshuba. It places its capabilities . . . within the framework of strengthening Lebanon . . . to be able to face the occupation and the danger and Israeli ambitions in our land and our wealth of water.[25]

Hizbullah claimed that a small piece of territory, the Shebaa Farms and the hills of Kafrshuba, remained (and still remains) under Israeli occupation.[26] The group has used the issue to justify its armed presence in southern Lebanon. Additionally, the control of water supplies was presented as an issue of contention between the two sides.

Hizbullah's unique understanding of territoriality sets a broader vision that incorporates concrete environmental proposals. The 2000 electoral programme had briefly proclaimed its goals as follows: developing and organising wastewater treatment plants and completing sewerage networks; preserving forest wealth; protecting afforestation in various regions to address the problem of desertification; enacting laws to protect this wealth and establish natural reserves; activating the role of municipalities in environmental activities; tightening control over how factories dispose of industrial waste; and enacting laws that protect the environment, especially rivers, the sea and groundwater, from pollution.[27] For the first time, Hizbullah provided a plan for the environmental protection of Lebanon. The document placed more emphasis on issues of growing public concern, such as sewage and wastewater management, desertification and pollution.

Subsequently, Hizbullah treated environmental protection as a local issue; its constituency is specific both socially and religiously. The 2004 municipal election programme outlined the following measures for local government: regular inspection of the environment by state agencies to determine the pollutants in sanitary sewers, drinking water, air and waste; keeping in touch with private companies, local ministries and foreign associations that specialise in executing projects capable of fighting pollution; spreading environmental awareness; planting trees and various plants as well as establishing public gardens and greenhouses; solutions to get rid of all kinds of garbage and pollutants to the environment, in co-ordination with the ministries concerned as well as competent international associations; preserving environmental and national heritage; and cleaning and protecting beaches and river banks.[28] Hence, the group attempted to lay the foundation for a more efficient management of environmental problems at the local level.

During the first decade of the twenty-first century, Hizbullah maintained its strong interest in environmental issues. The 2009 electoral programme dedicated a separate section to environmental matters. More specifically, it stated that 'the environment in Lebanon has been subjected to a wide process of destruction: from burning forests to indiscriminate cutting of trees, to the chaos of quarries and fractures, to pollution of rivers with sewage to the random dumping of solid waste'.[29] Hence, the group depicted the environmental situation as in critical need of attention. It proposed the following measures: adopting a scientific master plan; completing the construction of sewage plants in all regions; a modern study of the best means of disposal of solid waste to convert it into energy rather than burying in the ground; providing effective means for firefighting (aircraft etc.); preventing the warming of the environment; combating encroachment on sea shores and river banks; and launching a national campaign to renew the greening of Lebanon, in co-operation with all organisations and associations, local and foreign, interested in this matter.[30] Interestingly, the group did not exclude the engagement of foreign partners in tackling ecological problems. As distinct from previous programmes, the 2009 electoral programme adopted a strategic long-term vision for the environmental protection of Lebanon.

In the same year, Hizbullah published a new political manifesto to replace the Open Letter of 1985. This time, the document described American-led globalisation as a menace against Muslim-majority countries. In fact, it offered a neo-Marxist critique of globalised capitalism, claiming that it is a tool of hegemonic power in a divided world:

> The most dangerous aspect in the Western hegemony – the American one precisely – is that they consider themselves owners of the world and there-fore, this expanding strategy along with the economic-capitalist project has become a 'Western expanding strategy' that turned out to be an inter-national scheme of limitless greed. Savage capitalism forces – embodied mainly in international monopoly networks of companies that cross nations and continents, networks of various international establishments especially financial ones backed by superior military force – have led to more contra-dictions and . . . conflicts of identities, cultures, civilizations, in addition to the conflicts of poverty and wealth.[31]

Thus, Hizbullah does not isolate environmental problems from the complexity of international politics. It has identified Western capitalism as the main source of conflict in the Global South. In this way, the group has focused on environmental justice and human suffering. The absence of Islamic phraseology is indicative of Hizbullah's ideological flexibility regarding the assessment of global problems and challenges.

Nonetheless, regional developments have created new dynamics. The outbreak of the Arab Spring revolutions changed the broad political-environmental landscape in the Middle East. In Syria, Hizbullah's fighters have been involved in major military operations against the armed Sunni opposition to support the Assad regime.[32] Likewise, the group has supported the Houthi insurgency in Yemen by providing training and expertise.[33] In both cases, Hizbullah has allied with non-Twelver Shi'a leaderships despite their theological differences.[34] [35] If geographical proximity can explain the group's involvement in neighbouring Syria, it surely cannot explain its sup-port of Houthi rebels in remote Yemen. Therefore, Hizbullah's area of opera-tions is at least partly determined by sectarian affinity. It can be argued that the group is now embracing a sectarian extra-territoriality. Hizbullah's reach is supposedly defined by the totality of the Muslim world, but in reality it is only a fraction of it, that is, the pro-Iranian Shi'a.

In summary, the group has developed its own understanding of the environment, including not only physical surroundings (for example, land, water) but also the changing politico-religious space. The concept of territoriality has a fluid character that serves Hizbullah's political agenda well, depending on the circumstances. Still, consistent efforts are being made to address ecological challenges facing Lebanese society. This chapter now attends to three areas of environmental engagement: water management, tree-planting, and pollution and energy.

Water Management

Hizbullah's branch of social services, the Jihad al-Binaa Association (JABA), has strived to improve the living conditions of Shi'a Muslims. Since its establishment in 1988, the JABA has engaged in various environmental projects in certain areas of Lebanon. For example, following the end of the civil war, the JABA contributed to the water security of Beirut's Shi'a-populated southern suburbs by distributing water tanks. Also, it extended the existing water network with 15,000 metres of piping.[36]

The group has often claimed that Israel seeks control of Lebanon's water supplies. In this way, Hizbullah is entitled to act as the guardian of water supplies against a thirsty neighbour. It is well known that the forefathers of the Zionist movement envisioned the establishment of a Jewish state with natural borders. The northern border of the proposed state was along the River Litani for practical, not religious, reasons.[37] That initial plan has been used by Hizbullah for the purposes of propaganda. The environmentalisation of the Hizbullah–Israeli conflict provides the Lebanese group with additional justification for its armed struggle. The Israelis are presented as an evil opponent seeking the destruction of Lebanon's rich environment.

In May 1998, for instance, Sayyed Hassan Nasrallah claimed with knowing irony that 'Israel's borders extend to river sources and sea basins . . . that is the land of Israel. The waters of the Nile and the Euphrates, the mountains of Yemen, and the land of Khaybar are part of Israel's land. Is this not the dream?'[38] The mentioning of Khaybar is hardly a coincidence. It was an oasis inhabited by a Jewish tribe in the Arabian Peninsula which was conquered by the Prophet in the Battle of Khaybar in 628. According to a Shi'i tradition, Ali demonstrated enormous courage and bravery during the battle.[39] Thus, Nasrallah attempted to construct a conceptual bridge between the heroism of Ali against his Jewish foes and Hizbullah's resistance to the territorial expansion of modern Israel. In this way, he portrays modern Jews as vengeful and aggressive. They are an old enemy that can be defeated by the brave followers of Imam Ali.

The politicisation of water gradually took a domestic turn, reflecting increased scarcity and unreliability of supply. In 2010, Nasrallah described his water vision for Lebanon, which included technical, environmental and political aspects:

> We are a country rich in water. But unfortunately our water runs to the sea or goes deep into the earth. Simply, we may build a number of dams and collect this water. As the region is heading towards a water crisis, the issue of water if taken seriously might solve not only the water crisis in Lebanon, but water will be in the future among the most important state resources because it would be far more costly than oil . . . If time comes when we are able to sell water we will sell water. As we want to dig in the sea to extract oil and gas to cover for our debts, time will come when the worth of water will be more than the worth of gas and oil.[40]

From his perspective, water was not only a natural resource but a strategic commodity that could benefit the Lebanese economy. More importantly, Nasrallah tried to foster a sense of national pride by portraying Lebanon as the water reservoir of the region.

Indeed, water issues have been increasingly high on Hizbullah's political agenda. Its 2018 electoral programme, for example, called for 'the implementation of law to protect public and communal property, especially sources of natural resources associated with water (including underground)'.[41] Again, the group emphasised the importance of water resources for the well-being of the country and assigned a sense of collective responsibility.

At the same time, Hizbullah has viewed rivers as not merely bodies of water. They constitute markers of statehood and symbols of independence. Hizbullah has embraced the Palestinian slogan 'free from the river to the sea' (*horra min al-nahr ila al-ba'har*) partly because it has been an integral part of the Iranian understanding of the Palestinian issue. Following the US recognition of Jerusalem as capital of Israel in 2017, the current supreme leader of the Islamic Republic declared that 'Palestine . . . includes a country and a history, Palestine from the river to the sea and undoubtedly Jerusalem as its capital'.[42] The River Jordan is a natural boundary for an imagined homeland that must be liberated from the foreign yoke.

However, water is more than just a natural frontier. In his book *Hizbullah: The Story from Within*, Sheikh Naim Qassem discussed its religious importance:

> The Prophet concentrated on the importance of water as a means for achieving desired purity, and also defined the specifics of using water in order to achieve the cleanliness needed to complete certain forms of worship . . . [H]e left the possibilities open as to the methods to be followed for achieving general cleanliness and safety of the environment, be that through the use of water or other alternative cleaning means, and be it applied to houses, streets, agricultural pastures, seas or rivers.[43]

Here, Qassem focused on the concept of *tahara* (cleanliness) as a religious obligation. It is vital for the physical and spiritual purity of every believer. Additionally, he acknowledged the importance of environmental cleanliness in inhabited and uninhabited areas, but he held the opinion that it is a technical issue that can be dealt with flexibly. From Hizbullah's point of view, water is a strategic commodity, a source of growing tension and a religious symbol of purification.

Trees

Since the end of the civil war, Hizbullah has invested important resources in reforestation projects. As early as 1992, the JABA initiated the Good Tree Campaign to plant trees in certain areas of Lebanon. Consequently, it has planted millions of trees to restore the country's forests, which were destroyed by the 1975–90 civil war and the Israeli incursions. In 2010, the JABA launched a much-publicised campaign to plant one million trees (*hamlat milyun shajara*) in Lebanon. With the help of the Lebanese Ministry of Agriculture and local authorities, Hizbullah concentrated its efforts on those forests destroyed during the 2006 war. The group even produced a YouTube video showing Nasrallah planting and watering the millionth tree near his house.[44] By 2010, the JABA had planted 7.3 million trees throughout Lebanon.[45]

The reforestation campaign aligned with the JABA's long-term objectives, among which are the following: raising awareness of fighting the phenomenon of desertification; promoting organic farming; training farmers to adopt new techniques to reduce the phenomenon of land degradation; and rationalising the use of pesticides.[46] In effect, the JABA has advocated a new agricultural policy that creates a sustainable future for the Lebanese farming sector.

In addition, the JABA has supported farmers by promoting green agriculture. Indeed, it has established three centres for development and agricultural guidance, namely the Sayyed Abbas Moussawi Centre, the Jawad Centre and the Abu Zhar al-Ghafari Centre.[47] The JABA has organised relevant seminars and courses for farmers and cattlemen, while offering assistance in kind to farmers and livestock vaccination against contagious diseases.[48]

Hizbullah's preoccupation with agricultural activities can be partly explained by the demographics of its base of support. Many Shi'a live in predominantly rural areas in the south and the Bekaa Valley, as evidenced by the 2018 election results.[49] The group has apparently provided assistance without religious content. Yet Hizbullah's involvement in the field of agriculture implicitly reaffirms its devotion to the Islamic principles of *khilafa* (viceregency) and *mizan* (balance). In a way, it has aspired to act as the viceregent of vicegerents to maintain divine balance in nature.

Additionally, Nasrallah has used religious arguments to reinforce his environmental message about tree-planting. In his speech on marking the end of the Planting One Million Trees Campaign, he claimed that 'the biography of the great Prophet comprises important assertions on Muslims of that time – and this not limited to that era but it applies until Doom's Day – on the issue of agriculture and especially tree-planting, taking care of trees, protecting trees and on the greatness and nobleness of this occupation' (see appendix).[50] In the same speech Nasrallah used the word *sadaqa* several times to describe the planting of a tree as an act of charity. As opposed to *zakat*, which is obligatory, *sadaqa* is a voluntary act of charity. Additionally, he argued that there are two types of *sadaqa*: the instant act of charity like buying food for the poor and the ongoing charity. For this purpose, the leader of Hizbullah cited two famous *ahadith*:

> Every Muslim who sows a seedling or plants a plant from which a man, bird
> or a beast eats, but it was a charity (for which he is rewarded) through which
> he becomes closer to Allah Al Mighty.

> Whoever plants a plant which yields fruits, Allah would reward him equivalent to its fruits.[51]

Both *ahadith* imply that the planting of a tree could bring the believer closer to God, which remains the ultimate goal. According to the Qur'an, *sadaqa* should be given to certain groups of people (for example, the poor, the needy) or for the cause of spreading Islam.[52] The use of the word *sadaqa* clearly implies that followers of Hizbullah have a religious obligation to plant trees as a visible manifestation of their faith. It is a powerful religious concept that could mobilise devout Muslims to participate in the campaigns of reforestation.

In 2013, Green without Borders (*akhdar bela hodod*), another Hizbullah-affiliated NGO, was registered to develop reforestation projects in the country. During 2014/15, the organisation planted 160,000 trees with the help of 8,540 volunteers.[53] The NGO is also involved in cleaning forests, building public parks and fighting wildfires. Thus, tree-planting has been at the heart of Hizbullah's environmental efforts in Lebanon.

Pollution and Energy

Lebanon is faced with harsh and deteriorating environmental conditions due to urban pollution and resource depletion. It is a major problem particularly affecting poor Shi'a-populated suburbs in Beirut and other cities. Therefore, Hizbullah has paid growing attention to sewage management. During the Lebanese civil war, the group facilitated the distribution of electricity to south Beirut by using generators, collected garbage, and repaired sewage pipes.[54]

The 2000 and 2009 election programmes included provisions for sewage and wastewater management. In addition, the 2018 programme committed the group to following up 'the government's work on completing the implementation of sewage treatment projects on riverbeds, especially on the Litani and Assi'.[55] Also, Hizbullah has supported pollution prevention projects for Lake Qaroun.[56] The urgency of pollution control has prompted the group to appear proactive and responsive to public concerns.

Furthermore, Hizbullah has extended its environmental reach well beyond Lebanon. In fact, Nasrallah has discussed the problem of global warming:

What the world is witnessing today such as earthquakes, floods, torrents, serious climatic changes and fires that threatened millions and what is taking place now in India, China and especially in Pakistan is a human catastrophe in the whole sense of the word. These are the results of climatic changes. Today humanity is confronting this great and serious climatic threat.[57]

In contrast to deniers in the West, Nasrallah has supported the mainstream view that climate change is the result of human activities. Indeed, he has declared that 'the climate threat today is among the biggest threats faced by mankind in (terms of) peace, security, stability, and existence'.[58] Without proper conceptualisation of the context, the leader of Hizbullah has described a nexus of environment and security. His message is not religious or sectarian. The unit of identification is mankind, confronted with a challenge of enormous proportions.

Despite its sensitivities over climate change, Hizbullah has fiercely supported the exploration of offshore energy reserves. With new gas discoveries in the last few years containing significant reserves, the eastern Mediterranean will soon become the new gas frontier. More specifically, the Tamar field with estimated reserves of 9.7 trillion cubic feet (tcf) (275 billion cubic metres) was confirmed by the Israelis in 2009. In December 2010, the US company Noble Energy, as part of a consortium including Delek Drilling, Avner Oil and Ratio Oil, hailed the Leviathan gas field off the Israeli coast as a 'significant natural gas discovery' with a potential of 16 tcf (450 billion cubic metres).[59] In August 2010, Lebanon passed a law through parliament to survey and explore the eastern Mediterranean for energy resources, contesting ownership rights within Leviathan.

Hizbullah has not stayed aloof from the debate. In July 2011, Sheikh Naim Qassem warned that 'Lebanon will stand guard in order to protect all its rights, no matter the cost'.[60] It seems that the group has attempted to add a new issue to the Israeli–Lebanese confrontation. By claiming that Israel is stealing Lebanon's gas resources, Hizbullah has in effect further demonised its adversary, which is accused of energy imperialism. Such a claim resonates well with many Lebanese who perceive Israel as an aggressive neighbour that has not respected the territorial integrity of their country. Thus, Hizbullah could keep presenting itself as a determined and genuinely patriotic group fighting against Israel in the name of national independence and sovereignty.

During a televised speech marking the fifth anniversary of the 2006 war, Nasrallah did not hesitate to threaten Israel with a strike against its energy infrastructure: 'We warn Israel against extending its hands to this area and steal[ing] Lebanon's resources from Lebanese waters . . . Whoever harms our future oil facilities in Lebanese territorial waters, its own facilities will be targeted.'[61] Furthermore, Nasrallah has increasingly used the oil conspiracy theory to explain regional developments. In February 2018, for example, he claimed that 'the entire region has entered the oil and gas battle . . . The Americans don't want to withdraw from eastern Syria because the most important oil and gas fields are found there.'[62] He has also revealed the importance that Hizbullah attributes to the Mediterranean offshore reserves. In his words, 'the oil wealth in the South [the southern part of Lebanon's exclusive economic zone], like the rest of Lebanon's wealth, belongs to all Lebanon and will go to the state funds. The oil and gas reserves may be the only hope for economic relief.' More importantly, Nasrallah has argued that the cause of the Israeli–Lebanese conflict is not the land border, whose dispute can be easily resolved, but the maritime border.[63] This is an astonishing admission by the leader of Hizbullah, who has shifted the focus of the debate from territoriality to hydro-territoriality.

Following the May 2018 general elections, Hizbullah and its allies increased their representation in the Lebanese parliament. During a meeting of Hizbullah's political wing, Loyalty to the Resistance (Al-Wafa lil-Muqawama), MP Mohammad Raad confirmed the new position:

> Forty years after the sinful crime – that led to Imam Moussa Al-Sadr's vanishing along with his two companions – the Lebanese now witness that Imam Sayyed Moussa Al-Sadr is still present and influential in the Lebanese equation at the level of the nation, the state and the citizens. His vision continues to inspire the most powerful national political forces in Lebanon . . . The opportunities for Lebanon to invest in its water and oil resources require a national government that enjoys full prerogatives and provides protection, especially as the enemy continues its intensive looting of oil and gas fields.[64]

Thus, Imam al-Sadr has almost been elevated to the status of the hidden imam, reflecting a belief shared by many Lebanese Shi'a. Since he was the founder of Amal, Imam al-Sadr could serve as more than a source of inspiration for Hizbullah; his image is that of a unifying figure promoting pan-Shi'a solidarity. At the same time, Hizbullah's political wing stressed that the strategic significance of natural resources (for example, water, oil, gas) is linked with the dynamics of Israeli–Lebanese relations.

More recently, Lebanon's financial crisis has led to a severe shortage of fuel. In mid-September 2021, dozens of trucks carrying Iranian diesel entered Lebanon from Syria; Tehran had sent a shipment to the Syrian port of Baniyas. The operation was organised by Hizbullah, which distributed the fuel free of charge to hospitals, nursing homes, orphanages and the Lebanese Red Cross.[65] While the group avoided any religious rhetoric, its collaboration with Iran and Syria on this matter had a clear underpinning message: Lebanon had been saved by the Shi'a 'axis of resistance'.

Energy is more than oil and gas, though. For many years, Lebanon has faced a serious electricity crisis due to growing needs, mismanagement and corruption.[66] It is a problem of immense social and economic proportions that could not be ignored by Hizbullah. In August 2010, Nasrallah proposed the construction of a nuclear plant to tackle Lebanon's electricity crisis. In a speech during an *iftar* banquet organised by the women's division of the Islamic Resistance Support Organization at Al-Kawthar School, he claimed:

> The cost to build the nuclear plant of Bushehr which will provide a great amount of Iran's energy is far less than what Lebanon has so far spent on the electricity sector . . . Let's learn from the Iranians who are our friends. Iran has oil, gas and various other energy resources. Still what does the leadership in Iran say? It says that after 20, 30 or 40 years, when oil and gas are used up, how are we to provide people with electricity? Let's then secure peaceful nuclear energy . . . I seriously call on the Lebanese government to examine and discuss a plan to build a nuclear reactor for peaceful nuclear energy to produce electricity in Lebanon.

Here Nasrallah offered a radical solution to the country's electricity crisis, while supporting the Iranian nuclear programme. It was a gesture of political solidarity with Tehran, which remains Hizbullah's main sponsor. Without resorting to political or ideological arguments, he opened the public debate on a vital issue for Lebanese energy security. His words were carefully crafted with the intent to tackle an issue of growing public concern (that is, the electricity crisis) from a unique perspective. Once again, the leader of Hizbullah deliberately eschewed the use of any religious phraseology. Instead, he used technical language to make a proposal for the strengthening of the country's energy security.

The Role of Religion

Hizbullah has an ideological platform drawing on Ayatollah Khomeini's political theology and its interpretation of Shi'a terms. The group was established by Shi'a revolutionaries with ties to Iran to represent the community of the *mustad'afin* (oppressed) in Lebanon and elsewhere. In the words of its former secretary general Abbas al-Mussawi, Hizbullah is not a 'party in the traditional sense of the term. Every Muslim is automatically a member of Hizbullah, thus it is impossible to list our membership.'[67] Since Hizbullah is run by Shi'a clerics, it must act and must be seen to act in accordance with Islamic principles and ethics. While this is not always possible, the group has made a conscious decision to demonstrate piety and knowledge. Leaders and members must live according to high ethical standards. After all, this the party of God with a special mission on earth.

Contrary to this, the environmental policy of Hizbullah is pragmatic and hence contextualistic. Hizbullah's understanding of territoriality reveals the ambivalence of its environmental policy: the group has shifted between pan-Islamic (albeit sectarian) extra-territoriality, Lebanese territoriality and even hydro-territoriality. Initially, the main goal was the support of the Shi'i community in environmentally problematic areas. However, over the years, the group has shown interest in nationwide ecological challenges. From water issues and tree-planting to sewage problems and energy issues, Hizbullah has defended Lebanese interests as it perceives them. Despite its identification with Shi'a causes, the group has tried to craft environmentalist messages that resonate with the larger society.

Yet the group cannot deny its religious roots. Therefore, Hizbullah has been keen to utilise some Islamic concepts and principles for its proposed environmental policy. For instance, the JABA's mission statement reads:

> The environment is a system created by the Almighty Allah in a delicate balance, as said in the Holy Book . . . The creator of this system has deposited all the viable elements of life, and makes it serviceable to mankind to exploit its resources for its interests and benefit . . . Due to the increasing environmental risks that threaten this divine gift, in the absence of the local and integrated management to protect the environmental rights and how to defend them, we have adopted an organizational plan to develop a vision for the environmental life . . . that will achieve the safety and protection to the components of the system.[68]

Thus, Hizbullah seeks to inextricably intertwine its activities with Islamic environmental ethics. Not only does it adhere to the principles of vicegerent (*khalifa*) and balance (*mizan*), but it aspires to develop a vision for environmental sustainability.

Since the group has a sacred mission to follow God's path, the respect and protection of the environment are perceived as religious duties. A manifestation of this perception can be found in Hizbullah's reforestation projects. Like many Muslims, Hizbullah's members have attached important religious meaning to trees. The group has successfully used the Qur'an and *ahadith* to promote reforestation projects throughout the country. In this regard, it has significantly contributed to the protection of Lebanon's forests. Participation is portrayed as a religious obligation for Hizbullah's followers. Indeed, as mentioned earlier, Hassan Nasrallah has used the term *sadaqa* to describe the planting of a tree as an act of charity. In other words, there is some sincere interest in protecting nature and its resources that cannot be easily dismissed.

At the same time, Hizbullah has apparently avoided the use of religious rhetoric to address water-related issues. Although Shari'a covers water management and conservation, the group has proposed only non-religious solutions that are aligned with modern technological evolution. Hizbullah has accepted that Shari'a cannot replace the current legal system.

Hizbullah has also focused on the utilisation of offshore energy resources, which is a source of tensions with Israel. It has used nationalist rhetoric to claim that the neighbouring country constitutes a security threat for Lebanon. Given that the problem of climate change has generated wide public attention, Hizbullah feels obliged to engage in the relevant debate. As evidenced by Nasrallah's statements, the Lebanese group is concerned about rising global temperatures and aspires to contribute to the solution of the problem. Only then will it fulfil its long-term goal of representing the interests and viewpoints of most Muslims. It is an ambitious endeavour deriving perhaps from a strict sense of religious commitment.

Overall, Hizbullah has understood the environment as a contested space. Indeed, the group's uniqueness lies in the fact that it is a non-state armed actor with many state features; it functions as a proto-state in some parts of the country. The group seeks to protect the environment by collecting waste, cleaning forests, distributing water and planting trees. Hizbullah's environmentalism is anthropocentric, focusing on disenfranchised communities. This pragmatism keeps the group embedded in Lebanese society.

In any case, there is a paradox in Hizbullah's policy formulation. Although religion is the foundation of its ideology and praxis, the group does not always use theological evidence and argumentation for policy purposes. Although there is some Islamic influence in Hizbullah's environmental policy, the only occasional use of religious terms indicates the evolution of the group's identity. Still, Hizbullah remains a Shi'i organisation engaging in multiple policy contexts, albeit in different ways. It can be argued that religion is a source of inspiration, but not always; it clearly depends on the context.

Notes

1. Although the demographic composition of Lebanon is a contested issue, most analyses acknowledge that Twelver Shi'a Muslims constitute the second largest group as far as religious affiliation is concerned. See 'Lebanon', *The World Factbook*, 16 June 2022, https://www.cia.gov/the-world-factbook/countries/lebanon/ (accessed 20 June 2022).

2. Naim Qassem, *Hizbullah: The Story from Within* (London: Saqi, 2005), p. 76.

3. Currently, Hizbullah is under the political and spiritual supervision of Ayatollah Ali Khamenei, who is the *marja' al-taqlid*. See Joseph Alagha, 'Hezbollah's Conception of the Islamic State', in Sabrina Mervin (ed.), *The Shi'a Worlds and Iran* (London: Saqi, 2010), p. 93. The Occultation of the Mahdi, the twelfth imam, can be divided into two periods: the Minor Occultation (874–941), when he used his deputies to maintain contact with followers, and the Major

Occultation (since 941), when the hidden imam has not been in contact with the faithful.

4. Vali Nasr, *The Shia Revival: How Conflicts within Islam Will Shape the Future* (New York: W. W. Norton, 2007), p. 137.

5. Olivier Roy, 'The Impact of the Iranian Revolution on the Middle East', in Sabrina Mervin (ed.), *The Shi'a Worlds and Iran* (London: Saqi, 2010), pp. 29–30.

6. Imam Khomeini, *Islamic Government: Governance of the Jurist* (Tehran: Institute for Compilation and Publication of Imam Khomeini's Works, 2002), p. 30.

7. Imam Khomeini, *Islam and Revolution: Writings and Declarations of Imam Khomeini* (Berkeley, CA: Mizan Press, 1981), p. 50. It is a quote from Imam Ali's will to his sons after he was wounded in the Great Mosque of Kufa. See 'Letter 47: Will to Imam Hasan (a) and Imam Husayn (a) after he was wounded by Abd al-Rahman b. Muljam whilst offered the morning prayers in the mosque of Kufa', Al-Islam.org, https://www.al-islam.org/nahjul-balagha-part-2-letters-and-sayings/letter-47-will-imam-hasan-and-imam-husayn-after-he-was (accessed 20 June 2022).

8. Marvin Zonis and Daniel Brumberg, 'Shi'ism as Interpreted by Khomeini: An Ideology of Revolutionary Violence', in Martin Kramer (ed.), *Shi'ism, Resistance, and Revolution* (Boulder, CO: Westview Press, 1987), p. 57.

9. In 1974, Imam Musa al-Sadr founded Harakat al-Mahrumin (the Movement of the Dispossessed) to support the Lebanese Shi'a. The movement eventually evolved into a militia known by its acronym, Amal (Afwaj al-Muqawamah al-Lubnaniyyah – Battalions of the Lebanese Resistance). See Fouad Ajami, *The Vanished Imam: Musa al Sadr and the Shia of Lebanon* (Ithaca, NY: Cornell University Press, 1986).

10. On the Islamic Da'wa Party see Ranj Alaaldin, 'The Islamic Da'wa Party and the Mobilization of Iraq's Shi'i Community, 1958–1965', *Middle East Journal*, vol. 71, no. 1, 2017, pp. 45–65.

11. Qassem, *Hizbullah*, p. 20.

12. For a Shi'i perspective see Yasin T. al-Jibouri, *Kerbala and Beyond* (Qum: Ansariyan, 2002), pp. 42–57.

13. Qassem, *Hizbullah*, p. 45.

14. Ibid., p. 47.

15. The National Accord Document – The Taef Agreement, 1989, http://www.presidency.gov.lb/Arabic/LebaneseSystem/Documents/TaefAgreementEn.pdf (accessed 21 June 2022).

16. Magnus Ranstorp, 'The Strategy and Tactics of Hizballah's Current "Lebanonization" Process', *Mediterranean Politics*, vol. 3, no. 1, 1998, pp. 103–34.

17. See, for example, Amal Saad-Ghorayeb, *Hizbu'llah: Politics and Religion* (London: Pluto Press, 2002); Ahmad Nizar Hamzeh, *In the Path of Hizbullah* (Syracuse, NY: Syracuse University Press, 2004); Judith Palmer Harik, *Hezbollah: The Changing Face of Terrorism* (London: I. B. Tauris, 2004); Gilbert Achcar and Michel Warschawski, *The 33-Day War: Israel's War on Hezbollah in Lebanon and Its Consequences* (Boulder, CO: Paradigm Publishers, 2007); Eitan Azani, *Hezbollah: The Story of the Party of God – From Revolution to Institutionalization* (New York: Palgrave Macmillan, 2009); Matthew Levitt, *Hezbollah: The Global Footprint of Lebanon's Party of God* (Washington, DC: Georgetown University Press, 2013).

18. Antony Black, *The History of Islamic Thought: From the Prophet to the Present*, 2nd ed. (Edinburgh: Edinburgh University Press, 2011), p. 42.

19. Robert Gleave, 'Political Aspects of Modern Shi'i Legal Discussions: Khumayni and Khu'i on *ijtihad* and *qada''*, in B. A. Roberson (ed.), *Shaping the Current Islamic Reformation* (London: Frank Cass, 2003), p. 112.

20. Hamid Mavani, *Religious Authority and Political Thought in Twelver Shi'ism: From Ali to Post-Khomeini* (Abingdon: Routledge, 2013), p. 69.

21. Khomeini's concept of absolute guardianship was not widely accepted by other senior Shi'a clerics because it seems unorthodox and non-traditional. See Hamid Mavani, 'Analysis of Khomeini's Proofs for *al-Wilaya al-Mutlaqa* (Comprehensive Authority) of the Jurist', in Linda S. Walbridge (ed.), *The Most Learned of the Shi'a: The Institution of the Marja' Taqlid* (New York: Oxford University Press, 2001), pp. 183–210.

22. Dominique Avon and Anaïs-Trissa Khatchadourian, *Hezbollah: A History of the 'Party of God'* (Cambridge, MA: Harvard University Press, 2012), p. 106.

23. Qassem, *Hizbullah*, p. 273.

24. Hizbullah, للعام النيابية الانتخابات في الله لحزب الانتخابي البرنامج 2000 (2000 Electoral Programme), https://www.moqawama.org/essaydetails.php?eid=11255&cid=109 (accessed 21 June 2022).

25. Hizbullah, النيابية للانتخابات الله لحزب الانتخابي البرنامج 2009 (2009 Electoral Programme), https://www.moqawama.org/essaydetailsf.php?eid=14229&fid=45 (accessed 21 June 2022).

26. The area is claimed by Lebanon, but Israel has annexed it as part of the formerly Syrian-controlled Golan Heights. See Asher Kaufman, 'Who Owns the Shebaa

Farms? Chronicle of a Territorial Dispute', *Middle East Journal*, vol. 56, no. 4, 2002, pp. 576–95.

27. Hizbullah, 2000 Electoral Programme.

28. Joseph Alagha, *The Shifts in Hizbullah's Ideology: Religious Ideology, Political Ideology, and Political Program* (Amsterdam: Amsterdam University Press, 2006), p. 274.

29. Hizbullah, 2009 Electoral Programme.

30. Ibid.

31. 'The New Hezbollah Manifesto', November 2009, available at http://www.leba nonrenaissance.org/assets/Uploads/15-The-New-Hezbollah-Manifesto-Nov09 .pdf (accessed 18 July 2022).

32. See Marisa Sullivan, 'Hezbollah in Syria', Middle East Security Report 19, Institute for the Study of War, April 2014, http://www.understandingwar.org /sites/default/files/Hezbollah_Sullivan_FINAL.pdf (accessed 21 June 2022).

33. Daniel Sobelman, 'Hezbollah's friends in Yemen are trying to lure the Saudis into a ground war', *Foreign Policy*, 11 June 2015, https://foreignpolicy.com/20 15/06/11/yemens-rebels-are-stealing-a-page-from-hezbollahs-playbook-iran-sa udi-arabia/ (accessed 21 June 2022).

34. The Assad dynasty of Syria follows the Alawite branch of Shi'i Islam, whose doctrine and practices have integrated many non-Islamic elements. The founder of Amal, Musa al-Sadr, recognised Alawites as fellow Shi'a and Hizbullah has followed suit to maintain its close relationship with Damascus. According to Heinz Halm, Alawites believe that their souls were originally lights which rebelled against God. They were expelled from heaven, exiled on the earth and trapped inside human bodies. Alawites are condemned to metempsychosis unless they understand the essence (*ma'na*) of God, who is incarnated in Ali. See Heinz Halm, 'Nusayriyya', in Peri Bearman et al. (eds), *Encyclopaedia of Islam*, 2nd ed., Brill Online, 2012, http://dx.doi.org/10.1163/1573-3912_islam_COM_0876 (accessed 21 June 2022).

35. Although Yemen's Zaydi community is closer to Sunni jurisprudence, Hizbullah has chosen to ignore that affinity. Zaydis largely accept Sunni collections of *ahadith* and do not accept the infallibility of imams apart from Ali, Hassan and Hussein. See Wilferd Madelung, 'Zaydiyya', in Peri Bearman et al. (eds), *Encyclopaedia of Islam*, 2nd ed., Brill Online, 2012, http://dx.doi.org/10.1163 /1573-3912_islam_COM_1385 (accessed 21 June 2022); Barak A. Salmoni, Bryce Loidolt and Madeleine Wells, *Regime and Periphery in Northern Yemen: The Huthi Phenomenon* (Santa Monica, CA: RAND, 2010), pp. 287–95.

36. Harik, *Hezbollah*, p. 85.

37. Laura Zittrain Eisenberg, 'Israel's South Lebanon Imbroglio', *Middle East Quarterly*, June 1997, pp. 60–1.

38. Nicholas Noe (ed.), *Voice of Hezbollah: The Statements of Sayyed Hassan Nasrallah* (London: Verso, 2007), pp. 189–90.

39. Laura Veccia Vaglieri, 'Khaybar', in Peri Bearman et al. (eds), *Encyclopaedia of Islam*, 2nd ed., Brill Online, 2012, http://dx.doi.org/10.1163/1573-3912_islam_COM_0503 (accessed 21 June 2022).

40. 'Speech of Hezbollah secretary general Sayyed Hassan Nasrallah on Tuesday August 24, 2010', The Saker, 27 August 2010, http://thesaker.is/speech-of-hezbollah-secretary-general-sayyed-hassan-nasrallah-on-tuesday-august-24-2010/ (accessed 21 June 2022).

41. Hizb'allah, العام انتخابات لدورة حزب الله لحزب الانتخابي البرنامج 2018 (2018 Electoral Programme), 22 March 2018, https://alwafaabloc.org/post/14972/2018.-العام-انتخابات-لدورة-الله-لحزب-الانتخابي-البرنامج.

42. Imam Khamenei, الإمام الخامنئي: فلسطين من النهر إلى البحر وعلى الأمة الإسلامية منع تشكيل هامش أمن للكيان الصهيوني ('Palestine from the river to the sea'), 17 January 2018, https://www.moqawama.org/essaydetails.php?eid=34738&cid=202&st=%D9%86%D9%87%D8%B1 (accessed 21 June 2022).

43. Qassem, *Hizbullah*, p. 29.

44. 'Hezbollah leader Hassan Nasrallah plants in Beirut's suburbs', Hasan Almustafa/YouTube, 8 October 2010, https://www.youtu.be/dZZsM_Tj-CE (accessed 21 June 2022).

45. Local editor, 'One Million Tree Campaign: Culture of Nature', 8 October 2010, http://www.english.moqawama.org/essaydetailsf.php?eid=12310&fid=55

46. 'The Good Tree', Jihad al-Binaa Development Association, no date, https://jihadbinaa.org.lb/english/essaydetails.php?eid=64&cid=384#.XFOJg1z7Q2w

47. 'Agriculture', Jihad al-Binaa Development Association, no date, https://jihadbinaa.org.lb/english/essaydetails.php?eid=4&cid=274#.XFday1z7Q2w

48. Ibid.

49. '2018 Lebanese Parliamentary Elections: Results & Figures', UNDP Lebanon, 2018, http://www.lb.undp.org/content/lebanon/en/home/library/democratic_governance/2018LebaneseParliamentaryElectionsResultsandFigures.html (accessed 21 June 2022).

50. Hassan Nasrallah, 'Speech on marking end of planting one million trees campaign', 9 October 2010, https://english.alahednews.com.lb/12511/385 (accessed 18 July 2022).

51. Ibid.

52. The Qur'an mentions that 'charities are for the poor, and the destitute, and those who administer them, and for reconciling hearts, and for freeing slaves, and for those in debt, and in the path of God, and for the traveller in need – an obligation from God. God is All-Knowing, Most Wise' (9: 60).

53. انجازات جمعية اخضر بلا حدود خلال موسم تشجير ('Achievements of Green without Borders association during the 2014–15 afforestation season'), Green without Borders, http://akhdarbelahodod.blogspot.com/2015/04/2014-2015.html

54. Joseph Daher, *Hezbollah: The Political Economy of Lebanon's Party of God* (London: Pluto Press, 2016), p. 33.

55. Hizb'alla, 2018 Electoral Programme.

56. Sara Taha Moughnieh, 'Sayyed Nasrallah: after every victory we will witness US chemical play', Al Manar TV, 15 April 2018, http://english.almanar.com.lb/486385 (accessed 21 June 2022).

57. Nasrallah, 'Speech on marking end of planting one million trees campaign'.

58. Alistair Lyon, 'Go green, Hezbollah guerrilla chief tells Lebanese', Reuters, 11 October 2010, http://www.reuters.com/article/us-ba-lebanon-hezbollah-trees-idUSTRE69A2TW20101011 (accessed 21 June 2022).

59. 'What a gas!', *The Economist*, 11 November 2010, http://www.economist.com/node/17468208 (accessed 21 June 2022).

60. 'Hezbollah: Lebanon will not let Israel seize its natural gas', *Haaretz*, 14 July 2011, https://www.haaretz.com/2011-07-14/ty-article/hezbollah-lebanon-will-not-let-israel-seize-its-natural-gas/0000017f-e0bc-df7c-a5ff-e2fe70fc0000 (accessed 21 June 2022).

61. Hussein Dakroub, 'Nasrallah: hands off our waters', *Daily Star* (Lebanon), 27 July 2011, p. 1

62. 'Sayyed Nasrallah: We can disable Israel's offshore installations within hours', Al Manar TV, 16 February 2018, http://english.almanar.com.lb/447900 (accessed 21 June 2022).

63. Ibid.

64. 'Loyalty to resistance: Cabinet formation delay triggers new complications', Al Manar TV, 30 August 2018, http://english.almanar.com.lb/570953 (accessed 21 June 2022).

65. 'Hezbollah brings Iranian fuel into Lebanon to ease shortages', BBC News, 16 September 2021, https://www.bbc.com/news/world-middle-east-58583008 (accessed 21 June 2022).

66. Makram Rabah, 'Lebanon's electricity crisis fuelled by decades of

mismanagement', *Arab Weekly*, 12 August 2018, https://thearabweekly
.com/lebanons-electricity-crisis-fuelled-decades-mismanagement (accessed 21
June 2022).

67. Interview with Abbas al-Mussawi, *Revue du Liban*, 27 July 1985.
68. 'Introduction', Jihad al-Binaa Development Association, no date, https://jihad
binaa.org.lb/english/essaydetails.php?eid=14&cid=284#.XFOLqVz7Q2w

5

HAMAS AND THE ENVIRONMENT

The Palestinian group Harakah al-Muqawamah al-Islamiyyah (Movement of Islamic Resistance – Hamas) is an offshoot of the Muslim Brotherhood that was established in 1987 during the first Intifada.[1] The ideology of Hamas contains elements of Arab nationalism, Islamism and anti-Semitism. It was founded by seven members of the Ikhwan in the Gaza Strip, including Sheikh Ahmad Yassin and Abdel Aziz al-Rantisi. Both were of refugee origin whose families fled to Gaza from other parts of British-mandated Palestine after the 1948 Arab–Israeli war. Yassin served as the spiritual leader of Hamas, while al-Rantisi was its political leader.

The decision-making body of Hamas is the secretive Consultative Council (*Majlis al-Shura*), consisting of religious and political leaders. The Council elects the fifteen-member Political Bureau (*al-Maktab al-Siyasi*), where all important decisions are made. Although only lay members apparently participate in the Political Bureau, the influence of religious leaders remains significant. Yet Hamas does not have its own fatwa-issuing body.

From the beginning, the group had an uncompromising stance towards Israel that reflected a wider Islamist understanding of the conflict. For instance, the influential Palestinian-American Islamic thinker Ismail Raji al-Faruqi argued that '[Islam] imposes upon Muslims all over the world to rise like one man to put an end to injustice . . . [T]he Islamic position leaves no chance for the Zionist state but to be dismantled and destroyed, and its wealth confiscated to pay off its liabilities.'[2] Such views provided justification for Hamas to denounce the Arab–Israeli peace process and use violence against the Jewish State.

In February 1989, Hamas's military wing, the Izz ad-Din al-Qassam Brigades,[3] conducted their first attack against an Israeli target. Since then, the Qassam Brigades have claimed responsibility for dozens of suicide bombings and other attacks in Israel. In fact, the second Intifada was a Hamas-led armed uprising that began in September 2000 and ended almost five years later. In June 2006, its fighters attacked an Israel Defence Forces (IDF) outpost and captured an Israeli soldier. In December 2008, Hamas launched rocket attacks into Israel and provoked an IDF operation called Operation Cast Lead that lasted three weeks. In July 2014, Tel Aviv mounted a similar operation to stop Hamas from firing rockets against nearby Israeli towns.

Domestically, following the signing of the 1993 Oslo Accords, Hamas decided to boycott the newly established Palestinian institutions. Therefore, it refused to participate in the 1996 and 2005 presidential elections. Notwithstanding its violent tactics, Hamas eventually developed a political wing to participate in the embryonic Palestinian political system. In January 2006, Hamas won 74 out of the 132 seats for the Palestinian Legislative Council, while Fatah (the largest faction of the Palestinian Liberation Organisation) won only 45 seats.[4] The failure of the peace process and the growing frustration against the Israeli government certainly contributed to Hamas's victory.[5] In June 2007, Hamas managed to take over Gaza by staging a coup against the local branch of Fatah. The group has maintained control of the coastal enclave ever since, although there have been efforts to establish a Palestinian unity government.

Hamas is more than an armed group opposing Israel, though. It is an organisation with a complex structure that has been able to develop agendas and policies in many areas of responsibility. This chapter first details Hamas's general perspective on the environment, particularly the religious significance of Palestine. It then examines four areas of engagement: water management, tree-planting, animals, and pollution and energy. Finally, the chapter examines the role of religion in the emergence of Hamas's environmentalism.

Hamas's General Perspective on the Environment

At the heart of Hamas's general perspective on the environment is the sacred status of Palestine. The leaders of Hamas have viewed Palestine as an Islamic endowment (*waqf*) because it 'embraces within it the first of the two *qibla* [the direction of prayer towards Jerusalem] and the third most important mosque, which the Prophet visited during his *al-mi'raj* (night journey) to the Upper Heavens'.[6] The reference to the location of the first *qibla* reinforces the legitimacy of the group's claim on Jerusalem by utilising early Islamic history.[7]

Since Hamas originates from the Muslim Brotherhood, it has been influenced by the thinking of its founder. Hassan al-Banna declared that 'Palestine is not the case of a specific geographical entity; it is rather the case of the Islam that you embrace; Palestine is an injured part of the Islamic body; any part that doesn't feel the pain and suffering of Palestine doesn't belong to that body'.[8] Palestine has been portrayed as the cradle of the *umma* that must be defended at all costs. It is a symbol of Muslim unity.

Interestingly, the 1988 Hamas Charter attempted to blend nationalism and Islamism by claiming that 'nationalism is part and parcel of its religious creed. Nothing is loftier or deeper in nationalism than [waging] a holy war [jihad] against the enemy and confronting him when he sets foot on the land of the Muslims.'[9] This form of Islamic nationalism can mobilise devout Muslims, although Islam is generally against nationalism.[10] Hamas has portrayed the Palestinian nation as a vanguard of the *umma* that has engaged in a civilisational war against the Jews.

On 13 March 1988, for instance, it issued a leaflet that stated, 'Let any hand be cut off that signs [away] a grain of sand in Palestine in favour of the enemies of God . . . who have seized . . . the blessed land.'[11] On 18 August 1988, the group issued another leaflet, titled 'Islamic Palestine from the Sea to the River' (that is, from the Mediterranean to the Jordan), in which it stated that 'the Muslims have had a full (not partial) right to Palestine for generations in the past, present and future . . . [Y]ou must continue the uprising and stand up against the usurpers whenever they may be, until the complete liberation of every grain of the soil of . . . Palestine.'[12] The 2017 Document of General Principles and Policies, which revised the 1988 Charter, defined Palestine as the area 'which extends from the River Jordan in the east to the Mediterranean in the west and from Ras Al-Naqurah in the north to Umm Al-Rashrash in the south' (see appendix).[13] Hence, the Palestinians are the rightful inhabitants of the land for historical and religious reasons. In contrast, those who occupy Palestine are designated as 'enemies of God' who deserve severe punishment.

While Hamas still has an active armed wing, it has also become the governing party in the Gaza Strip. This means that the group is now accountable to the Palestinian citizens, whose living conditions have dramatically worsened in recent years. In particular, the environmental situation in Gaza has been described by the United Nations as 'serious . . . due to underinvestment in environmental systems, lack of progress on priority environmental projects and the collapse of governance mechanisms'.[14] According to Hussam Abdulhadi, director of the Hamas Information Office's Foreign Media Unit, 'being part of the Palestinian people, Hamas highly considers environmental issues since they have considerable positive impacts on the lives of the Palestinians'.[15]

The urgency of Gaza's environmental problems has forced Hamas to formulate an environmental agenda. The electoral campaign platform 'List for Change and Reform', drafted in the autumn of 2005 during Hamas's campaign for the Palestinian legislative elections, mentioned for the first time that 'the environment is to be protected . . . Small farms will get credits to effectively make use of the land. The use of insecticides should be regulated for full benefits.'[16] Hamas elaborated further on the proposed environmental policy in its 2006 legislative election programme. It committed to creating

> a clean environment through developing the culture of general cleaning, and planting trees in roads and public parks; and encouraging the setting up of private and public gardens . . . protect[ing] the environment and stop[ping] the Palestinian environmental deterioration, through coordination with international organisations. Moreover, resisting the continuing environmental pollution of Palestinian lands, resulting from the occupation and the Zionist settlements . . . keeping Gaza sea beach clean and beautiful and valid for tourism . . . stopping environmental pollution resulting from turning sewers water to seawater.[17]

The programme gives us some insight into how Hamas views environmental issues. First, it seeks to develop a 'culture of general cleaning', implying that the current situation is the result of public ignorance. Second, the

Palestinian group makes an interesting case for the environmental protection of Gaza's coast by highlighting its tourist potential. Isolated by both Israel and Egypt, Hamas has become more pragmatic because tourism could be a lucrative business. Despite its problematic relationship with the international community, Hamas does not deny the importance of international organisations in protecting the environment.

Since them, the group has intensified its criticism against Israel regarding the blockade of Gaza. Hamas has even accused the Israeli authorities of preventing the entry of medical supplies into the enclave to battle the Covid-19 pandemic.[18] While the physical space has remained the same, the human environment is deteriorating significantly. Thus, the Gaza of Hamas is under mental and military siege.

In summary, Hamas's general perspective on the environment is defined by its confrontation with Israel. From its point of view, Palestine is the sacred land of Muslims that the group is destined to liberate. This is a central tenet of its ideology that inevitably sets the limits of its emerging environmentalism. The chapter now turns to the water management policy of Hamas.

Water Management

The Gaza Strip has suffered from a severe lack of drinking water. United Nations agencies and international NGOs have claimed that the enclave will soon become unliveable.[19] The quality of the drinking water is poor due to contamination of the aquifer by sewage and seawater.[20] To make matters worse, Gaza uses most of the available water for agriculture.[21] As a result, many Palestinians no longer have access to clean water, a health and ecological problem with serious political implications.

Given the situation, Hamas has been forced to address water issues in Gaza. In general, Hamas has maintained that 'the Islamic principles recommend all Muslims not to waste water and to save it as much as they can'.[22] Yet the water deficit is a symptom of the ongoing Hamas–Israeli conflict. In March 2001, the group accused the Israeli authorities of weaponising water against Gaza. A statement claimed that

the Zionists have flooded the Shajaiya neighbourhood with some wastewater after opening huge reservoirs in which water is gathered from within the borders of occupied Palestine adjacent to the Gaza Strip, causing a humanitarian disaster that has affected homes, livestock and farms and disrupted the life of our people in the area.[23]

The 2006 legislative election programme explains how Hamas views water policy; it called for 'encouraging land reclamation, and supporting its cultivating and irrigation', as well as 'monitoring the performance of Coast Water authority, to achieve the interest of nation and citizens'.[24] It was probably the first hint that Hamas considers water management not only as part of the Israeli–Palestinian conflict, but also as a domestic political issue that can undermine the credibility of the governing Fatah party.

Nevertheless, the Palestinian administration was paralysed after the 2007 takeover of Gaza by Hamas. The group started to purge Fatah from administrative structures in the area to solidify its power. As a result, staff members from the Environmental Quality Authority and the Palestinian Hydrology Group were asked not to resume their responsibilities or take data and information with them.[25] It is not clear why Hamas decided to dismiss the existing personnel from these agencies. One possible explanation is that the group fundamentally distrusted those working for the Palestinian Authority and sought to replace them with Hamas loyalists.

The situation was worsened by the Israeli bombing during the 2014 Gaza conflict when the enclave's water supply network was greatly damaged. The Palestinian Water Authority announced that thirty-two water wells were completely or partially damaged, and 17 kilometres of water supply networks were destroyed.[26] While the IDF have never admitted that the targeting of water infrastructure is a deliberate policy, the level of the destruction indicates otherwise. It is likely that the Israeli leadership has sought to collectively punish the civilian population for supporting Hamas.

Indeed, Hamas has claimed that the Israeli government has imposed a water siege on the inhabitants of the enclave. According to Hussam Abdulhadi, the organisation

is deeply concerned about [the water crisis] because the techniques used by the Israeli occupation to deprive the Palestinians [of] adequate amounts of water fit for human use are alarming . . . Not only do [the Israelis] prevent water flow from [the] North to access [the] Gaza Strip through [the] Gaza

Valley, but they also thwart the Palestinians' tries [sic] to enjoy groundwater available in areas surrounding Gaza.[27]

It is not easy to verify Hamas's allegations, but the scarcity of water has certainly created tensions between the two sides.

In any case, Hamas shares some of the blame for Gaza's water crisis. For instance, it has not been able to eradicate overextraction. The area has 10,000 wells, including 300 municipal wells, 2,700 agricultural wells and 7,000 unlicensed wells.[28] Even the group itself has acknowledged the urgency of the water crisis. A report published by the Political Department of Hamas's International and Foreign Affairs Unit in December 2017 claimed that 'nearly 100 percent of drinking water in Gaza is polluted and unfit for human use and does not meet international health standards . . . [T]he absence of electricity for long periods of time and shortages of fuel have affected Gaza's clean water supply system.'[29] This description provides an accurate picture of the situation. Nevertheless, Hamas has not provided a detailed plan for solving the water problem.

The apparent failure of Hamas has encouraged the Fatah-controlled Palestinian Authority to pursue its own water policy. In July 2017, it agreed to a deal to buy from Israel 32 million cubic metres (mcm) of water at a reduced price; the plan is to consume 22 mcm in the West Bank, and the rest would go to Gaza.[30] One month later, the Palestinian Authority accused Hamas of hindering the building of a desalination plant in the Gaza Strip.[31] Palestinian officials have also proposed the construction of a pipeline to carry water from Gaza to the West Bank via Israel.[32] The main explanation for Hamas's reluctance to start these projects is that they would require some co-operation with Israel. In late August 2021, however, the Hamas administration issued a ban against digging water wells in Gaza to stop the overexploitation of the aquifer.[33]

At the same time, Gaza's water crisis has allowed Hamas to participate in a public debate about Palestinian human rights. Mustafa Barghouti, a member of the Palestinian Legislative Council and general secretary of the Palestinian National Initiative Party, has declared:

> It is our duty to struggle for our right to our water, because the right to water equals the right to life. It is our right to expose and fight against

using water as a weapon of racial discrimination. Palestinians will never leave (their land) no matter how much Israelis master racial discrimination, even if we are forced to squeeze cactus trees to look for water to quench our thirst.[34]

While Barghouti is not a political ally of Hamas, he aptly describes the Palestinian position. Most Palestinians have blamed Israel for the lack of water in Gaza and the West Bank. Since access to water is a human right, the Israeli side has been accused of installing a 'water apartheid' by favouring the Jewish population at the expense of Palestinians.[35] Hamas has capitalised on these public perceptions to maintain its animosity against Israel.

Trees

Hamas has developed its own policy regarding the management of Gaza's flora. To begin with, former minister of agriculture Mohamad Alagha once stated that the slogan of his policy was 'Toward building a resilient agricultural economy', which could be part of a resistant society.[36] The Hamas official envisioned a self-sufficient economy that can survive on its own, without any interactions with or dependencies on Israel. Therefore, the planting of trees has been part of a greater effort to gain self-sufficiency.

In October 2010, Hamas prime minister Ismail Haniyeh launched a campaign to plant one million olive trees in Gaza.[37] The ambitious project was directed by the Ministry of Agriculture to provide jobs, increase agricultural production and support political independence.[38] Additionally, Hamas has planted a further 18,000 apple trees, 4,000 peach trees, 70,000 mango trees, and 3,000 lemon trees.[39] Some foreign Islamic charities have launched their own plantation projects. In 2015, for instance, the Al-Imdaad Foundation planted 3,000 olive trees in Gaza.[40]

Hamas has accused Israel of conducting ecological warfare against the Palestinians by destroying olive trees, which are a symbol of 'Palestinian steadfastness' against occupation. Moreover, it has been claimed that 'the olive tree is a blessed tree and belongs to the Palestinian citizens . . . [T]he Zionist forces are targeting this tree with a deliberate and systematic plan to uproot it and deprive the Palestinians of its benefits.'[41] According to Tayseer al-Tamimi, supreme judge in the West Bank, the Israeli army has deliberately uprooted thousands of productive olive trees because 'they are the historic source of livelihood for tens of thousands of Palestinian families'.[42] The 2008 war led to the destruction of 2,000 hectares of agricultural land and 305 agricultural wells.[43] In addition, the Palestinians accused the Israelis of destroying 140,965 olive trees, 136,217 citrus trees, 10,365 date trees, 22,745 other fruit trees, and 8,822 other trees.[44]

This is an issue of immense political and economic importance for the Palestinians because it is linked to their livelihood as a people. Moreover, it has fuelled anti-settler sentiments in the West Bank. Hamas has argued, with regard to the destruction of trees, that 'is not new to witness such acts and we profoundly realise the underlying motives of the Israeli settlers, which include the following: confiscating the lands and livelihoods of the Palestinians, especially farmers; vanishing the Palestinian identity of the land; and generating disturbance and poisoning the lives of the Palestinians'.[45] Hence, the group has claimed that the destruction of trees aims at the physical, psychological and cultural annihilation of the Palestinian population.

For Hamas, trees have also an important religious meaning that cannot be ignored. In its 1988 Charter, Hamas cited a famous *hadith* that states:

> The time will not come until Muslims will fight the Jews (and kill them); until the Jews hide behind the rocks and trees, which will cry: O Muslim! There is a Jew hiding behind me, come on and kill him! This will not apply to the Gharqad, which is a Jewish tree.[46]

The group mentioned this *hadith*, which was narrated by Imam al-Bukhari, to prove the predetermined outcome of the battle between Muslims and Jews for the control of Palestine. In this way, Muslims would be supported even by trees, which are a manifestation of the divine creation.[47] There is speculation about what this mythical tree may look like, but thorns are believed to be a part of it. Indeed, there is a widespread rumour among Palestinians that Israelis have planted thorny trees around their houses to protect themselves from the rage of Muslims.[48]

Additionally, Hamas has used other types of trees to support its claims against Israel. In July 2017, for example, the first deputy speaker of the Hamas-controlled Palestinian Legislative Council, Ahmed Bahar, stated that 'Gaza's population will remain deep-rooted in their motherland as a palm tree is in its soil ... The Palestinian people will forever remain faithful to their native soil until every inch of it is liberated.'[49] While the palm tree is not a symbol of Palestine, it has important religious significance for Muslims. It is mentioned by the Qur'an in twenty verses of sixteen chapters, which is more than any other tree. The palm tree is part of the garden of paradise, as stated in the Qur'an: 'Which then of the bounties of your Lord will you deny? Therein are fruits and palms and pomegranates' (55:67–8). Hamas has often asked young Palestinians to die as martyrs, and the palm tree is divine and perfect because it waits for them in the afterlife. It is a manifestation of God's reward for those who follow the path of jihad.

Since trees have such a positive connotation, Hamas has even described itself as a strong-rooted tree. Ismail Haniyeh has compared Hamas to 'a good tree planted by the best people. On top of them is the martyr Ahmad Yassin.'[50] Like a big tree, Hamas has grown strong roots within Palestinian society. What makes the group unique is its self-perceived moral superiority that lies in the martyrdom of its leaders and members.

In summary, trees have persistently featured in Hamas's discourses. Due to their religious significance, trees can function as cognitive reference points for devout Muslims, who make up the core constituency of Hamas. Depending on the circumstances, trees can be a symbol of resilience, a valuable military asset, an ally against the archenemy, a sign of heaven, or even a representation of Hamas's grassroots.

Animals

The official position of Hamas is that it 'takes animals' welfare and rights into consideration because Islam recommends us to do so'.[51] Nonetheless, the isolation of Gaza from the outside world has created a siege mentality affecting, among other things, Hamas's perception of animals. In August 2015, for instance, a Palestinian newspaper reported a bizarre story about the naval unit of Hamas's military wing capturing a dolphin that was allegedly being used by the Israelis as a spy; it was claimed that the mammal was equipped with spying cameras and a device capable of firing arrows.[52] While dolphins and other marine mammals have been trained by Russia and the United States for military purposes, it is doubtful whether the IDF have such capability. Indeed, no photographs of the dolphin were released by Hamas.[53] It should be noted that there have been similar claims about Israeli use of animals for espionage and other purposes throughout the region. In December 2010, the South Sinai governor had speculated that a series of shark attacks in the Red Sea could have been the work of Mossad 'to hit tourism in Egypt'.[54]

On the other hand, Hamas has used donkeys laden with explosives to carry out attacks against Israeli forces.[55] According to the IDF, the first such attack involving a donkey took place in June 1995.[56] During the second Palestinian Intifada (2000–05), Hamas and other Palestinian militant groups continued the weaponisation of animals.[57] In Sunni Islam, donkeys do not have a great religious significance. In contrast, Shiʻa traditions have described the close relationship between the Prophet and his donkey Yaʻfur, which probably was either a gift from Cyrus, the patriarch of Alexandria, or a spoil of war from Khaybar.[58] The military use of donkeys implicitly reveals the Sunni character of Hamas, which perceives them only as expendable beasts of burden.

Also, the Palestinian group has targeted dogs as being dangerous and impure. In May 2017, Hamas banned owners of dogs from walking them in public places such as open markets and beaches. The spokesman of the Hamas-controlled police, Ayman al-Batniji, explained that 'it is neither of our culture nor of our traditions . . . [W]e are not against dogs, we use dogs in our work – the ban is simply to protect our women and children.'[59] While the group justified its decision on the basis of public safety, it is clear that the Islamic perception of dogs was deliberately mentioned to demonstrate the rightness of the ban.

Another indication of Hamas's anti-dog prejudice is the use of the word 'dog' as a derogatory term against the Jews. For example, a pro-Hamas preacher once stated that the Jews 'used to be a dog that frightened the entire neighbourhood with its barking. This dog begot a pup which was more wicked than its father. The Jews are always the same . . . Both dogs and pups bark and bite, and both are impure. That is the truth about the Jews.'[60] Such words indicate that dogs are viewed as inherently untrustworthy and aggressive. Thus, they can be compared to the Jews, who supposedly have the same characteristics.

Likewise, Hamas has targeted pigs not only as unclean, but also as a tool of Jewish conspiracy against the Palestinians. The group has used, for instance, the outbreak of swine flu in 2009 as a metaphor to describe the 'danger of Zionism'. In the words of Yunis al-Astal, Hamas MP and cleric,

> people who are afraid of the bestial swine flu should be even more afraid of the measures taken by the Zionist devils, which are more lethal to humanity than pigs . . . The fact that some countries slaughtered their pigs constitutes a modest measure in confronting this danger, as long as those countries maintain intimate, strong ties with the Zionists, whom Allah has decreed to be the brothers of apes and pigs.[61]

Not only did al-Astal condemn countries affected by the swine flu that have maintained relations with Israel (for example, Egypt), but he used a verse from the Qur'an to dehumanise the Jews: 'Say: Should I inform you of those worse than this in retribution from Allah? They are those whom Allah has cursed and upon whom He brought His wrath and of whom He made apes and swine, and who serve the devil' (5:60). Once again, Hamas used the Qur'an as a basis of legitimacy for its propaganda against the Jews.

Finally, the group has used animals for propaganda purposes. Hamas's TV channel Al-Aqsa has broadcast the children's show *The Pioneers of Tomorrow*, which features animal characters. For example, Farfour the Mouse once proclaimed that 'we, tomorrow's pioneers, will restore to this nation to its glory and we will liberate the Muslim countries, invaded by murderers. We will liberate al-Aqsa with Allah's will and we will liberate Iraq.'[62] This character was later replaced by Nahoul the Bee, who was featured abusing animals in one episode; it flung cats by the tail and threw stones at lions in Gaza Zoo.[63] Following Nahoul's 'martyrdom', Assud the Bunny became the main animal character in the show. Assud introduced itself as follows: 'I come from the diaspora, carrying the Key of Return . . . Allah willing, we will use this key to liberate our al-Aqsa mosque . . . [W]e are all martyrdom-seekers.'[64]

The Pioneers of Tomorrow has portrayed animals and insects as aggressive and violent. These animal characters are fiercely committed to the liberation of Palestine and use hateful language against the Jews. The choice of animals and insects is not always coincidental. The sixteenth chapter of the Qur'an is named after the bee, mentioned in verses 68 and 69:

And thy Lord revealed to the bee: Make hives in the mountains and in the trees and in what they build. Then eat of all fruits and walk in the ways of thy Lord submissively. There comes forth from their bellies a beverage of many hues, in which there is healing for men. Therein is surely a sign for a people who reflect.

Thus the bee serves as an example of dedication, determination and eventual success.

The Qur'an does not mention mice but there are some *ahadith* which state that the killing of mice is permissible. For example, a *hadith* narrated by al-Bukhari maintains that 'there are five animals for which there is no blame on the one who kills them: crows, kites, mice, scorpions and mad dogs'.[65] Hence, the appearance of Farfour the Mouse seems unorthodox because it is a rodent that has a negative image in Islam. Farfour clearly resembles the iconic American cartoon character Mickey Mouse, which has already been attacked by conservative *'ulama*. In the words of the Saudi cleric Muhammad al-Munajid, 'according to Islamic law, the mouse is [a] repulsive, corrupting creature . . . [they] have become wonderful and are loved by children . . . Mickey Mouse has become an awesome character, even though according to Islamic law Mickey Mouse should be killed in all cases.'[66] Hamas has ignored a mainstream Muslim belief about mice probably because Farfour the Mouse proved very popular among young viewers.

Of all the animals that appeared in the show, rabbits are the least theologically important. The Qur'an does not mention rabbits, whose meat is halal for Sunnis.[67] In contrast, most Shi'a consider rabbits to be unclean. For example, Grand Ayatollah Ali al-Sistani has argued that 'it is haram to eat the meat of rabbit, elephant, bear, monkey, jerboa, mouse, snake, hedgehog, and crawling animals and insects'.[68] However, the selection of Assud the Bunny did not have any religious meaning for Hamas; it was chosen probably only because it looked more appealing to children. In other words, Hamas's *Pioneers of Tomorrow* was less religion-driven and more politics-focused.

In summary, animals have been instrumentalised by Hamas for political purposes. They can be either allies (for example, bees, mice, rabbits, donkeys) or enemies (for example, dolphins, pigs, apes). This dichotomous logic reflects the reality of permanent war in Gaza.

Pollution and Energy

Pollution has been an issue of public concern because it has dramatically affected the quality of life in Gaza. During the May Day celebration on 1 May 2011, for example, Hamas's members and sympathisers participated in the cleaning of streets in Gaza City.[69] The cleaning campaign was inexpensive, but politically beneficial. Such events usually attract young participants who could be mobilised later as needed. More importantly, the campaign was designed to prove to many within and outside the Gaza Strip that Hamas is not just another armed group; it is a movement that cares about the well-being of its supporters.

Initiatives of this kind could hardly solve the pollution problem. Sewage and wastewater management systems require regular maintenance and pumping. Due to the power crisis in the Gaza Strip, Hamas has claimed that 'sewage pumps operate only occasionally, and subsequently, sewage water floods the houses of the Palestinian people or is discharged into Gaza Sea through undesignated channels. [As a result] groundwater and seawater are polluted by wastewater, which, in turn, make water unfit for human use or even for swimming.'[70] This is an accurate description of the current situation in the area. Additionally, air pollution has been a problem of growing importance because municipal solid waste is burned in open areas due to lack of waste-handling facilities.[71]

Additionally, Hamas has shown some interest in energy issues. Gaza has faced a serious electricity crisis since 2008. Its daily electricity needs are estimated at around 430 megawatts, but the area receives only half of that.[72] The electricity deficit has been exacerbated by the growing tensions between Hamas and the Fatah-dominated Palestinian Authority. The latter is financially responsible for the import of electricity from Israel and Egypt, but due to the post-2007 Israeli–Egyptian blockade, Gaza's only functioning power plant has often run out of fuel.[73] Yet Hamas has accused only the Israeli government of committing a crime against humanity.[74]

Gaza's energy dependence on Israel and Egypt has prompted Hamas to explore other options. During the late 1990s, the Marine gas field was discovered about 30 kilometres off the Gaza coast. It contains approximately 1 trillion cubic feet (28 billion cubic metres) of gas.[75] In 1999, President Yasser

Arafat negotiated an agreement with British Gas (BG), in which the latter took a 55 per cent share. In 2016 BG sold its share to Royal Dutch Shell. The rivalry between the Palestinian Authority and Hamas just two years later forced the company to give up its stake in the undeveloped offshore field.[76] Following the 2006 election victory, Hamas minister of finance Ziad Zaza had dismissed the Palestinian Authority's agreement with BG as 'an act of theft'.[77]

The lack of progress in resource exploration has fuelled new tensions in the area. Apart from Fatah, Hamas has blamed the Israeli government for the stagnation in exploration activities. In August 2014, the armed wing of Hamas fired two rockets at the Israeli Noa gas field, which is close to Gaza.[78] Although they missed the target, it was the first time that Hamas had attempted to destroy an Israeli gas installation. Gas exploration is perceived by the group as a zero-sum game with winners and losers. However, the current electricity crisis facing Gaza is bound to increase Hamas's interest in gas exploration and transportation.[79]

The Role of Religion

Hamas has promoted the religionisation of the environment by invoking Islamic sources of authority. It has often utilised Qur'anic verses and *ahadith* to highlight the religious significance of Palestine and to condemn the Jews as a people. Additionally, pro-Hamas *'ulama* have issued fatwas forbidding the concession of any part of Palestine.[80] It serves Hamas's political objectives to claim that there is a cosmogonic battle between Islam and Judaism. The *hadith* about the gharqad tree is indicative of the use of religion to support a politicised environmental agenda.

Nonetheless, the group has become increasingly pragmatic regarding the physical control of the environment. In January 2004, the Hamas leader Sheikh Hassan Yussef offered a ten-year truce conditional upon a Palestinian state being established in Gaza and the West Bank, with East Jerusalem as its capital; prisoners were to be released and Palestinian refugees allowed to return.[81] Hamas has repeated its offer of truce without success. In fact, the group has used the Islamic term *hudna* to describe its proposed truce. The first *hudna* was the Treaty of Hudaybiya, which was signed between the Prophet Muhammad and the Quraysh tribe of Mecca in March 628. It affirmed a ten-year period of peace, although it did not prevent the eventual resumption of hostilities. Most jurists hold the opinion that the maximum period of peace with an enemy should not exceed ten years, as this was the duration provided by the Treaty of Hudaybiya.[82] In December 2006, however, Hamas's leader Ismail Haniyeh called for a twenty-year truce with Israel that clearly deviates from the Islamic legal tradition.[83]

But Hamas does not believe in perpetual peace with Israel, which remains its archenemy. In this regard, the group's understanding of conflict is perhaps shaped by Abdullah Azzam, a Palestinian Islamic scholar who fought in Afghanistan against the Soviets and acted as the mentor of Osama bin Laden. He argued that peace with Israel is not possible because 'the land of Islam belongs to no one, therefore [no one] can make negotiations over it. Such a condition nullifies the treaty because the land belongs to Allah and to Islam.'[84] Theologically speaking, this is debatable.

Andrea Nüsse has observed that the Qur'an mentions only the towns of Mecca and Medina as sacred, whereby non-Muslims are not allowed to enter them.[85] In fact, Palestine theologically constitutes just another part of *Dar al-Islam* (that is, the Abode of Islam). Thus, the religious significance attached to Palestine by Hamas represents a departure from the Qur'anic perception of divine territory. Yet, the group has largely utilised Islamic evidence to support its claim to Palestine. In the 1988 Charter, for example, it used the following *hadith* narrated by al-Tabarani: 'The people of Sham (that is, Greater Syria) are God's whip on His earth; with them He takes revenge on who He pleases of His servants. It is forbidden for the hypocrites to rule over the believers, and they will die in worry and darkness.'[86] The *hadith* refers to Greater Syria, which historically and geographically includes Palestine.

Also, Hamas officials have used the Qur'an to justify their unwillingness to recognise Israel as a legitimate state. In March 2017, for example, one of Hamas's leaders in Gaza, Mahmoud al-Zahhar, argued that the Qur'an commands Muslims to 'drive them out from where they drove you out' (2:191). 'From where did the Jews drive us out? From within the 1967 borders or the 1948 borders? From within the 1948 borders . . . Hence, removing the Jews from the land they occupied in 1948 is an immutable principle, because it appears in the Book of Allah.'[87] In this way, the Qur'an is used as an authoritative source to justify Hamas's anti-Jewish stance. According to Jeroen Gunning, the interpretation of religion sets the parameters; yet the latter are not static but change in a dynamic process due to the constant interplay between religion and politics.[88]

The religionisation of the environment is neither consistent nor complete, however. There have been occasions on which the group has depicted Palestine as a primordial and eternal entity without any religious connotations. In the words of Ismail Haniyeh, 'our steadfast people in the occupied territories of 1948 . . . face the bare policy of demolition and annexation and attempts to empty the land of their rightful owners . . . [Our people] stand like the mountains of Galilee, Triangle and Mengerson in their land.'[89] Haniyeh evokes the notion of rightful land ownership to counter Jewish claims to the land. His metaphor about the Palestinians and mountains intends to demonstrate the resilience and endurance of his people. The message is clear: we are here to stay, as the mountains of Palestine do. Hamas claims that Israel intends to destroy the environment in which Palestinians live because it wants to uproot them from their ancestral land. From its point of view, this is the continuation of the war by other means.

Therefore, Palestinians have commemorated Land Day (*Yom al-Ard*) annually since 1976, when Israeli plans to expropriate land in the region of Galilee were met with massive protests. It is a day of national pride for the Palestinians and Hamas has participated in the commemorations of the events. On the forty-first anniversary of Land Day, it issued a statement that claimed:

> Above all are the rights to resist, to liberate our land and holy places and to enable refugees to return to their lands. These constitute the steps to achieving self-determination needed to establish our independent state on the entire land of Palestine with Jerusalem as its capital where all Palestinians can live in dignity and equally enjoy all rights and liberties without any discrimination.[90]

Here, the group adhered to the broader nationalist narrative about the liberation of historic Palestine, the return of refugees from the 1948 and 1967 wars, and the establishment of a new, presumably secular, state with Jerusalem as its capital.

Simultaneously, Hamas has formulated an environmental policy to tackle certain issues in Gaza. The group has launched a tree-planting programme in the Palestinian enclave without a religious reasoning. Although the group is apparently aware that the conservation of water is a religious duty, it has not developed any large-scale initiatives to promote a Shari'a-compliant system of water management. The understanding of animals has been influenced only to a certain extent by religion. Finally, Islam plays no role in pollution control and energy development.

Hamas has not attempted to promote faith-based solutions to ecological problems, although many Palestinians support a public role for Islam. In April 2013, a Pew Research Centre survey found that 89 per cent of Palestinians favour making Shari'a the official law in the Palestinian Territories.[91] At the same time, Hamas is aware of the competition it faces from other Islamist groups. For instance, Hizb ut-Tahrir has accused Hamas of losing its Islamic identity.[92] This paradox implies that other factors have also shaped the environmentalism of Hamas.

Notes

1. There is an extensive literature on Hamas. See, for example, Matthew Levitt, *Hamas: Politics, Charity, and Terrorism in the Service of Jihad* (New Haven, CT, and London: Yale University Press, 2006); Zaki Chehab, *Inside Hamas: The Untold Story of the Militant Islamic Movement* (New York: Nation, 2007); Beverley Milton-Edwards and Stephen Farrell, *Hamas: The Islamic Resistance Movement* (Cambridge: Polity, 2010); Azzam Tamimi, *Hamas: A History from Within* (Northampton, MA: Olive Branch Press, 2011); Paola Caridi, *Hamas: From Resistance to Government* (New York: Seven Stories Press, 2012); Björn Brenner: *Gaza under Hamas: From Islamic Democracy to Islamist Governance* (London and New York: I. B. Tauris, 2017).

2. Ismail Raji al-Faruqi, 'Islam and Zionism', in John L. Esposito (ed.), *Voices of Resurgent Islam* (New York: Oxford University Press, 1983), pp. 261–2.

3. Izz ad-Din al-Qassam was a Syrian Islamic preacher and resistance fighter who was killed by the British police in the northern West Bank in 1935.

4. 'The Second 2006 PLC Elections: The Final Distribution of PLC Seats', Central Elections Commission Palestine, 2006, http://www.elections.ps/Portals/0/pdf/The%20final%20distribution%20of%20PLC%20seats.pdf (accessed 28 June 2022).

5. Khaled Hroub, *Hamas: A Beginner's Guide* (London: Pluto Press, 2006), p. xvii.

6. 'The Islamic Resistance Movement (Hamas)', memo prepared by Hamas Political Bureau in 2000, in Azzam Tamini, *Hamas: Unwritten Chapters* (London: Hurst, 2007), p. 279.

7. The change of *qibla* occurred sixteen or seventeen months after the departure from Mecca. According to the Qur'an, the Prophet received a revelation to pray in the direction of the Sacred Mosque (that is, the Kaaba in Mecca) (2:144). However, antagonism with the Jews of Medina could possibly explain the decision. See Arent Jan Wensinck and David A. King, 'Kibla', in Peri Bearman et al., *Encyclopaedia of Islam*, 2nd ed., Brill Online, 2012, http://dx.doi.org/10.11 63/1573-3912_islam_COM_0513 (accessed 22 June 2022).

8. Mohsen Saleh, 'Hassan Al Banna's centenary . . . Attitude towards Palestinian cause', IkhwanWeb, 13 June 2007, http://www.ikhwanweb.com/article.php?id =820 (accessed 22 June 2022).

9. Khaled Hroub, *Hamas: Political Thought and Practice* (Washington, DC: Institute of Palestine Studies, 2000), p. 274.

10. In his Final Sermon (*Khutbatu l-Wada*), the Prophet Muhammad declared that 'all mankind is from Adam and Eve. An Arab has no superiority over a non-Arab nor [does] a non-Arab [have] any superiority over an Arab; also a white [person] has no superiority over a black [person], nor does a black [person] have any superiority over a white [person], except by piety and good action. Learn that every Muslim is a brother to every Muslim and that the Muslims constitute one brotherhood.' See Carolyn Moxley Rouse, *Engaged Surrender: African American Women and Islam* (Berkeley, CA: University of California Press, 2004), p. 101.

11. Shaul Mishal and Avraham Sela, *The Palestinian Hamas: Vision, Violence, and Coexistence* (New York: Columbia University Press, 2006), p. 51.

12. Ibid.

13. 'A Document of General Principles & Policies', Hamas, May 2017, https:// hamas.ps/ar/uploads/documents/06c77206ce934064ab5a901fa8bfef44.pdf (accessed 22 June 2022).

14. United Nations Environment Programme, *Environmental Assessment of the Gaza Strip Following the Escalations of Hostilities in December 2008–January 2009* (Nairobi: UNEP, 2009), p. 6.

15. Email interview with Hussam Abdulhadi, director of Foreign Media Unit, Hamas Information Office, 29 January 2018.

16. 'Hamas – Electoral Campaign Platform 2006', Britannica ProCon, 12 March 2007, https://israelipalestinian.procon.org/background-resources/hamas-2006-electoral-campaign-platform/ (accessed 22 June 2022).

17. 'Text of Hamas Legislative Elections Program', IkhwanWeb, 30 January 2006, http://www.ikhwanweb.com/article.php?id=4921 (accessed 22 June 2022).

18. تصريح صحفي حول تهرب قطاع غزة تجاه مسؤولياته من الاحتلال' ('A press statement about the occupation evading its responsibilities towards the suffering of the Gaza Strip'), Hamas, 20 November 2020, https://hamas.ps/ar/post/12689/ تصريح-صحفي-حول-تهرب-الاحتلال-من-مسؤولياته-تجاه-معاناة-قطاع-غزة (accessed 22 June 2022).

19. See 'Gaza conditions "unliveable" 10 years into siege: UN', Al Jazeera, 12 July 2017, http://www.aljazeera.com/news/2017/07/living-conditions-worsen-10-year-gaza-siege-170712045047448.html (accessed 22 June 2022).

20. Nidal al-Mughrabi, 'Gaza's water shortage worsening, no easy solutions seen', Reuters, 26 January 2017, https://www.reuters.com/article/us-palestinians-gaza-water/gazas-water-shortage-worsening-no-easy-solutions-seen-idUSKBN15A1FC (accessed 22 June 2022).

21. Seth M. Siegel, *Let There Be Water: Israel's Solution for a Water-Starved World* (New York: St Martin's Press, 2015), p. 179.

22. Email interview with Hussam Abdulhadi, 29 January 2018.

23. بيان صحفي حول إغراق الاحتلال حي الشجاعية بمياه بعضها عادمة' ('A press release about the occupation of the Shajaiya Neighbourhood by water, some of which is wastewater'), Hamas, 27 March 2001, http://hamas.ps/ar/post/367/ بيان-صحفي-حول-إقدام-الاحتلال-على-إغراق-حي-الشجاعية-بالمياه-وبعضها-مياه-عادمة (accessed 22 June 2022).

24. 'Text of Hamas Legislative Elections Program'.

25. Irna van der Molen and Nora Stel, 'Multi-Stakeholder Partnerships in Fragile Political Contexts: Experiences from the Palestinian Water and Waste Sector', in Cheryl de Boer et al. (eds), *Water Governance, Policy and Knowledge Transfer: International Studies on Contextual Water Management* (Abingdon: Routledge, 2013), p. 158.

26. 'Authority: $34.4 million worth of damages to Gaza water sector', Marsad, 17 August 2014, https://www.marsad.ps/en/2014/08/17/authority-34-4-million-worth-of-damages-to-gaza-water-sector/?doing_wp_cron=1657916595.74809 69429016113281250 (accessed 18 July 2022).

27. Email interview with Hussam Abdulhadi, 29 January 2018.

28. Rasha Abou Jalal, 'How long can Gaza survive with no water?', Al-Monitor,

4 August 2017, http://www.al-monitor.com/pulse/originals/2017/08/palesti ne-gaza-strip-water-crisis-unlicensed-wells-shortage.html#ixzz533IDGtqA (accessed 22 June 2022).

29. 'Siege of Gaza: Until When!', Hamas, December 2017, p. 9, http://hamas.ps/en /post/1086/siege-of-gaza-until-when? (accessed 22 June 2022).

30. 'Israel, Palestinian Authority reach water-sharing deal', Al Jazeera, 13 July 2017, https://www.aljazeera.com/news/2017/7/13/israel-palestinian-authority-reach -water-sharing-deal (accessed 22 June 2022).

31. Dalit Halevi, 'Hamas won't allow a desalination facility', Israel National News, 3 August 2017, https://www.israelnationalnews.com/News/News.aspx/233374 (accessed 22 June 2022).

32. Siegel, *Let There Be Water*, p. 182.

33. Rasha Abou Jalal, 'Gazans fear worst after Hamas bans water wells', Al-Monitor, 31 August 2021, https://www.al-monitor.com/originals/2021/08/gazans-fear - worst-after-hamas-bans-water-wells (accessed 22 June 2022).

34. Mustapha al-Barghouthi, 'Water is a weapon in the battle of racial discrimi- nation', Palestinian Information Center, 30 June 2016, https://english.palinfo .com/articles/2016/6/30/Water-is-a-Weapon-in-the-Battle-of-Racial-Discrimin ation (accessed 22 June 2022).

35. Mersiha Gadzo, 'How Israel engages in "water apartheid"', Al Jazeera, 21 October 2017, http://www.aljazeera.com/news/2017/10/israel-engages-water -apartheid-171013110734930.html (accessed 22 June 2022).

36. Wael Abdelal, *Hamas and the Media: Politics and Strategy* (Abingdon: Routledge, 2016), p. 56.

37. 'Government in Gaza launches olive planting campaign', Middle East Monitor, 20 February 2014, https://www.middleeastmonitor.com/20140220-govern ment-in-gaza-launches-olive-planting-campaign/

38. حماس تهدف لاستزراع مليون شجرة زيتون في غزة ('Hamas aims to cultivate one million olive trees in Gaza'), Islam Times, 12 November 2010, http://islamtimes.org/ar/ doc/news/43733/حماس-تهدف-لاستزراع-مليون-شجرة-زيتون-في-غزة

39. 'Hamas has made for itself the "Garden of Eden" in Gaza', Addustour. com, 14 August 2010, https://addustour.com/articles/324390-حماس-صنعت- لنفسها-«جنة-عدن»-في-غزة

40. Al-Imdaad Foundation, 'Olive trees feedback', 8 February 2021, https://www.fa cebook.com/watch/?v=1065468347271403 (accessed 18 July 2022).

41. تعزيزًا لمفهوم الاقتصاد الزراعي المقاوم ('In order to promote the concept of a resil- ient agricultural economy'), Palestinian Information Center, 30 August 2009,

https://www.palinfo.com/news/2009/8/30/-مليون-زيتونة-في-إطار-مواجهة-حرب
-الاحتلال-على-الشجرة-المباركة-في-فلسطين--تقرير (accessed 22 June 2022).

42. Amelia Smith, 'The olive tree: a symbol of palestinian steadfastness, subject to systematic destruction', *Middle East Monitor*, 11 May 2014, https://www.mid dleeastmonitor.com/20140511-the-olive-tree-a-symbol-of-palestinian-steadfast ness-subject-to-systematic-destruction/amp/ (accessed 22 June 2022).

43. Sara Roy, *Hamas and Civil Society in Gaza: Engaging the Islamist Social Sector* (Princeton, NJ: Princeton University Press, 2013), p. 241.

44. Ibid.

45. Email interview with Hussam Abdulhadi, 29 January 2018.

46. Charter of Hamas, translated and annotated by Raphael Israeli, Hebrew University, 1988, https://fas.org/irp/world/para/docs/880818.htm

47. Anne Marie Oliver and Paul Steinberg have observed that this hadith has been interpreted not only literally, but also allegorically. During the Intifada, for example, the imam of Jericho's main mosque Sheikh Isma'il Jamal, claimed that the Gharqad tree represented 'the collaborator who doesn't want to say 'Here is a Jew!'. See Anne Marie Oliver and Paul F. Steinberg, *The Road to Martyrs' Square: A Journey into the World of the Suicide Bomber* (New York: Oxford University Press, 2006), p. 21.

48. Adnan Oktar, 'Gharqad tree myth still continues to stir enmity against Jews in the Muslim world', JerusalemOnLine, 27 March 2016, https://web.archive .org/web/20180813071200/http://www.jerusalemonline.com/news/middle-ea st/the-arab-world/op-ed-gharqad-tree-myth-still-continues-to-stir-enmity-again st-jews-20091 (accessed 22 June 2022).

49. 'Bahar: Gazans as deep-seated in their motherland as palm trees', Palestinian Information Center, 13 July 2017, https://english.palinfo.com/news/2017/7/13 /Bahar-Gazans-as-deep-seated-in-their-motherland-as-palm-trees (accessed 22 June 2022).

50. 'Hamas renews its twentieth rejection of the principle of recognizing Israel as a state', Mareb Press, 16 December 2007, http://marebpress.net/mobile/news_de tails.php?sid=8738

51. Email interview with Hussam Abdulhadi, 29 January 2018.

52. Inna Lazareva, 'Israeli "spy dolphin" caught off Gaza coast', *The Telegraph*, 19 August 2015, http://www.telegraph.co.uk/news/worldnews/middleeast/israel /11813322/Israeli-spy-dolphin-caught-off-Gaza-coast.html (accessed 22 June 2022).

53. 'Hamas "seizes Israeli spy dolphin" off Gaza', BBC News, 20 August 2015,

http://www.bbc.co.uk/news/world-middle-east-34001790 (accessed 22 June 2022).

54. Yolande Knell, 'Shark attacks not linked to Mossad says Israel', BBC News, 7 December 2010, http://www.bbc.co.uk/news/world-middle-east-11937285 (accessed 22 June 2022).

55. Robert Tait, 'Donkey suicide bomb stopped by Israeli troops in Gaza', *The Telegraph*, 18 July 2014, https://www.telegraph.co.uk/news/worldnews/middle east/israel/10977818/Donkey-suicide-bomb-stopped-by-Israeli-troops-in-Gaza .html (accessed 22 June 2022).

56. 'Hamas attacks Israeli soldiers with explosive donkey', Israel Defence Forces, 19 July 2014, https://www.idf.il/en/minisites/hamas/hamas-attacks-israeli-soldiers -with-explosive-donkey/ (accessed 22 June 2022).

57. Ibid.

58. In the latter scenario, Ya'fur was able to speak to the Prophet and explained that it belonged to a line of donkeys serving prophets, including Jesus. See Khalid Sindawi, 'The Donkey of the Prophet in Shi'ite Tradition', *Al-Masaq*, vol. 18, no. 1, 2006, pp. 90–3.

59. Greg Wilford, 'Hamas bans dog walking through the Gaza Strip to "protect women and children"', *The Independent*, 20 May 2017, https://www.indepen dent.co.uk/news/world/politics/hamas-gaza-strip-occupied-palestinian-territori es-facebook-israel-dogs-dog-walking-a7746101.html (accessed 22 June 2022).

60. 'On Hamas TV Friday sermon: calls to annihilate the Jews, who are compared to dogs', Memri TV, 3 April 2009, https://www.memri.org/tv/hamas-tv-friday -sermon-calls-annihilate-jews-who-are-compared-dogs (accessed 22 June 2022).

61. 'Hamas MP and cleric Yunis al-Astal on swine flu and "the brothers of apes and pigs"', Memri TV, 15 May 2009, https://www.memri.org/tv/hamas-mp-and -cleric-yunis-al-astal-swine-flu-and-brothers-apes-and-pigs (accessed 22 June 2022).

62. Hamas Mickey Mouse teaches terror to kids', MediaMayhem, 8 May 2007, https://youtu.be/gi-c6lbFGC4 (accessed 18 July 2022).

63. 'Hamas' bee Nahoul abuses cats and lions at Gaza Zoo and calls to liberate al-Aqsa Mosque', Memri TV, 10 August 2007, https://www.memri.org/tv/hamas -bee-nahoul-abuses-cats-and-lions-gaza-zoo-and-calls-liberate-al-aqsa-mosque (accessed 22 June 2022).

64. 'Hamas' children TV with a terrorist Jew eating rabbit', The Evil Israel/YouTube, no date, https://www.youtu.be./0YU__vFw_0E (accessed 22 June 2022).

65. Muhammad Saed Abdul-Rahman, *Islam: Questions and Answers, vol. 17: Manners* (London: MSA, 2007), p. 26.

66. 'Islam wants to kill Mickey Mouse', inei9j43710hd83k34/YouTube, 27 December 2009, https://youtu.be/6cTZ9-TCvMc (accessed 22 June 2022).

67. See 'Eating rabbit', Fatwa 84598, IslamWeb, 29 July 2002, http://www.islamw eb.net/en/ fatwa/84598 (accessed 22 June 2022).

68. 'Dialogue on slaughtering and hunting', Al-Sayyid Ali Al-Husseini Al-Sistani website, http://www.sistani.org/english/book/49/2413/ (accessed 22 June 2022).

69. 'Thousands of Hamas members take on massive cleaning up of streets', AP Archive/YouTube, 30 July 2015, https://www.youtu.be/k3WWssNsGYo (accessed 22 June 2022).

70. Email interview with Hussam Abdulhadi, 29 January 2018.

71. Ibid.

72. Peter Beaumont, 'Gaza electricity crisis: "It is the worst I can remember – but we expect it to get worse"', *The Guardian*, 10 July 2017, https://www.theguar dian.com/world/2017/jul/10/gaza-electricity-crisis-it-is-the-worst-i-can-remem ber-mahmoud-abbas (accessed 22 June 2022).

73. Diana B. Greenwald, 'Who is responsible for solving Gaza's massive electricity crisis?', *Washington Post*, 5 February 2018, https://www.washingtonpost.com /news/monkey-cage/wp/2018/02/05/who-is-responsible-for-solving-gazas-mas sive-electricity-crisis/?noredirect=on&utm_term=.f17b287a750d (accessed 22 June 2022).

74. Hamas, الكهرباء أزمة وتفاقم الحصار استمرار حول صحفي تصريح ('A press statement about the continuation of the siege and the exacerbation of the electricity crisis'), 18 August 2020, https://hamas.ps/ar/post/12370/تصريح-صحفي-حول-استمرار-الحصار-وتفاقم-أزمة-الكهرباء (accessed 22 June 2022).

75. 'Eastern Mediterranean natural gas exploration focused on the Levant Basin', US Energy Information Agency, 20 August 2013, https://www.eia.gov/today inenergy/detail.php?id=12611 (accessed 22 June 2022).

76. 'PA: Shell pulls out of Gaza's gas field', Al Jazeera, 6 March 2018, https://www .aljazeera.com/news/2018/03/pa-shell-pulls-gaza-gas-field-180306124715796 .html (accessed 22 June 2022).

77. Nafeez Mosaddeq Ahmed, 'Israel's war for Gaza's gas', *Le Monde Diplomatique*, 28 November 2012, https://mondediplo.com/outsidein/israel-s-war-for-gaza-s-gas (accessed 22 June 2022).

78. 'Hamas says fired rockets at off-shore Israeli gas well', Reuters, 20 August 2014,

https://www.reuters.com/article/uk-mideast-gaza-gas/hamas-says-fired-rockets-at-off-shore-israeli-gas-well-idUKKBN0GK1BH20140820 (accessed 22 June 2022).

79. On the Gaza electricity crisis see 'UN releases $2.5 million from pooled fund to tackle energy crisis in Gaza', Sustainable Development Goals, 24 August 2017, http://www.un.org/sustainabledevelopment/blog/2017/08/un-releases-2-5-million-from-pooled-fund-to-tackle-energy-crisis-in-gaza/ (accessed 22 June 2022).

80. Hroub, *Hamas: A Beginner's Guide*, p. 186.

81. Scott Atran, 'Hamas may give peace a chance', *New York Times*, 18 December 2004, http://www.nytimes.com/2004/12/18/opinion/hamas-may-give-peace-a-chance.html (accessed 22 June 2022).

82. On *hudna* see Majid Khadduri, 'Hudna', in Peri Bearman et al. (eds), *Encyclopaedia of Islam*, 2nd ed., Brill Online, 2012, http://dx.doi.org/10.1163/1573-3912_islam_SIM_2933 (accessed 22 June 2022).

83. 'Haniyeh calls for formation of Palestinian state on 1967 lines', *Haaretz*, 19 December 2006, https://www.haaretz.com/1.4941383 (accessed 22 June 2022).

84. Abdullah Azzam, 'Defence of the Muslim Lands: The First Obligation after Imam', 2002, p. 46, https://islamfuture.files.wordpress.com/2009/11/defence-of-the-muslim-lands.pdf (accessed 22 June 2022).

85. Andrea Nüsse, *Muslim Palestine: The Ideology of Hamas* (Amsterdam: Harwood Academic, 1998), p. 48.

86. Hroub, *Hamas: Political Thought*, p. 275.

87. 'Hamas official Mahmoud al-Zahhar: The Qur'an tells us to drive the Jews out of Palestine in its entirety', Memri TV, 7 March 2017, https://www.memri.org/tv/hamas-official-mahmoud-al-zahhar-quran-tells-us-drive-jews-out-palestine-its-entirety (accessed 22 June 2022).

88. Jeroen Gunning, *Hamas in Politics: Democracy, Religion, Violence* (London: Hurst, 2007), p. 125.

89. نص خطاب رئيس المكتب السياسي لحركة حماس إسماعيل هنية ('The text of the speech of the president of the Political Bureau of Hamas Ismail Haniyeh'), Hamas, 6 July 2017, http://hamas.ps/ar/post/7588/نص-خطاب-رئيس-المكتب-السياسي-لحركة-حماس-إسماعيل-هنية (accessed 22 June 2022).

90. 'Press release issued by Hamas on the 41st anniversary of Palestinian Land Day', Hamas, 31 March 2017, http://hamas.ps/en/post/601/press-release-issued-by-hamas-on-the-41st-anniversary-of-palestinian-land-day (accessed 22 June 2022).

91. See 'The World's Muslims: Religion, Politics and Society', Pew Research Center,

30 April 2013, http://www.pewforum.org/2013/04/30/the-worlds-muslims-20 13-2/ (accessed 22 June 2022).

92. Yahya Nisbet, 'Liberating the whole of Palestine is the Islamic solution for al-Quds', Hizb ut-Tahrir Britain, 6 December 2017, http://www.hizb.org .uk/media/press-releases/liberating-whole-palestine-islamic-solution-al-quds/ (accessed 22 June 2022).

6

THE JIHADI-SALAFI MOVEMENT AND
THE ENVIRONMENT

The US invasion of Afghanistan in October 2001 led to the franchising of al-Qaeda.[1] While its top leadership found refuge in Pakistan, the organisation spread its operations into various Middle Eastern countries. For this purpose, Osama bin Laden collaborated with Abu Musab al-Zarqawi, a Jordanian of Palestinian origin, who had visited Afghanistan after establishing the Organisation of Monotheism and Jihad (*Jama'at al-Tawhid wal-Jihad*). In March 2003, the toppling of Saddam Hussein by the US military paved the way for the expansion of al-Zarqawi's organisation into Iraq. In October 2004, al-Zarqawi pledged allegiance to bin Laden and took over the local branch of al-Qaeda.

However, he did not remain obedient to the central leadership. Despite bin Laden's objections, al-Zarqawi initiated an anti-Shi'a campaign that brought the country to the brink of civil war. In June 2006, he was killed in a US air strike and was replaced by Abu Hamza al-Muhajir. The new leader reverted to al-Qaeda's orbit, but he was killed in a joint US–Iraqi operation in April 2010.

Abu Bakr al-Baghdadi then became the head of the local branch of al-Qaeda, which had changed its name to the Islamic State of Iraq. The rise of al-Baghdadi coincided with the outbreak of the Arab Spring revolutions. While fighting against the Shi'a-dominated regime in Baghdad, al-Baghdadi decided to expand into Syria sometime in 2011.[2] As a result, the al-Qaeda-affiliated Support Front for the People of Syria (*Jabhat al-Nusra li Ahl al-Sham*) was established in north-western Syria by Abu Mohammed al-Julani. In April 2013, al-Baghdadi attempted to take over the Syrian branch; al-Julani referred the issue to the new leader of al-Qaeda, Ayman al-Zawahiri, who had been chosen after the killing of bin Laden by US forces. While he ruled against the merger of the two branches, al-Baghdadi ignored the mother organisation and attempted to absorb the Syrian branch by establishing the Islamic State of Iraq and Syria (*ad-Dawlah al-Islamiyah fi l-Iraq wa-sh-Sham*).[3] In June 2014, he declared himself a caliph in Mosul.

Although al-Qaeda and ISIS are two different organisations, they have shared many common features. First, both groups have adhered to the ideology of jihadi-Salafism. The Salafi movement demands that modern Muslims embrace the authentic Islam of the Prophet Muhammad and his Companions, the *salaf* or 'ancient ones'.[4] Salafis have claimed that the first three generations of Muslims learned Islam directly from the Prophet or those who knew him. According to a *hadith*, the Prophet stated that 'the people of my own generation are the best, then those who come after them, and then those of the next generation'.[5] Therefore, Salafis have recognised only the Qur'an, the *ahadith* and the consensus of the Companions (*ijma' al-sahaba*) as valid sources of Islamic law. Salafis accept the teachings of the four *madhahib* (that is, Hanafi, Hanbali, Maliki and Shafi'i), as long as they are based on the Qur'an and the *Sunna*.

According to Mohamed Hafez, the ideology of jihadi-Salafism is characterised by five features: the prominence of the oneness of God (*tawhid*); the emphasis on God's sovereignty (*hakimiyyat Allah*); the rejection of innovation (*bid'a*); the permissibility and necessity of *takfir* (that is, declaring a Muslim as apostate); and the centrality of jihad against adversaries.[6] Most jihadi-Salafis have denounced Shi'a Muslims as heretics and have called them rejectionists (*rawafid*) because they do not recognise the legitimacy of the first three caliphs.

On the other hand, al-Qaeda and ISIS have different *modi operandi* and organisational cultures. The former has acted as an umbrella organisation for different branches in the Muslim world, whereas the latter has evolved into a hierarchical organisation with command and control. Moreover, al-Qaeda has pursued a global borderless jihad, while ISIS has largely launched insurgencies in the greater Middle East. As a result, there are constant tensions between al-Qaeda and ISIS that have occasionally led to armed confrontation in northern Syria and elsewhere. In reality, the two groups have competed for ideological supremacy and political influence. With the fall of the last ISIS stronghold in Syria in March 2019, al-Qaeda could come to dominate the jihadi-Salafi movement once again.

This chapter first describes jihadi-Salafism's general perspective on the environment, focusing on general and particular understandings of territoriality. It then outlines how jihadi-Salafis have politicised and weaponised water in the Middle East. The chapter further analyses their perspectives on animal-related issues, pollution and energy. Finally, the chapter examines the role of religion in the emergence of jihadi-Salafi environmentalism.

Jihadi-Salafism's General Perspective on the Environment

The jihadi-Salafi understanding of the environment is polemical. The opinion of the radical Egyptian preacher Abu Hamza al-Masri is probably indicative of the confrontational nature of the movement:

> In this day and time, the earth is in one of its most extreme phases of turmoil . . . Some have stated that the earth cannot continue to hold the amount of people that are being born. Others are saying that arable land is scarce, thus widespread starvation is coming to all countries. Due to this, other countries are also fighting for space. Country after country is going to war, jockeying for position, striving to preserve their land boundaries, fighting for food and water, which is essential for survival.[7]

Hence, Abu Hamza has adopted an alarmist approach to environmental issues that almost resembles that of radical environmentalists. Humanity is faced with important challenges, such overpopulation, scarcity of arable land and competition over resources. Overall, he portrays the future as dark and violent. In this context, the jihadi-Salafi movement must strive to protect those Muslims who adhere to its version of authentic Islam.

Identity and territory are often linked together by complex interactions. Marco Antonsich defines the term 'territoriality' as an important 'link between society and space in terms of identity, concentration of activities and exclusion of undesirable outsiders'.[8] It is hardly a coincidence that al-Qaeda has viewed the Muslim world as a unified space that is under siege. In his 1996 Declaration of Jihad against the Americans Occupying the Land of the Two Holy Sanctuaries, Osama bin Laden claimed that Muslim 'blood has been spilt in Palestine and Iraq . . . [M]assacres have taken place in Tajikistan, Burma, Kashmir, Assam, the Philippines, Fatami, Ogaden, Somalia, Eritrea, Chechnya, and Bosnia-Herzegovina.'[9] The declaration sketches the borders of an imaginary Muslim nation that struggles for survival. Thus, only places of conflict and war are worth mentioning. The rest of the (presumably peaceful) Muslim world does not fit the narrative. Consequently, al-Qaeda has constructed its own *Dar al-Harb/Dar al-Islam* dichotomy to justify the reach of its operations. The Muslim world is now the land of war.

Al-Qaeda has been very consistent in terms of ideological content. In spring 2013, following the Boston Marathon attacks, the editor of the al-Qaeda magazine *Inspire* declared:

> The act of the two great brothers, Tamerlan and Dzokhar, is but the true image reflected by the bloody deeds of your hands, reflected by the oppressive policies of your downtrodden regimes . . . [Y]ou will never enjoy peace until we live it practically in Palestine and all the infidel forces leave the Peninsula of Muhammad and all other Muslim lands.[10]

From its point of view, there is a permanent war between Islam and the West. The Boston bombings and other similar attacks were supposedly defensive actions for the liberation of Muslim-populated lands that are under occupation or the influence of the West. Palestine and the Arabian Peninsula are at the epicentre of al-Qaeda's clash of civilisations. The former constitutes the primary battlefield against the Jews, who are viewed as the eternal enemy of Muslims. The latter is the birthplace of Islam, which must remain beyond foreign influences.

Although ISIS is a breakaway group of al-Qaeda, it has embraced a different approach to territoriality. Indeed, ISIS has attempted to build an exclusive identity by imposing new norms of Islamic piety and targeting those viewed as a threat to the Muslim faith. The new identity has a territorial component because the group has aspired to build a polity based on sectarian affiliation. Following the declaration of the new caliphate, the group called upon Sunni Muslims to perform a new *hijra*:

Amirul-Mu'minin said: 'Therefore, rush O Muslims to your state. Yes, it is your state. Rush, because Syria is not for the Syrians, and Iraq is not for the Iraqis. The earth is Allah's ("Indeed, the earth belongs to Allah. He causes to inherit it whom He wills of His servants. And the [best] outcome is for the righteous" (7:128)). The State is a state for all Muslims . . . O Muslims everywhere, whoever is capable of performing hijrah to the Islamic State, then let him do so, because hijrah to the land of Islam is obligatory.'[11]

The self-declared caliphate was supposedly an Islamic utopia on earth where all pious Sunni Muslims were obliged to immigrate. Moreover, ISIS has idealised the land of Sham (that is, Syria) as a sacred battleground between Islam and the West. In fact, it first named its magazine after Dabiq, a small town in northern Syria, because the place is mentioned in a famous *hadith*:

The Hour will not be established until the Romans land at al-A'maq or Dabiq . . . Then an army from al-Madinah of the best people on the earth at that time will leave for them . . . Then one third of them [the Muslims] will flee; Allah will never forgive them. One third will be killed; they will be the best martyrs with Allah. And one third will conquer them; they will never be afflicted with fitnah [strife within Islam]. Then they will conquer Constantinople. While they are dividing the war booty, having hung their swords on olive trees, Shaytan will shout, 'The [false] Messiah has followed after your families [who were left behind].' So they will leave [for their families], but Shaytan's claim is false.[12]

Here ISIS uses a *hadith* that prophesies the end of the world following the final battle between a selected group of Muslims and Westerners, who are the modern descendants of the Romans. The battle is conceptually bound by territory because it can happen only in northern Syria. The reconquest of Constantinople (that is, the Turkish city of Istanbul) is a highly symbolic act of prevalence against those who do not adhere to ISIS's version of authentic Islam. The *hadith* also conveys an image of Mediterranean life because Satan would attempt to mislead the believers who rest under olive trees.

It can be argued that the world of ISIS is strictly defined by a concept of subjective territoriality. The group views territory as a space of political belonging that surpasses the nation-state.[13] As a result, ISIS has been keen to emphasise its denouncement of the post-First World War order in the Middle East. Like many other Islamist groups, it has not recognised the existing borders established by the Sykes–Picot agreement in 1916. In an article published by one of its journals, ISIS explained its rationale for coming out against the agreement:

> It was 98 years ago that the Allies of WWI forged a secret agreement to carve up the territories of the Muslim lands . . . The areas of Iraq, Sham, and some neighbouring regions were divided into four sections . . . A fifth region in the area of Palestine was carved out as an international zone . . . Years after the agreement, invisible borders would go on to separate between a Muslim and his brother, and pave the way for ruthless, nationalistic *tawaghit* [transgressing rulers] to entrench the ummah's division rather than working to unite the Muslims under one imam carrying the banner of truth.[14]

In other words, the group has viewed the Middle East as a single region without borders that could form the nucleus of the new caliphate.

While occupying large parts of Syria and Iraq, ISIS attempted to impose a form of religious nationalism on the populace. In 2013, for instance, the group clarified that 'our war with Kurds is a religious war. It is not a nationalistic war . . . We do not fight Kurds because they are Kurds . . . The Muslim Kurds in the ranks of the Islamic State are many.'[15] Therefore, ISIS has aimed at eliminating not only geographical borders but also different identities.

Simultaneously, the group has attempted to offer an Islamic justification for its insurgencies in certain areas of the Muslim world. For example, it has claimed that its campaign of terror in the Sinai Peninsula against the Egyptian government and its perceived local allies is a religious obligation because

> Al-Qurtubi said in his tafsir [exegesis] of the verse . . . a tree issuing from the Tur of Sinai which produces oil and food for those who eat (23:20), The Tur of Sinai is from the land of Sham. It is the mountain where Allah spoke to Musa [Moses] . . . And 'tur' means mountain in the language of the Arabs.[16]

Thus, Sinai is important for ISIS because it links back to the sacred land of Syria and the history of the Arabs. It is a claim with theological underpinnings which could determine future expectations.

Additionally, the group has tried to mobilise support for its operations in the area by invoking anti-Semitism. It has stated that

> Sinai is . . . a front against the Jews, an important step towards the liberation of Bayt al-Maqdis [that is, al-Aqsa Mosque]. This expansion brings the battle where the Jews hide behind their Gharqad trees closer to the Muslims, by ridding the path of the obstacles manifested in the apostate [Egyptian] regime and army of Fir'awn [Pharaoh].[17]

In this way, ISIS has seen Sinai as part of a triangle that includes Syria and Palestine where Muslims fight an existential war against their Jewish enemies and Muslim 'apostates'. The mention of al-Aqsa Mosque is meant to evoke collective memories of a glorious past, while reaffirming a sense of religious duty.

At the same time ISIS attempted unsuccessfully to formulate an environmental policy for the areas under its control in Syria and Iraq. Hence, the group established three ministries (*dawawin*) dealing with different environment-related policy areas. The Diwan of Agriculture was 'responsible for the agricultural and animal resources and for maintaining food security for the subjects of the Islamic State'; the Diwan of Resources was 'responsible for the exploitation of oil, gas, and mineral resources'; and the Diwan of Services was 'responsible for supplying water and electricity, paving and maintaining roads, and supervising and maintaining the public utilities in the Islamic State'.[18] Yet ISIS did not manage to evolve into a state in the Westphalian sense of the term.

In summary, jihadi-Salafi groups have largely perceived the lands of the greater Middle East as a symbolic battleground in which Islam confronts its enemies. But al-Qaeda and ISIS have dissimilar understandings of territoriality deriving from their political strategies. The organisation of Osama bin Laden and now Ayman al-Zawahiri has aimed at establishing a deterritorialised community of fighters that can fight a generational war. In contrast, al-Baghdadi's caliphate had borders, albeit contested. This chapter continues with an investigation of four areas of jihadi-Salafi environmentalism, namely water management, trees, animals, and pollution and energy.

Water Management

Despite the emphasis that the Muslim faith has placed on water conservation, jihadi-Salafis have almost completely ignored the relevant Shari'a rules and environmental ethics. To begin with, ISIS was the first jihadi-Salafi group to systematically use water as a weapon against its perceived enemies. In early 2014, the group managed to control the Tabqa Dam near Raqqa, which includes a hydroelectric power station and holds back Lake Assad. The dam is more than 4 kilometres long and 60 metres high.[19] Initially, ISIS used the facility to gain support by increasing the supply of electricity to areas which had previously been neglected.[20] In May 2017, US-supported forces liberated the dam after striking a deal with ISIS fighters who had threatened to destroy it.[21]

According to Tobias von Lossow, ISIS weaponised water in three ways. First, it cut off supplies to districts or towns that were deemed hostile. In June 2014, for example, ISIS stopped the supply of water to the Christian town of Qaraqosh in northern Iraq.[22] Second, the group used dams to flood areas, thereby killing its enemies. In April of the same year, it used the Falluja Dam in central Iraq to flood neighbouring areas controlled by government forces.[23] Third, ISIS occasionally poisoned water resources to intimidate its enemies. In December 2014, the group contaminated drinking water with crude oil in the Balad district of central Iraq.[24]

Simultaneously, water has often been used metaphorically by ISIS to propagate messages. The second issue of *Dabiq*, titled 'The Flood', offered a modern interpretation of the story of Noah and his Ark:

> For the flood was the result and consequence of opposing the truth . . .
> They would have also realized that the mountain was the sign of protection and safety from the punishment for those who believed and followed the truth, and that the ark would always be a witness to two important facts. The first is that only those who agreed with and followed the truth would be saved from the punishment in the dunya [the temporal world], in contrast to those who opposed it. The second is that in every time and place, those who are saved from the punishment are a small group, whereas the majority are destroyed.[25]

Here ISIS invokes the story of the Great Flood to draw a parallel with the situation in Syria and Iraq. Like the Ark, ISIS protects the chosen ones at a time of great upheaval and will bring them to the self-declared caliphate, which is the modern Mount Ararat. There they will feel safe and protected. The rest of the Muslims and non-Muslims will be punished by God for their sins. In other words, ISIS presents water as an enduring metaphor for life or death.

Additionally, ISIS has used symbolism to convey messages about large bodies of water. For example, the Mediterranean Sea represents both a physical barrier and a virtual bridge between Islam and the West. In February 2015, ISIS released a video depicting the brutal murder of twenty-one Egyptian Coptic Christians who had been kidnapped in the Libyan city of Sirte. In the video the narrator declared that 'the sea you've hidden Sheikh Osama bin Laden's body in, we swear to Allah we will mix it with your blood . . . [W]e will conquer Rome, by Allah's permission,' pointing his knife towards the sea.[26] Despite its antagonism towards al-Qaeda, ISIS has attempted to immortalise bin Laden as a hero who gave his life for a greater cause, namely the expansion of Islam to Europe. The body of the martyr sanctified the water and metamorphosed the sea into a bridge of invasion for God's righteous warriors. In this way, the polysemy of images captures the ambiguity of water in the world of ISIS.

Al-Qaeda has also used water metaphorically to describe the state of society. In *The Management of Savagery*, Islamist strategist Abu Bakr Naji has argued, '[L]ike stagnant water, nothing rises to the surface of stagnant societies except decay, algae, and moss . . . As for the mujahid society, it is like moving water and the flowing river which refuses to bear decay or to have scum floating on its surface.'[27] Hence, water can symbolise both conformity and resistance depending on the socio-political context. It is a source of decaying stagnation or radical change.

In summary, some jihadi-Salafis have perceived water as a weapon that can coerce adversaries. At the same time, it is a metaphor that can explain complexities and dilemmas. In fact, the duality of water echoes the reality of a war conducted in the name of religious supremacy. Water is both an instrument of salvation and a dispensable resource to gain advantage.

Trees

The flora of many Muslim-populated countries has suffered enormous damage due to wars and conflicts. In recent years, Islamist groups have paid increased attention to the protection of forests. Al-Qaeda has apparently not produced any material addressing the use of trees. Yet, the al-Qaeda-allied and Deobandi-oriented Taliban movement has expressed its concern over the destruction of flora. In January 2011, for example, the Taliban claimed that US forces had destroyed the greenery of Band-e-Sarda, a district that is part of Ghazni province. They argued the following:

> The deforestation and destruction of fruit bearing trees by American forces is not only limited to the Andar district, in the past years countless number of trees have been cut down that were along the Kabul Kandahar highway in the areas of Maydan, Saidabad, Ghazni and Zabul. But sadly, neither it was reported by any news agency nor was it taken into consideration by any environment protecting organization. If the cruel operations like 'the Kandahar operation' and Band-e-Sarda terror continue to happen it might cause a long-lasting damage to the beautiful and natural environment of Afghanistan. The natural environment in Afghanistan which has been basically harmed by the use of chemical weapons, years of drought and fighting, such planned and deliberate acts will worsen the catastrophe.[28]

The Taliban not only accused US troops of destroying the environment by cutting down trees, but also criticised the international media and NGOs for allegedly ignoring the environmental problems of Afghanistan.

One week later, the Taliban issued a statement accusing the US forces of destroying the country's environment together with President Karzai. The group claimed, '[A]ccording to [Karzai], the Taliban have to be blamed for the destruction of the trees not the Americans because they ambush the Americans from there, firing at them. The Americans had no way to respond except resorting to bombardment or cutting down trees and orchards.'[29] Thus, the Taliban accused Karzai of colluding with Washington in committing 'environmental crimes' against the country. Such an allegation undermined Karzai's legitimacy and the credibility of the US government.

In February 2017, the Taliban launched their own reforestation project in areas under their control. The new leader of the movement, Mawlawi Hibat Allah Akhund Zadah, issued a statement in which he explained the rationale behind the initiative:

> Allah Almighty has interconnected the lives of human beings with plants. Plants live off soil while humans and animals off plants . . . Tree planta-tion is considered one of the greatest good deeds in Islam and is labeled Sadaqa Jariya (continuous charity) . . . The Islamic Emirate – just as it is actively engaged in a struggle against foreign invaders and their hirelings for the attainment of true peace and security – works within the limits of its resources for the prosperity, economic welfare, development and self-reliance of its beloved countrymen. Therefore, as spring approaches, it calls on its Mujahideen and every individual of its devout nation to plant one or several fruit or non-fruit trees for the beautification of earth and for the benefit of Almighty Allah's creations.[30]

In this way, the Taliban offer an Islamic justification for the plantation programme in parts of the country that are under their control. The call for individual participation does not only target their members and sympathis-ers; they try to reach out to a larger audience of Muslims who share a sense of responsibility for the protection of the environment. Moreover, the Taliban seek to portray themselves as environmentally conscious and active for the benefit of all Afghans. While the timing of the decision may be coincidental, it is possible that the Taliban were influenced by Jamaat-e-Islami, which has also invested politically in deforestation.[31] Indeed, a trend is rising among Islamist groups to announce measures to tackle such problems. In July 2018, for example, the Somali group al-Shabaab declared a ban on single-use plastic bags because they are 'a serious threat to both humans and livestock' and banned the logging of rare trees in the areas under its control.[32]

On the other hand, ISIS has issued fatwas that authorise the destruction of trees and crops during fighting with enemies. Fatwa no. 15 states that 'it is allowed on necessity, need, or interest to burn the fortresses of the enemies by fire, destroy their homes, bring them down upon them, and cut their trees, and ruin their agriculture, when in that there is breaking their thorn, weaken-ing their determination, and dispersing their gathering'.[33] The Research and

Fatwa Issuing Committee (*Diwan al-Ifta' wa al-Buhuth*) has provided the necessary evidence from the Qur'an, according to which God Almighty has said, 'Whatever palm-tree you cut down or leave it standing upon its roots, it is by Allah's permission, and that he may abase the transgressors' (59:5).[34] The Qur'anic reference describes an incident when the Prophet and his army attempted to expel the Jewish tribe of Banu Nadir from Medina.

Nevertheless, there is Islamic evidence pointing in a different direction. The first Caliph, Abu Bakr, advised his army commander Usama Ibn Zayd before invading Palestine, 'Do not cut down fruit-bearing trees, do not destroy buildings; do not slaughter a sheep or a camel except for food; do not burn or drown palm trees.'[35] As a result, Muslim jurists have differing views on the issue. Some claim that Abu Bakr gave that advice because he knew that the Prophet's order was later abrogated, while others believe that it is permissible to destroy trees during the course of fighting.[36] Yet ISIS has viewed trees as collateral damage of the war against those who do not submit to its will.

Animals

Animal life has not featured much in al-Qaeda's or ISIS's discourses, which are almost exclusively anthropocentric. However, some of the articles published by ISIS fighters offer a rare glance at their perceptions of animals. One of the men describes his experience of companionship with a stray cat in the battlefield as follows:

> It was a very cold day on *ribat* (frontier-guarding) near the Layramun industrial zone during the winter sometime between late 2012 and early 2013 ... using night vision goggles ... [S]uddenly something moved nearby ... I noticed it was a cat, cold like myself. It observed me for a few seconds as I observed it. It appeared to consider whether or not I was an aggressive or compassionate soul, then advanced towards me, leaped on my lap, and began purring ... It was a creature, with a soul, able to observe another creature ... and then determine if the other creature would be welcoming or not, and finally decide to take the risk of intruding upon this other creature's lap for the sake of comfort and warmth. How great is He who created both of these creatures and facilitated for them a means of communication not fathomable by either of them![37]

In this short autobiographical story, the author describes his emotions and thoughts eloquently. The encounter with a stray cat made him realise the wholeness of God's order in creation. At a time of war, he had a moment of clarity about the essence of life. This moment presented an opportunity to rethink his relationship with animals. The mention of a cat is hardly a coincidence, regardless of its factual or fictional character. According to the Islamic tradition, the Prophet was fond of cats, his favourite being Muezza (see Chapter 1). This carefully crafted story connects the glorious past with the embattled present.

Additionally, jihadi-Salafis have instrumentalised some animals for the purposes of propaganda. For instance, the horse has been featured in many videos and other visual images of jihadi propaganda because it evokes connotations of religious battles during Islam's early history.[38] In their imaginary final battle, horses would be ridden by the pious Muslim knights. It is equally important that horses are mentioned favourably in the Qur'an, as explained in Chapter 1.

Moreover, both al-Qaeda and ISIS have called their killed members lions to stress their bravery and courage. In 2014, al-Qaeda's Global Islamic Media Front declared:

> May Allah protect the Islamic lions in Chechnya who are resisting the Russian occupiers for four and a half centuries. May Allah protect the Islamic lions in East Turkistan who have been defending their religion, honour, and dignity . . . May Allah protect the Islamic lions in Iraq who are resisting the Safavid government that is backed by America, which is causing bloodshed to the Sunnis.[39]

Likewise, the ISIS fighters who attacked Paris in 2015 were said to be 'the lions of Islam [that] have avenged our Prophet. Let these crusaders be scared because they should be.'[40] Following the capture of the Division 17 army base outside ar-Raqqa, *Dabiq* stated that 'the lions of the Islamic State advanced and continued capturing one position after another until the entire base fell under their control in less than two days'.[41]

The Qur'an briefly mentions the lion as an animal to be feared, explaining, 'What is then the matter with them, that they turn away from the Reminder, as if they were frightened asses fleeing from a lion?' (74: 49–51).

The Prophet's paternal uncle and companion Hamza was given the nickname 'Lion of God' (*Asad Allah*) because he fought bravely in the Battle of Badr in 624. Thus, al-Qaeda and ISIS follow a deep-rooted tradition of identifying brave warriors with lions.

Furthermore, jihadi propaganda has used animals to ridicule its enemies. In June 2012, for example, Fuad Muhammad Khalaf of the al-Shabaab group in Somalia made an offer after Friday prayers: 'Whoever reveals the hideout of the idiot Obama will be rewarded with 10 camels, and whoever reveals the hideout of the old woman Hillary Clinton will be rewarded 10 chickens and 10 roosters.'[42] Apparently, the choice of animals reflected socio-economic realities in the country, as well as a local hierarchy whereby camels are more important than chickens.

Overall, animals represent symbols of determination and power which have been derived from the Islamic tradition. However, from the jihadi-Salafi point of view, the relationship between humans and animals is largely symbolic and not particularly potent.

Pollution and Energy

Jihadi-Salafi groups have increasingly paid attention to issues like global warming and climate change. In this regard, Osama bin Laden was the pioneer thinker of the movement. Following the US invasion of Afghanistan in October 2002 and the retreat to the Pakistani tribal areas, al-Qaeda attempted to broaden its political agenda. Instead of focusing only on US foreign policy, the group started emphasising the ills of capitalism and the necessities of ecology.

In 2002, the founder of al-Qaeda published a letter to the American people, accusing them of destroying 'nature with your industrial waste and gases more than any other nation in history. Despite this, you refuse to sign the Kyoto agreement so that you can secure the profit of your greedy companies and industries.'[43] Clearly, he was aiming more at confronting the American government and society than raising awareness about global warming.

In September 2007, bin Laden repeated his criticism against the United States: 'The life of all of mankind is in danger because of the global warming resulting to a large degree from the emissions of the factories of the major corporations; yet despite that, the representative of these corporations in the White House insists on not observing the Kyoto accord.'[44] This time he blamed only President Bush and mentioned a conspiracy theory of a government-industrial complex controlling US environmental policy, although he did not really provide any evidence.

Despite the predominance of political and security themes, al-Qaeda continued to discuss climate change. In an audiotape statement released on 29 January 2010, bin Laden argued that

> speaking about climate change is not a matter of intellectual luxury – the phenomenon is an actual fact. All of the industrialized countries, especially the big ones, bear responsibility for the global warming crisis . . . George Bush Junior, preceded by Congress, dismissed the [Kyoto] agreement to placate giant corporations. And they are themselves standing behind speculation, monopoly and soaring living costs . . . They are also behind globalisation and its tragic implications.[45]

He used global warming as the prism through which to make larger observations about the nature of capitalism. His emphasis on the issues of market speculation, corporate monopoly and rising living expenses clearly pointed to neo-Marxist influence. He also perceived globalisation as a negative force.

Following the election of Barack Obama, bin Laden wrote another letter to the American people asking them to help the new president make 'a rational decision to save humanity from the harmful gases that threaten its destiny'.[46] The undated letter was seized by the US special forces during the operation to kill bin Laden in his Pakistani compound in 2011 (see appendix). It was never published for unknown reasons. Nevertheless, the letter reveals his persistent concern about global ecological crises, as well as an unexpected acknowledgement of America's special role in the world.

The Taliban have not openly discussed the problem of global warming, but they have raised the problem of pollution in Central Asia. In September 2010, for example, the then leader of the movement, Mullah Mohammed Omar, issued a statement in which he claimed that 'our upcoming system of government . . . will cooperate with regional countries in all common problems of the region like . . . narcotics, *environment pollution* [emphasis added], commercial and economic problems'.[47] The Taliban tried to emphasise their 'governability', if ever they returned to power.

Global warming and climate change are not known as topics of extensive discussion for ISIS. These issues are not of great importance for the group, although the Middle East has suffered from the impacts of rising temperatures. As an organisation with a territorial base, ISIS is probably more interested in controlling land and population. As a result, global issues and problems have not attracted its attention. Since ISIS does not aspire to enter the international community, it has been indifferent to global environmental problems and hostile to global environmental solutions.

At the same time, jihadi-Salafi groups have focused on the energy industry because it remains a key sector of the economy in many Muslim-majority countries. Since there is state ownership of oil and gas reserves, the energy industry is usually plagued by corruption and a lack of transparency. Most oil-rentier states of the Middle East have relied on Western powers for their defence against external threats.[48] Indeed, Arab regimes often have been seen as obedient allies of Western powers.

In his statements and videos, Osama bin Laden analysed the political and security implications of the energy trade for Arab countries. In July 1996, he first mentioned energy during an interview with *The Independent*. He argued, 'The ordinary man knows that [Saudi Arabia] is the largest oil producer in the world, yet at the same time it is suffering from taxes and bad services. Now the people understand the speeches of the 'ulama in the mosques – that our country has become an American colony.'[49] Three months later, bin Laden declared his jihad against the United States and its allies. Once again, he brought up the energy dimension of the conflict by arguing that 'as a result of the policy imposed on [Saudi Arabia] . . . [oil] production is restricted or expanded and prices are fixed to suit the American economy'.[50] In March 1997, he elaborated on the importance of the oil industry:

Since 1973, the price of petrol has increased only 8 dollars per barrel while the prices of other items have gone up three times. The oil prices should also have gone up three times but this did not happen . . . We are suffering a loss of 115 dollars per barrel every day. Only Saudi Arabia produces 10 million barrels oil per day and thus the loss is one billion dollar[s] per day . . . In the past 13 years, the United States has caused us a loss of more [than] 1,100

billion dollars. We must get this money back from the United States . . .
Muslims are starving to death and the United States is stealing their oil.[51]

Thus, bin Laden offered a rationale for targeting the oil industry, a highly
profitable sector of the economy in the region. He claimed that the oil price
was not fair for the producing Arab countries because Washington was able
to keep it low.

Consequently, al-Qaeda and groups affiliated to it have attacked energy
infrastructure (such as pipelines and power plants) in North Africa and the
Middle East. On 6 October 2002, for example, the French-owned oil tanker
Maritime Jewel was hit by a suicide bomber. Al-Qaeda claimed responsibility and explained that 'by striking the oil tanker in Yemen with explosives,
the attackers struck at the umbilical cord of the Christians, reminding the
enemy of the bloody price they have to pay for their continued aggression
on our nation and robbing our riches'.[52] Hence, the group attacked the
tanker to damage Western oil interests and defend the *umma* against external
aggression.

Moreover, there have been efforts to theorise the attacks against energy
facilities. In June 2004, Shaykh Abdullah bin Nasser al-Rashid, the so-called
al-Qaeda minister of propaganda, elaborated on the targeting of oil infrastructure. In *The Laws of Targeting Petroleum-Related Interests and a Review of
the Laws Pertaining to the Economic Jihad*, he claimed the following:

1. The targeting of oil infrastructure is a legitimate means of economic
   jihad against the opponents.
2. The infidels do not own what they have seized from the ummah, because
   it is still its property.
3. The destruction of infidel property as part of jihad is legitimate, as long
   as the benefits outweigh the costs of such action.
4. It is acceptable to destroy Muslim property if infidels have seized control
   of it, or if there are fears that something like this may happen.
5. There are four types of oil related interests: oil wells, pipelines, oil facilities, oil business executives.[53]

Interestingly, al-Rashid attempted to draw an analogy between al-
Qaeda's targeting of energy infrastructure and the Prophet Muhammad's

'Medinan strategy'. Following his departure from Mecca and the establishment of the first Islamic state in Medina, the Prophet and his followers launched attacks against caravan routes to gain booty and harm the Meccan economy. This 'Medinan strategy' has apparently been adopted by al-Qaeda to 'bleed America economically'.[54]

ISIS has been less keen to attack the energy industry, probably because oil-smuggling was one of its main sources of funding. It exploited oil fields in eastern Syria and northern Iraq, and utilised existing networks of smugglers to sell crude oil to neighbouring countries. In this way, the group was able to offer good salaries to its fighters.[55] In November 2014, ISIS even attempted to recruit oil specialists and managers from the open market.[56] The group was able to sell oil to regime- and opposition-controlled areas.[57] In October 2015, ISIS produced an estimated 34,000–40,000 barrels per day, which were sold at $25–40, generating $1.5 million.[58] In reality, ISIS established its own oil production and distribution business in parts of Syria and Iraq. In the words of a local businessman, 'everyone here needs diesel: for water, for farming, for hospitals, for offices. If diesel is cut off, there is no life here . . . Isis knows this [oil] is a winning card.'[59] Additionally, the group controlled eight electricity power plants, including three hydroelectric facilities, in Syria.[60]

What is absent from al-Qaeda's and ISIS's approach to energy issues is any concern about the environmental impact of the oil and gas industry. While other Islamist groups like the Muslim Brotherhood have discussed the growing importance of renewables, the jihadi-Salafis have not shown any sincere interest in alternative forms of energy. Their understanding of energy is oil- and gas-centric because their main goal is to defeat Arab regimes and harm Western interests in the region.

The Role of Religion

Typically, jihadi-Salafism has been identified with acts of violence and terror in the Middle East and elsewhere. It is true that the movement has been preoccupied with the imposition of Shari'a and the punishment of 'apostates' or 'disbelievers'. Nevertheless, jihadi-Salafis have increasingly addressed issues that have an environmental component.

Religious commitment can partly explain the seemingly unlikely engagement of al-Qaeda and ISIS with ecological and related matters. It is true that militants superciliously claim to represent the authentic Islam of the Prophet Muhammad and his Companions. As a result, it is imperative for them to offer a religious justification for their decisions and positions. In some cases, such justification is possible and straightforward. Thus, al-Qaeda has used the example of the Prophet's strategy of economic warfare against Mecca to justify the targeting of the energy industry, despite the potential environmental consequences. Equally, ISIS has issued its own fatwa to justify the destruction of trees for military purposes and the Taliban have invoked the Islamic principle of continuous charity (*sadaqa jariya*) to encourage the planting of trees in Afghanistan.

Jihadi-Salafi groups have often been trapped into a metaphysical understanding of land, however. According to their worldview, the cosmos consists of three realms: the heavens, *Dar al-Harb* (the Abode of War) and *Dar al-Islam* (the Abode of Islam). The status of land is determined by divine command; any challenger can be deemed an enemy of God. It is with ease that al-Qaeda and ISIS could dehumanise whole communities of different religious beliefs. Thus, land is more than a prize to be fought over and claimed. It is the place of salvation or condemnation.

This metaphysical essentialism does not lead to the sacralisation of nature. Despite its religious significance, the use of water as a weapon indicates a scorched-earth approach to warfare that bears no Islamic reasoning. Trees have been perceived as either vital to life or just collateral damage. Non-humans only exist to serve human needs. From a jihadi-Salafi perspective, energy is a new field of political antagonism. Al-Qaeda's focus on climate change has not been based on Islamic teachings and principles, although Muslim scholars have convincingly offered a religious perspective on the issue.[61] Instead, Osama bin Laden used neo-Marxist arguments to explain the urgency of the global warming problem. Whether it was through lack of knowledge or purposeful, an iconic figure of the movement used secular language to articulate his thoughts and sent a message.

Since al-Qaeda and ISIS claim to represent authentic Islam, their environmental approach should be faith-inspired. Indeed, their statements have often used Qur'anic verses to justify attacks, while their videos usually offer a visual representation of collective and emotionally charged Islamic symbols (for example, Ka'ba in Mecca and al-Aqsa Mosque in Jerusalem). The art of jihadi propaganda is evocative and emotive, shaping perceptions and attitudes in Muslim societies and communities.[62] The nominal religionisation of the environment has co-occurred with the environmentalisation of conflicts in the Middle East. Thus, the achievement of military victory remains the main objective for those who subordinate religion to politics.

Jihadi-Salafi groups have been able to mobilise supporters throughout the world by building exclusive identities based on confrontation and division. Most of their senior members do not have formal religious education, but al-Qaeda and ISIS have issued their own fatwas to justify the legality of their operations. By offering certain Islamic evidence, they have prioritised jurisprudence over ethics. Their environmentalism submits to the logic of perpetual conflict with those who are perceived as enemies.

In summary, Islamist militants have formed a cognitive and operational nexus between the environment, religion and politics. Religion is a source of legitimacy for jihadi-Salafi environmentalism, which is based on an arbitrary synthesis of Islamic beliefs and practices. The main goal is not the pursuit of knowledge and truth, but the achievement of power. Although Islamic cosmology advocates a symbiosis of the sacred and the material, the jihadi-Salafi version of Islamist environmentalism is narrow and superficial.

Notes

1. See, for example, Marc Sageman, *Leaderless Jihad: Terror Networks in the Twenty-First Century* (Philadelphia: University of Pennsylvania Press, 2008); Frazer Egerton, *Jihad in the West: The Rise of Militant Salafism* (Cambridge: Cambridge University Press, 2011); Fawaz A. Gerges, *The Rise and Fall of Al-Qaeda* (New York: Oxford University Press, 2011); Mitchell D. Silber, *The Al Qaeda Factor: Plots against the West* (Philadelphia: University of Pennsylvania Press, 2012); Michael W. S. Ryan, *Decoding Al-Qaeda's Strategy: The Deep Battle against America* (New York: Columbia University Press, 2013); Abdel Bari Atwan, *After Bin Laden: Al-Qaeda, the Next Generation* (New York: New Press, 2013).

2. On the Syrian civil war see David W. Lesch, *Syria: The Fall of the House of Assad* (New Haven, CT: Yale University Press, 2012); Emile Hokayem, *Syria's Uprising and the Fracturing of the Levant* (Abingdon: Routledge, 2013).

3. See, for example, Michael Weiss and Hassan Hassan, *ISIS: Inside the Army of Terror* (New York: Regan Arts, 2015); Jessica Stern and J. M. Berger, *ISIS: The*

State of Terror (London: William Collins, 2015); Patrick Cockburn, *The Rise of Islamic State: ISIS and the New Sunni Revolution* (London and New York: Verso, 2015); Joby Warrick, *Black Flags: The Rise of ISIS* (New York: Doubleday, 2015); Abdel Bari Atwan, *Islamic State: The Digital Caliphate* (London: Saqi, 2015).

4. On Salafism see Richard Gauvain, *Salafi Ritual Purity: In the Presence of God* (Abingdon: Routledge, 2013); Henri Lauzière, *The Making of Salafism: Islamic Reform in the Twentieth Century* (New York: Columbia University Press, 2016).

5. Sahih al-Bukhari, *To Make the Heart Tender*, Hadith 18, http://sunnah.com /bukhari/81/18 (accessed 23 June 2022).

6. Mohammed M. Hafez, *Suicide Bombers in Iraq: The Strategy and Ideology of Martyrdom* (Washington, DC: United States Institute of Peace Press, 2007), pp. 65–70.

7. Abu Hamza al-Masri, *Allah's Governance on Earth*, 1999, p. 9, https://www.ka lamullah.com/Books/Allah%20Governance%20on%20Earth.pdf (accessed 23 June 2022).

8. Marco Antonsich, 'Territory and Territoriality' in Douglas Richardson (ed.), *The International Encyclopedia of Geography: People, the Earth, Environment and Technology* (New York: Wiley-Blackwell, 2017), p. 6991.

9. Bruce Lawrence (ed.), *Messages to the World: The Statements of Osama Bin Laden* (London and New York: Verso, 2005), p. 25.

10. 'Letter from the editor', *Inspire Magazine*, Spring 2013, p. 1.

11. 'A call to hijrah', *Dabiq*, no. 1, 2014, p. 10.

12. 'Introduction', *Dabiq*, no. 1, 2014, p. 4.

13. Antonsich, 'Territory and Territoriality', p. 6996.

14. 'Smashing the Borders of the Tawaghit', *Islamic State Report: An Insight into the Islamic State*, no. 4, 2013, p. 1.

15. Official Spokesman for the Islamic State, 'Indeed your Lord is ever watchful', *Dabiq*, no. 4, 2013, p. 9.

16. 'Remaining and expanding', *Dabiq*, no. 5, 2014, pp. 28–9.

17. Ibid.

18. Haroro J. Ingram, Craig Whiteside and Charlie Winter, *The ISIS Reader: Milestone Texts of the Islamic State Movement* (New York: Oxford University Press, 2020), p. 239.

19. Kieran Cooke, 'Islamic State makes its last dam stand', *Middle East Eye*, 30 March 2017, http://www.middleeasteye.net/columns/makes-its-last-dam-stand -1339950924 (accessed 23 June 2022).

20. Kieran Cooke, 'Destruction of dams: will IS carry through its threats?', *Middle*

East Eye, 3 November 2016, http://www.middleeasteye.net/columns/fears-dam
-collapse-remain-raging-battles-1410255276 (accessed 23 June 2022).

21. Lizzie Dearden, 'ISIS gives up Tabqa Dam in exchange for fighters' lives in deal
with US-backed forces advancing on Raqqa', *The Independent*, 12 May 2017,
http://www.independent.co.uk/news/world/middle-east/isis-syria-raqqa-offens
ive-advance-tabqa-dam-deal-sdf-kurds-ypg-us-led-coalition-deal-deserted-a773
3101.html (accessed 23 June 2022).

22. Tobias von Lossow, 'Water as Weapon: IS on the Euphrates and Tigris', SWP
Comment 3, January 2016, p. 2, https://www.swp-berlin.org/fileadmin/conten
ts/products/comments/2016C03_lsw.pdf (accessed 23 June 2022)

23. Ibid.

24. Ibid.

25. Abu Amr al-Kinani, 'The flood is a refutation of the pacifists', *Dabiq*, no. 2,
2014, p. 9.

26. Jared Malsin, 'Beheading of Coptic Christians in Libya shows ISIS branching
out', *Time*, 15 February 2015, http://time.com/3710610/libya-coptic-christians
-isis-egypt/ (accessed 23 June 2022).

27. Abu Bakr Naji, *The Management of Savagery: The Most Critical Stage through
Which the Umma Will Pass* (Cambridge, MA: John M. Olin Institute for
Strategic Studies, Harvard University, 2006), p. 181.

28. 'New statement from the Islamic Emirate of Afghanistan: "The greenery of
Band-e-Sarda, fallen prey to the American terror"', Jihadology, 26 January
2011, http://jihadology.net/2011/01/26/new-statement-from-the-islamic-emi
rate-of-afghanistan-the-greenery-of-band-e-sarda-fallen-prey-to-the-american
-terror/ (accessed 23 June 2022).

29. 'New statement from the Islamic Emirate of Afghanistan: "Destruction of trees
will not turn American defeat into victory"', Jihadology, 2 February 2011,
http://jihadology.net/2011/02/02/new-statement-from-the-islamic-emirate-of
-afghanistan-destruction-of-trees-will-not-turn-american-defeat-into-victory/
(accessed 23 June 2022).

30. 'New release from the Islamic Emirate of Afghanistan's Mawlawi Hibat Allah
Akhund Zadah: "Special message regarding tree plantation"', Jihadology, 26
February 2017, http://jihadology.net/2017/02/26/new-release-from-the-isla
mic-emirate-of-afghanistans-mawlawi-hibat-allah-akhund-zadah-special-messa
ge-regarding-tree-plantation/ (accessed 23 June 2022).

31. The Pakistani Islamist group has focused on deforestation and forest degradation, which is an issue of great concern for the country. For example, its senior

official Maulana Abdul Akbar Chitrali has campaigned against deforestation in parts of Pakistan, arguing that trees protect the environment from global warming. See 'Unchecked deforestation in Chitral District', *The News International*, 4 July 2011, https://www.thenews.com.pk/archive/print/309854-unchecked-de forestation-in-chitral-flayed

32. Bethan McKernan, 'Al Shabaab bans single use plastic bags because of threat to people and livestock', *The Independent*, 3 July 2018, https://www.independent .co.uk/news/world/africa/al-shabaab-somalia-ban-single-use-plastic-bags-terror -environment-livestock-a8428641.html (accessed 23 June 2022).

33. 'The Archivist: Unseen Islamic State fatwas on jihad and sabaya', Jihadology, 25 September 2015, http://jihadology.net/2015/09/25/the-archivist-unseen-is lamic-state-fatwas-on-jihad-and-sabaya/ (accessed 23 June 2022).

34. Ibid.

35. Ahmed Al-Dawoody, *The Islamic Law of War: Justifications and Regulations* (New York: Palgrave Macmillan, 2011), p. 127.

36. Ibid.

37. Abul-Harith ath-Thaghri, 'Contemplate the Creation', *Dabiq*, no. 15, 2016, pp. 8–9.

38. Afshon Ostovar, 'The Visual Culture of Jihad', in Thomas Hegghammer (ed.), *Jihadi Culture: The Art and Social Practices of Militant Islamists* (Cambridge: Cambridge University Press, 2017), p. 94.

39. 'O Victorious Ummah, Carry Your Arms, Wage Jihad, and Rejoice', *An-Nafir*, no. 1, 2014, p. 4, https://web.archive.org/web/20180923075525/https://aze lin.files.wordpress.com/2014/07/al-qc481_idah-22al-nafc4abr-122-en.pdf (accessed 28 June 2022).

40. Ian Black, 'Charlie Hebdo killings condemned by Arab states – but hailed online by extremists', *The Guardian*, 7 January 2015, https://www.theguardian.com /world/2015/jan/07/charlie-hebdo-killings-arab-states-jihadi-extremist-sympat hisers-isis (accessed 23 June 2022).

41. 'The capture of Division 17', *Dabiq*, no. 2, 2014, p. 42.

42. 'Al Qaeda group says Obama, Clinton worth only chickens, camels', Reuters, 10 June 2012, https://www.reuters.com/article/us-usa-somalia-reward/Al-Qa eda-group-says-obama-clinton-worth-only-chickens-camels-idUSBRE85901E2 0120610 (accessed 23 June 2022).

43. Lawrence, *Messages to the World*, p. 168.

44. '"The Solution": a video speech from Usama bin Laden addressing the American people on the occasion of the sixth anniversary of 9/11 – 9/2007', SITE

Intelligence Group, 7 September 2007, http://www.csun.edu/~hfspc002/442 /txt/20070911_OBL.pdf (accessed 23 June 2022).

45. Suzanne Goldenberg, 'Osama bin Laden lends unwelcome support in fight against climate change', *The Guardian*, 29 January 2010, http://www.guardi an.co. uk/environment/2010/jan/29/osama-bin-laden-climate-change (accessed 23 June 2022).

46. Jessica Chasmar, 'Osama bin Laden called for Americans to help Obama fight climate change', *Washington Times*, 2 March 2016, https://www.washington times.com/news/2016/mar/2/osama-bin-laden-called-for-americans-to-help-obama/ (accessed 23 June 2022).

47. 'Message of felicitation from Mulla Muhmmad 'Umar, on the eve of 'Id al-Fitr', Jihadology, 8 September 2010, http://jihadology.net/2010/09/08/message-of -felicitation-from-mulla-mu%E1%B8%A5mmad-umar-on-the-eve-of-id-al-fi %E1%B9%ADr/ (accessed 23 June 2022, emphasis added).

48. On the rentier states of the Middle East see Hazem Beblawi and Giacomo Luciani, *The Rentier State* (New York: Croom Helm, 1987).

49. 'Interview with Saudi dissident Osama bin Ladin', *The Independent*, 10 July 1996, p. 14.

50. 'Bin Laden's fatwa', PBS Newshour, 23 August 1996, http://web.archive.org /web/20121013022756/http://www.pbs.org/newshour/updates/military/july -dec96/fatwa_1996.html (accessed 23 June 2022).

51. Interview with Osama bin Laden by Hamid Mir, editor of *Daily Pakistan*, 18 March 1997.

52. 'Excerpts of purported statement by Bin Laden', 15 October 2002, available at https://scholarship.tricolib.brynmawr.edu/bitstream/handle/10066/4766/OBL 20021014P.pdf (accessed 23 June 2022).

53. 'Al Qaeda in Saudi Arabia: Excerpts from "The Laws of Targeting Petroleum-Related Interests"', Global Terror Alert, March 2006, http://web.archive.org /web/20111202105333/http://azelin.files.wordpress.com/2010/08/al-qaida -in -saudi-arabia-excerpts-from-e2809cthe-laws-of-targeting-petroleum-related -interests.pdf (accessed 23 June 2022).

54. Marisa Urgo and Jack F. Williams, 'Al Qa'ida's Medinan Strategy: Targeting Global Energy Infrastructure', *CTC Sentinel*, May 2008, pp. 17–18, https://ctc .westpoint.edu/al-qaidas-medinan-strategy-targeting-global-energy-infrastructu re/ (accessed 23 June 2022).

55. Fazel Hawramy, Shalaw Mohammed and Luke Harding, 'Inside Islamic State's oil empire: how captured oilfields fuel Isis insurgency', *The Guardian*, 19

November 2014, https://www.theguardian.com/world/2014/nov/19/-sp-isla
mic-state-oil-empire-iraq-isis (accessed 23 June 2022).

56. Jack Crone, 'Wanted – experienced oil plant manager, pay £140,000 p.a. . . .
send CV to ISIS: jihadists advertising for skilled professionals to man its failing
oil fields after string of fatal accidents', *Mail Online*, 1 November 2014, http://
www.dailymail.co.uk/news/article-2816755/Wanted-experienced-oil-plant-ma
nager-pay-140-000-p-send-CV-ISIS-Jihadists-advertising-skilled-professionals
-man-failing-oil-fields-string-fatal-accidents.html (accessed 23 June 2022).

57. Amr al-Faham, 'Fighting ISIS and the regime with renewable energy', Atlantic
Council, 12 May 2016, http://www.atlanticcouncil.org/blogs/syriasource/fight
ing-isis-and-the-regime-with-renewable-energy (accessed 23 June 2022).

58. Erika Solomon, Robin Kwong and Steven Bernard, 'Inside Isis Inc: the journey
of a barrel of oil', *Financial Times*, 29 February 2016, https://ig.ft.com/sites/20
15/isis-oil/ (accessed 23 June 2022).

59. Erika Solomon, Guy Chazan and Sam Jones, 'Isis Inc: how oil fuels the jihadi
terrorists', *Financial Times*, 14 October 2015, https://www.ft.com/content/b82
34932-719b-11e5-ad6d-f4ed76f0900a (accessed 23 June 2022).

60. Erika Solomon and Ahmed Mhidi, 'Isis Inc: Syria's "mafia-style" gas deals with
jihadis', *Financial Times*, 15 October 2015, https://www.ft.com/content/92f4e
036-6b69-11e5-aca9-d87542bf8673 (accessed 23 June 2022).

61. See, for example, 'Islamic Declaration on Global Climate Change', 18 August
2015, https://www.ifees.org.uk/wp-content/uploads/2020/01/climate_decla
rationmmwb.pdf (accessed 20 June 2022).

62. See Thomas Hegghammer, 'Introduction: What Is Jihadi Culture and Why
Should We Study It?' in Thomas Hegghammer (ed.), *Jihadi Culture: The Art and
Social Practices of Militant Islamists* (Cambridge: Cambridge University Press,
2017), pp. 1–11.

7

UNDERSTANDING ISLAMIST
ENVIRONMENTALISM

The Muslim Brotherhood, Hizb ut-Tahrir, Hizbullah, Hamas and al-Qaeda/ISIS have been increasingly preoccupied with environmental and environment-related themes. Consequently, Islamists have been addressing land and water issues, tree-planting, animal rights, pollution control and energy. They have offered proposals and suggestions to tackle problems that are affecting the environment and the population's quality of life. It is a clear trend indicating a change of direction for political Islam, which is becoming more responsive and engaging. However, each group has adopted a different scale of environmental engagement depending on its priorities and areas of operation. The priorities are set by electoral programmes or other documents, and the areas of operation are determined by ideology and circumstances. Hence, there are three types of Islamist environmentalism: localised, globalised and glocalised.

To begin with, the Muslim Brotherhood has formulated a localised agenda focusing on Egypt's ecological challenges. Notwithstanding its pan-Islamic claims and credentials, the organisation has not addressed global environmental problems (for example, climate change, ocean pollution). In fact, the Brotherhood's environmental policy is bound by geography. Pan-Islamism is in reality an elusive construct. This is hardly a surprise since the Brotherhood was founded and developed in Egypt. The Ikhwan aspired to come to power and succeeded in doing so; control of the state has been their ultimate political goal. Thus, the Brotherhood's scale of environmental engagement is local. The ban of the Muslim Brotherhood in 2013 has not changed its priorities: the group still concentrates on Egyptian affairs.

Likewise, Hamas has maintained an interest in local environmental matters. Although the group claims to represent all Palestinians, the confrontation with Israel has changed its perceptions and priorities. Hamas is now trapped, both physically and cognitively. Despite its pan-Palestinian rhetoric, the group has increasingly focused on the area under its control. Since coming to power in 2007, the formulation of Hamas's environmental policy has been due to the deteriorating conditions in Gaza. Consequently, Hamas's scale of environmental engagement is local.

ISIS has also shown interest in local issues only. The group claims to fight a regional war that is sanctioned by God. In this context, water can be used as a weapon and trees can be destroyed to undermine the enemy's willingness and ability to fight. It may or may not be permissible, but it is necessary. Nature is the battlefield that will determine victory or defeat. All this amounts to a new military strategy that serves the eventual goal of establishing an Islamic utopia on earth. In other words, ISIS's scale of environmental engagement is local in content.

In contrast, Hizb ut-Tahrir has promoted a globalised agenda that can reach audiences in different countries. Due to its universal membership, the group has focused on a wide range of issues of global concern (for example, animal-poaching). This is consistent with its goal of re-establishing the Caliphate, a political union of all Muslims. Only such a universal state could solve universal problems. Given that Hizb ut-Tahrir has embraced pan-Islamism in the form of neo-caliphatism, its scale of environmental engagement is global. Yet, 'global' is not meant here as covering the whole planet; rather, it implies the whole of the Muslim world.

Al-Qaeda has also followed a globalised approach by focusing on problems like climate change, for instance. Since it is a deterritorialised organisation that claims a global audience, it is oriented towards environmental issues that concern many different societies. The personality of Osama bin Laden can partly explain the organisational focus on global ecological challenges. He was a cosmopolitan Saudi who lived in different regions (for example, north Africa, the Middle East, central and south Asia) and married women from different countries (for example, Saudi Arabia, Syria, Yemen). Under his successor, Ayman al-Zawahiri, al-Qaeda has shown less interest in global warning and other problems of major concern.

Between the localised and the globalised Islamist environmentalists stand some groups like Hizbullah. The Lebanese group has acknowledged the significance of climate change, while mostly engaging in local activities. This reflects Hizbullah's duality of being simultaneously active inside and outside Lebanon. The group is not bound by national borders because it is situated in between different contexts and geographies. This inherent contradiction of Hizbullah can be attributed to two dissimilar ideologies: Lebanese nationalism and pan-Islamism, which really means pan-Shi'ism. Their combination can explain Hizbullah's inconsistencies in policy positions. Hence, its scale of environmental engagement is glocal.

Despite the different preferences, Islamist groups have the flexibility to focus on what matters to their supporters. The Brotherhood utilised gas exports as a political weapon to support fellow Ikhwan in Jordan. African and Asian branches of Hizb ut-Tahrir have often focused on local problems affecting Muslim communities. Hence, the scale of environmental engagement is more an orientation than a telos or destiny. Indeed, many Islamists constantly negotiate between global influences and local realities. Consequently, the notion of the environment is both broad and narrow because it is subject to situational factors, rather than predetermined conceptual frameworks. The elasticity of the environment is proportional to the scale of engagement; localised agendas incorporate narrower understandings of the environment than globalised ones. In reality, however, Islamist environmentalism is increasingly glocal in its outlook because there is a fusion of local and global issues.

Islamists do not always share the same view on a specific environmental issue because they represent different communities and pursue different goals. In fact, there is a diversity of views, indicating the heterogeneous nature of political Islam. The relationship between Islamist groups is not vertical but horizontal; they co-exist but often prefer to ignore each other. There are several examples of such disagreement.

Hizb ut-Tahrir perceives the Paris Agreement as a 'Western plot' to prevent Muslim-majority countries from becoming industrialised, while

Hizbullah and Osama bin Laden's al-Qaeda have a positive view of it. The Muslim Brotherhood, Hamas and Hizbullah have also welcomed the involvement of international organisations in environmental protection efforts, whereas Hizb ut-Tahrir and al-Qaeda typically view them as entities that conspire against Muslims. Hizbullah has ignored animal issues, although the Brotherhood, Hizb ut-Tahrir and Hamas have addressed them. Hizbullah and Hamas have been keen to engage in reforestation projects, while Hizb ut-Tahrir, al-Qaeda and ISIS have overlooked the issue.

At the same time, there are striking similarities among Islamist environmentalists. The question of water supply has been addressed one way or another by all groups. Since Middle Eastern countries have suffered from desertification and lack of clean water, many Islamists are preoccupied with the management of river eco-systems. Al-Qaeda and ISIS are the notable exceptions. Additionally, sewage management and pollution control have become policy priorities for most Islamists under study. On the related issue of energy, however, Islamist groups have proposed different policies with respect to supply, consumption and efficiency. Finally, Islamist environmentalists tend to ignore issues that are not relevant to them (for example, space debris). Hence, their actions and interventions are bound by the borders of the Muslim world.

These similarities and differences indicate the variety of Islamist environmental policies and approaches. The remainder of the chapter summarises the role of religion in Islamist environmentalism and examines three more factors prompting Islamists to pay attention to green issues: alliance-building, political and military expediency, and ideological realignment.

Is Islamist Environmentalism Religion-driven?

The Qur'an and the Prophet have called upon Muslims to be careful and gentle towards the environment. In this way, the believer can come closer to the divine. It is both a spiritual and doctrinal obligation to obey the divine rules and respect the godly order. However, Islamist environmentalists rarely provide sophisticated insights into Islamic eco-theology. They do not refer to Islamic theosophy (the nature of divinity), cosmology (the origin of the universe) or ontology (the nature of mankind). This omission is rather puzzling because many Islamist groups were established by Islamic scholars and even today are run by them, as in the case of Hizbullah and Hamas. These religious leaders are accustomed to using Islamic evidence as the foundation of their arguments.

The previous chapters explored whether religion is a source of knowledge or legitimisation for Islamist environmental policies. The former indicates a constant flow of knowledge and ideas feeding into policy suggestions. In this case, the relationship between religion and policy is vertical. The latter implies that religion offers concepts and principles that can inspire certain policy proposals. Consequently, the relationship is neither horizontal nor vertical but can still be noticeable.

The variable that indicates the 'Islamicness' of policy is the influence of Shari'a and Islamic environmental ethics. While rules and ethics are not synonymous, there is an overlapping element between them: both are based on the Qur'an and the *Sunna*. While many Islamist environmentalists have foreseen a particularly important role for Islam as a spiritual guide for mankind, very few have offered a legalistic, ethical framework for the resolution of the environmental crisis.

Indeed, Islamist groups have viewed the protection of the environment as a vehicle to achieve short-term aims. While it is true that sometimes they have a genuine religious interest in environmental issues, most of the time the pursuit of politics takes precedence over the fulfilment of a religious obligation. Islamists have not even engaged in dialogue with Muslim eco-scholars, although some of them are known for their pro-Islamist sympathies or tolerance (for example, Tariq Ramadan, Mustafa Abu-Sway, Ali Bulaç). Islamist environmentalism often has a contextualised relationship with the Muslim faith. Although Islamists sometimes do use religious rhetoric and arguments, this study of the five groups and movements does not reveal a depth of knowledge that is consistent.

The Muslim Brotherhood and Hamas want to offer solutions to problems that matter. Religious knowledge does not make a difference in this case. Hizb ut-Tahrir's environmentalism seeks some theological guidance in its effort to deal with ecological issues. Hizbullah's environmentalism incorporates a few religious and many non-religious elements. Al-Qaeda's and ISIS's approach to the environment is as simply another tool in their military toolkit. Overall, religion tends to be a powerful instrument of legitimisation.

Islamist environmentalism has often, but not always, an anti-state character because Islamists are usually in opposition to, or in competition with, authorities. Islamist environmentalism is politicised and confrontational. It is neither 'theocentric', for politics takes precedence over religious conformity, nor ecocentric, as nature is not protected for its own sake. In fact, Islamist environmentalism tends to be hyper-anthropocentric and non-spiritual. The Islamist perspective on water is indicative of this aspect. Although it has exercised full control over Gaza, Hamas has not enforced Shari'a rules regarding the use of water. ISIS's tactics contradict the spirit of Islam, which forbids wastage and monopoly of water. Despite its claim to Islamic authenticity, Hizbullah has ignored Islamic law and tradition regarding the management of water resources.

Nonetheless, the influence of religion on Islamist environmentalism cannot be dismissed easily. It is true that Islamists identify themselves as devout Muslims who follow the tenets of the Qur'an and the *Sunna*. The linkages between Islam and political Islam are debatable but undeniable, at least for political scientists. Bassam Tibi, for instance, has defined political Islam as the 'mobilization of religion for political ends'.[1] Yet, this modernity has taken place in the era of secular modernisation.

Peter Berger argued that modernity has five dilemmas, namely abstraction, futurity, individuation, liberation and secularisation.[2] Harvey Cox wrote about the pillars of modernity, including nationalism, technology, bureaucracy, profit maximisation and secularisation.[3] At first sight, the persistence of the Muslim faith seems to defy the Weberian thesis of secularisation.[4] *In the Protestant Ethic and the Spirit of Capitalism*, Max Weber argued that 'the people filled with the spirit of capitalism today tend to be indifferent, if not hostile, to the Church. The thought of the pious boredom of paradise has little attraction for their active natures; religion appears to them as a means of drawing people away from labour in this world.'[5] Thus, he claimed that religion will decline with the spread of capitalism. However, Berger has argued that the secularisation thesis is Eurocentric since the influence of religion has spread in other parts of the world.[6]

Islamist environmentalism is perhaps a postsecular phenomenon. Postsecularism, as espoused by Jürgen Habermas, was initially meant to explain the public influence and relevance of religion in European societies.[7] Yet Mariano Barbato has argued that the Arab Spring revolutions were postsecular revolutions because religion played an important role.[8] In fact, it could be argued that Islam – in its different manifestations – has always been involved in politics. Moreover, postsecularism does not necessarily equal anti-secularism. It is a rather multivocal phenomenon, as James Diamond suggested.[9]

Hence, Islamist environmentalism entails the construction of new dichotomies: tradition versus modernity and local versus global. The former is a constant struggle for identity and purpose, while the latter is the dialectic relationship between the tangible and the abstract. However, both must encounter normative isomorphic pressures deriving from the evolution of Muslim life in the Middle East and beyond. Islamists often need to address the concerns of their constituencies. They espouse an environmentalism that has only a superficial relationship with religion and seeks pragmatic solutions. These actors consider political and social realities, rather than religious beliefs and practices.

In any case, it is fair to argue that Islamist environmentalism is neither coherent nor monolithic. It is not just the engagement of Islamist actors with environmental and environment-related issues, as initially suggested in the Introduction. It is also a set of ideas, practices and outcomes that have come to shape policies and programmes. The various versions have similarities and differences because they seek to address the needs of many audiences. In effect, the diversity of understandings about the environment illustrates the complexity of contemporary Islamism.

Non-religious Factors Explaining Islamist Environmentalism

If religion does not play a dominant role in Islamist environmentalism, there must be some non-religious factors explaining the phenomenon. The study of five groups and movements have revealed three such factors: alliance-building, political and military expediency, and ideological realignment.

Alliance-building

Islamist environmentalists have formulated strategies of alliance-building to survive and possibly prosper politically. They are aware that constitutional and other political constraints prevent them from gaining power. Building a political alliance can save them from repression or help them to grow their constituency. This factor can explain why the Muslim Brotherhood, Hizbullah and Hamas have been keen to reach out to political parties and movements in their countries. However, political engagement often brings more willingness to compromise. Indeed, the moderation thesis has been supported by a growing number of scholars.[10] It claims that Islamists become more moderate when they enter the political system of their country. As a result, the more they participate in the public arena, the more co-operative they are.

Environmentalism as an ideology and practice has spread across the Muslim world. The degradation of eco-systems and biodiversity has affected human life in different social, economic, cultural and environmental aspects. Climate change has been viewed as one of the most serious global issues in many Muslim-majority countries.[11] As a result, environmental protection is widely perceived as a noble cause worthy of dedication. Care for the environment indicates ethical and responsible political behaviour. Simultaneously, the environment could become a political bridge between movements.

Since the outbreak of the January 2011 revolution, the Ikhwan have faced intense competition from Salafi groups. The al-Nour Party came second in the 2011 Egyptian parliamentary elections, receiving 27.8 per cent of the vote.[12] For many years, Salafis prioritised education and family issues over other areas of public policy but gradually developed a comprehensive strategy for environmental protection and sustainability. The 2011 electoral programme of al-Nour observed that

> it is clear that the pollution of the environment in Egypt is a vast problem. The main reason for this is the lack of religious belief that has caused officials and citizens alike to pollute the environment according to their location. There is no difference between a citizen throwing dirt in the street and factories dumping chemical waste in a river'.[13]

In other words, the Salafis of al-Nour blamed secularism for the current environmental crisis in Egypt.

Nevertheless, al-Nour proposed several measures to improve the environmental security of the country that lack any religious reasoning. The party called for the transfer of environmentally polluting industries outside the cities; the teaching of methods of environmental protection in schools and universities; the production and use of renewables and clean energy; the recycling of organic and agricultural waste; the enactment of laws protecting the environment from air and water pollution, as well as visual and audio pollution; the protection of beaches from pollution; the creation of green spaces in and around cities; and finally, the reclamation of land to stop desertification.[14] The Salafi environmental policy proposals clearly resembled those put forward by the Brotherhood's 2007 electoral programme for the Shura Council (see Chapter 2). They look reasonable and scientifically sound. The similarity between them indicates a convergence of environmental understandings on the part of major Islamist actors in Egypt. Despite their competition, the field of environmental protection has been one of the few areas seemingly immune to inter-Islamist competition.[15]

Furthermore, the Brotherhood has used environmental issues to reach out to Egyptians outside its traditional constituency. It should be noted that the Mubarak regime was criticised for lacking 'a clear environmental policy at any level'.[16] Currently, more and more people are aware of the environmental problems facing the country, and a growing number of NGOs and local initiatives (for instance, the Association for the Protection of the Environment and the Arab Office for Youth and Environment) are focusing on the protection of the environment. Consequently, the green movement in Egypt has managed to mobilise people around issues that can affect their lives. Quinn Mecham has observed that Islamist organisations could take advantage of political opportunities only if they diluted the religious content in their political platform.[17] Thus, the new reality of growing awareness could easily explain the non-religious content of the Brotherhood's environmentalism.

Hizbullah has embraced the cause of environmentalism because concerns over deforestation, water security and pollution have proliferated and gained broad legitimacy in recent decades. Its one-million-trees campaign attracted wide publicity and positive feedback from environmental NGOs in Lebanon. For instance, Ali Darwish, the general secretary of the Lebanese NGO Green Line argued, 'If two institutions, the church and the mosque, could unite on greening Lebanon, we would be much better off.'[18] This opinion was shared by Nada Zaarour, vice-president of Lebanon's Green Party, who believed that Sayyed Hassan Nasrallah 'has charisma, so if he plants trees, everyone who follows him might plant a tree ... [I]t's a good cause ... [L]et him plant.'[19] Hizbullah has hoped to reach out to non-Shi'a Lebanese, like the educated and urbanised Christians and Sunnis who tend to perceive the group as sectarian and militant.

Hizbullah has also accused Israel of stealing Lebanon's gas riches and plotting to do the same with its water supplies. Indeed, Israel has been portrayed as a greedy imperialist power. Following the unilateral Israeli withdrawal from south Lebanon in 2000, Nasrallah declared that 'what Israel cares about in Lebanon and this whole region is its own interests, its own purpose and ambitions; in the eyes of these Zionists, we Christians and Muslims are mere servants and slaves to God's chosen people'.[20] Thus, he has attempted to build a united Christian–Muslim front by invoking traditional anti-Semitism that has its roots in Christian and Islamic theology.

Although the group has built alliances with non-Muslim political forces, its core target audience remains the Shi'i community. Hence, it is obliged to use – even if only occasionally – traditional Islamic discourses to recontextualise policy decisions, as it did with the reforestation campaign. In this way, its environmental initiatives could serve as a mobilisation tool for engaging with the larger Shi'i community in the country. Indeed, the promotion of an environmentally friendly agenda could make Hizbullah more attractive in comparison to Amal, the other major Shi'i group in the country. The founder of Amal, Imam Musa al-Sadr, promoted what Karim Makdisi described as 'the environmentalism of the poor'.[21] Al-Sadr's approach was proto-environmentalist, not genuinely environmentalist. He campaigned for social and environmental justice in the form of Shi'a communal rights. Currently, there is more unity than division between the two groups.[22] Still, Hizbullah has sought to be pioneering and proactive in tackling new challenges.

In the case of Hamas, the adoption of environmentalism could be part of a broader strategy to improve its image as an organisation that cares for the well-being of all Palestinians. It has been accused by secular Palestinians of harbouring a hidden agenda to impose its conservative Islamic norms on the population.[23] The group understands that the promotion of environmentalism could ease tensions with non-Hamas Palestinians in Gaza and elsewhere.

Furthermore, Hamas is conscious that concerns over environmental issues have attracted increased global attention in recent years. Consequently, the embrace of environmental issues could enable Hamas to develop international links. In effect, its environmentalism can create a bridge with international social movements like the International Jewish Anti-Zionist Network (IJAN), which has an environmental component.[24] This is not the first time that Hamas has reached out to groups that are ideologically dissimilar. In October 1991, Hamas and leftist Palestinian groups (for example, the Revolutionary Palestinian Communist Party, the Popular Struggle Front) issued a declaration regarding the formation of the Ten Resistance Organizations.[25] The birth of this alliance was announced by the leaders of those organisations, who met concurrently with the International Conference on the Islamic Revolution's Support for the People of Palestine, which was convened in Tehran in October 1991.[26] Thus, Hamas has demonstrated flexibility in its effort to advance its cause and build alliances. The adoption of a hybrid environmentalism could be part of a broader strategy of internationalisation.

It is clear that alliance-building as a factor can be found in the contexts of political competition. The Muslim Brotherhood, Hizbullah and Hamas have participated in the electoral process by forming political parties. It is a game-changing development compelling them to seek political allies. Environmental problems are largely viewed as politically neutral in the sense of being equally harmful to all citizens. Therefore, the environmental policies of the Brotherhood, Hizbullah and Hamas are designed to build ties even with non-members and non-sympathisers. In contrast, Hizb ut-Tahrir, al-Qaeda and ISIS are Islamist groups operating on their own in different regions and countries. Since they do not seek allies, these groups have used polemical language excluding other political actors.

Political and Military Expediency

Political expediency is a critical contextual factor shaping or determining decisions. Islamist groups think and act politically because they address public issues and engage with wider society. It is the nature of politics to focus on what is important for the supporters. Hence, Islamists care more about popularity than religious rigidity. In this way, power derives from the size of the support base. As environmental issues become increasingly important, Islamists must be seen as active agents. They cannot afford to ignore the new reality if they want to remain relevant and appealing. If they do not adjust to the conditions of the present time, they risk marginalisation and alienation from the rest of society. Therefore, the pursuit of environmental goals often disguises political and sometimes even military intentions.

The environmentalism of the Muslim Brotherhood is partly the outcome of political expediency, rather than just an ethical endeavour to protect nature and its components. The Ikhwan have suggested certain policy measures to ease the life of their supporters who face ecological challenges and economic uncertainties. The Brotherhood has its own political constituency in small towns and villages of the Nile Delta. It is a region that has suffered from many environmental problems, including pollution, lack of clean water and coastal erosion.[27] To make matters worse, land ownership issues have sparked serious tensions in the Nile Delta. In 1992, President Mubarak managed to reverse the 1952 land reform that gave certain rights to tenant farmers; as a result, about six million Egyptians were negatively affected by the new legislation, which included the tripling of rent.[28] The indebted farmers have been evicted by landlords from their farms. In 2012, these people voted for Mohamed Morsi because the other candidate, Ahmed Shafiq, had served as a minister under Mubarak and was largely viewed as a stooge of the previous regime. However, Morsi's voters were not necessarily more religious than those of Shafiq.[29] Thus, the interplay between environment and class could explain why certain areas of the Nile Delta voted for Morsi in the 2012 presidential elections.

In this context of bottom-up social pressure for reform, the Brotherhood must demonstrate its ability to constantly provide solutions to new challenges. It is this political necessity that has prompted the Brotherhood to develop an environmental policy. This policy could offer cost-effective solutions to urgent environmental problems. For instance, irrigation problems have escalated in recent years due to mismanagement. The Brotherhood's pragmatic proposals on water management have aimed to address the needs of rural communities in the Nile Delta area.

The Clean Homeland Campaign of 2012 is another manifestation of political expediency. It served more aims than simply protecting the environment.

The timing of the decision – one month after Morsi's inauguration – indicated hidden political motives. The environmental campaign was destined to be popular among urban dwellers, particularly the educated middle-class Egyptians who had serious reservations about the Muslim Brotherhood's ability to govern the country. Morsi attempted to offer a new vision of patriotism which included social responsibility and environmental protection.

In July 2013, the military coup against President Morsi interrupted the implementation of the Brotherhood's environmental policy. Nonetheless, the organisation has maintained a strong interest in certain issues (for example, the country's rights over the Nile) because they can bring political benefits against the el-Sisi regime. Indeed, Egypt's ecological crisis has offered new opportunities for the Brotherhood to gain influence and position itself against competitors. Hence, the Brotherhood's environmental policy reflects power dynamics and strategic calculus shaped by local and national socioeconomic and political contexts.

Unlike the Muslim Brotherhood, Hizbullah has a military wing that has been active since the early to mid-1980s. The Lebanese group fought against the Israel Defence Forces (IDF) during the 1980s and 1990s, started a new war against the Jewish State in 2006, and is currently involved in the Syrian civil war. Yet Hizbullah has managed to participate in the political life of the country; it has sought legitimacy through political impact.

Although Hizbullah initially declared its intention to establish an Iranian-style Islamic republic, it gradually came to change its position. The group has recognised Lebanon as a legitimate state. In 1992, Hassan Nasrallah gave an interview to the pan-Arabic newspaper *Al-Watan al-Arabi*, where he explained Hizbullah's pragmatism as a political necessity. He stated:

> We have never proposed the idea of imposing an Islamic Republic on Lebanon by force, and will not do that in the future . . . This government would not be able to govern according to Islamic principles, or indeed survive, in the absence of overwhelming popular support. An Islamic government is an ideological entity committed, by virtue of its religious teachings – as well as legislatively and legally – to follow divinely inspired rules.[30]

His words revealed a pragmatic understanding of Lebanese intercommunal relations and politics. Military force cannot substitute for political action.

A massive organisation with a grassroots ethos could not ignore the state of the environmental situation in Lebanon. After years of community-based engagement and outreach, Hizbullah has built patronage networks in Shi'a-populated areas of the country. There is a kind of social contract between many Shi'a Muslims and the organisation. Hizbullah provides social and environmental services (for example, sewage and wastewater management, water supply) to the community, which in return supports the organisation's goals and objectives.

Political patronage is only one of the manifestations of political expediency. From Hizbullah's point of view, politics is the continuation of war by other means. Therefore, its officials have not hidden the military implications of reforestation. According to Mohammed Hajj, general manager of the Jihad al-Binaa Association (JABA), trees and forests are military assets for Hizbullah because they provide shelter and cover for its fighters against Israel.[31] In the summer of 2020, the Hizbullah-affiliated NGO Green without Borders initiated a reforestation project that sparked tensions with the IDF. The lines of trees planted by the NGO along the Israeli–Lebanese border almost blocked Israeli surveillance cameras in an apparent effort to stop further Israeli attacks.[32]

Despite its participation in the democratic process, Hizbullah has refused to give up its arms. Its military strategy is largely based on deception and ambush that depends on the effective use of natural resources. In fact, the combination of forests, hills and gorges make southern Lebanon an ideal place to conduct guerrilla warfare. Nasrallah has aptly summarised the military rationale behind the planting of trees by the JABA:

> It is the need of dealing with trees, tree-planting, woods, forests and even trees on roads and in front of houses as part of the Lebanese national security. So it is not only an environmental, health, climatic, aesthetic aspect of a green country. Lebanon is in need of this tree. Lebanon protects it so that it protects Lebanon. Notice that all around the world – even in military studies, military sciences, geography and demography – nature gives defensive characteristics which at times might be very important . . . [C]ombating in deserts differs from fighting in mountains which in its turn differs from battling in valleys.[33]

Interestingly, Nasrallah attempted to explain the relevance of military geography as a component of a national defence strategy. Indeed, Hizbullah's environmentalism reinforces the image of a noble group willing to resist real or imaginary invaders. Thus, political expediency does not necessarily imply non-violent forms of environmental engagement. On the contrary, it can determine a group's strategy for confronting its enemies. In effect, this amounts to a form of military expediency.

The tree-planting campaign of Hamas, described in Chapter 5, was apparently a duplicate of Hizbullah's campaign in Lebanon. Consequently, there is a military dimension to tree-planting. Although the group has largely operated from urban areas, olive trees have significant military impor-tance because they provide shelter for Palestinian fighters and their rocket-launching sites. Just like Hizbullah, Hamas has evolved into an organisation with multiple activities ranging from militancy to political participation. Indeed, the group's uniqueness lies in the fact that it is a non-state armed actor with many state features; it functions as a quasi-state. Since it became the governing party in Gaza, Hamas has struggled with new realities in the enclave. Many inhabitants demand from Hamas a better life because it now runs the government.[34] Thus, the group considers only environmental issues of growing importance for the local population.

Hamas is aware of the competition it faces from the emerging civil soci-ety. In recent years, a growing number of Palestinian NGOs have run envi-ronmental projects in the area. For example, the Palestinian branch of the Arab Youth Climate Movement has initiated an awareness campaign for the protection of Wadi Gaza, a natural reserve in the coastal enclave.[35] This emerging green movement has offered solutions and has implicitly challenged Hamas's efficiency in dealing with ecological challenges. In this context, the group cannot afford to ignore the mounting problems of pollution, water shortages and energy security. Environmental degradation is a problem that affects social and economic life in Gaza.

Hizb ut-Tahrir has remained politically introvert, although political cal-culations have taken precedence over professed religious commitments. In Palestine, Pakistan, Malaysia and Indonesia, Hizb ut-Tahrir has competed against other Islamist groups for the same pool of potential members. It has tried hard to retain the image of a devout group that can provide theological evidence to support its arguments. Consequently, it has dismissed similar efforts by other Islamists as superficial and secularist. In the words of a senior member of the British branch, 'in the 1950s, Shaikh Nabhani . . . built an understanding on an Islamic worldview – this meant looking at how Islam addresses human problems. Other Muslim groups and thinkers did not always discipline themselves in this way, so they understood general principles, so often end[ed] up copying left-wing policies on things.'[36]

Nevertheless, the group has not been involved in everyday politics. It has recruited from specific social and professional groups, such as medical doctors and engineers, students and academics, businessmen, and occasionally even members of the political and military elites. Hence, Hizb ut-Tahrir has been conservative in its recruitment strategy. Compared with other Islamist groups, Hizb ut-Tahrir has a rather unique relationship with its members. There is no expectation from members to vote for Hizb ut-Tahrir because it does not participate in elections.[37] The group engages mostly in intellectual work, while its activism is limited and selective. Hizb ut-Tahrir is not involved in the management of environmental problems and does not deliver any environmental services. Its proposals are theoretical in nature because the group has never gained power. Thus, political expediency does not play a significant role in Hizb ut-Tahrir's environmentalism.

Finally, the protection of the environment could serve as a source of legitimacy for jihadi-Salafi groups. In an era in which most Muslims and non-Muslims alike view jihadi-Salafism as a morally perverse ideology and movement, concerns over environmental degradation could change the public image of militants. Like other Islamist groups, al-Qaeda and ISIS have addressed an audience of people who have environmental concerns. In September 2010, for instance, Adam Gadahn, senior al-Qaeda operative, stated that 'this year, millions of Muslims in Pakistan, Afghanistan and neighbouring countries are spending Ramadhan as homeless . . . refugees. Some of them are refugees due to the devastating floods, resulting from the extraordinarily heavy monsoon rains.'[38] Nonetheless, al-Qaeda has never tried to engage in environmental activism like cleaning streets or planting trees. Its transnational, decentralised and violent nature does not allow the group to engage in such earthly activities.

In contrast, the Taliban have taken environmental initiatives, such as limited reforestation, that could benefit the eco-system of Afghanistan. These activities cannot come as a surprise since the Taliban has remained a Deobandi-oriented movement with a clear goal. Despite their quasi-adherence to jihadi-Salafism, they aspire to rule the country and normalise their relationship with the international community.[39] Afghan society has also become more environmentally aware in spite of its relative isolation.[40] Thus, political expediency could explain why the Taliban made the decision to invest resources in green issues.

In the case of ISIS, caring for animals could politically benefit the militants, who are often portrayed by the media, with justification, as sadistic and ruthless. Animals like cats, horses and lions are popular among children and adults alike. Consequently, they have served as an asset for the propaganda machine of ISIS, which has fought for power and recognition.

Political expediency is a factor contributing to the rise of Islamist environmentalism, but not for all groups at the same degree of intensity. The Muslim Brotherhood, Hizbullah and Hamas have become vote-sensitive because they either participate in elections (Hizbullah, Hamas) or hope to do so again (Muslim Brotherhood). In contrast, Hizb ut-Tahrir is less exposed to political expediency because it remains an intellectualist group engaging in low-level activism. Finally, jihadi-Salafi groups have sought popularity and support by either engaging in environmental activities or adopting environmentalist rhetoric. In the case of Hizbullah, Hamas and jihadi-Salafi groups, military expediency is a sub-factor that should be accorded some weight too.

Ideological Realignment

The concept of ideology is contested since it has itself become thoroughly ideologised.[41] For example, Antonio Gramsci argued that ideologies are antagonistic since they have a class character.[42] In the context of social movements, John Wilson defines 'ideology' as 'a set of beliefs about the social world and how it operates, containing statements about the rightness of certain social arrangements and what action would be undertaken in light of those statements'.[43] Ideology usually provides a critical analysis of the current situation, while suggesting a better future. Yet the Islamist ideology is not as coherent as it is often assumed. Nathan Brown has argued that Islamist movements are highly ideological, but their ideologies are fairly general.[44] In fact, groups and movements have promoted different versions of Islamism incorporating elements from various intellectual traditions.

The rise of Islamist environmentalism has been partly the result of ideological realignment, which is characterised increasingly by a process of rationalisation. The latter term refers to the 'the socially shared content of ideology' seeking to explain the 'social world by making it seem rational'.[45] The rationalisation of the social world cannot easily be done with the help of religion, which lacks the analytical tools.

Consequently, many Islamists have borrowed ideas and beliefs from secular ideologies, fusing Islamism with nationalism and neo-Marxism. Most Islamist environmentalists have blamed capitalism for the ills of the world, including environmental disasters. They have been particularly vocal in their criticisms of free-market mechanisms and their propensity to self-destruct. From the Islamist environmentalists' point of view, capitalism is identified with exploitation, racism, colonialism and human suffering. In effect, these Islamists seek to represent the deprived communities of the Global Muslim South.

The Muslim Brotherhood has embraced only Egyptian nationalism, while maintaining a conspiratorial and confrontational view of Israel. Certain issues, such as gas exports to Israel and the water dispute with Ethiopia, were perceived as an opportunity to strengthen the image of the Ikhwan as defenders of national interests. Historically, Egypt's relationship with both Israel and Ethiopia has been marked by tension and distrust. The former is viewed as a hostile country occupying Arab territories, whereas the latter has antagonised Cairo over water resources. The Brotherhood has capitalised on deep-rooted suspicions against the two countries to increase its appeal. Concurrently, gas exports became a political weapon against the Jordanian leadership, which confronted local Islamists. While embracing nationalism, the Brotherhood has espoused a form of pan-Islamism which can be better described as pan-Ikhwanism (that is, solidarity among different branches of the Brotherhood).

At the same time, the Ikhwan's ideological stance contains some self-contradicting elements. The Brotherhood's interest in environmental matters partly derives from its willingness to gain more acceptability in the West.

Due to its location and the significance of the River Nile, Egypt has attracted the attention of international environmental NGOs.[46] Additionally, international financial institutions, such as the European Bank for Reconstruction and Development, have funded various initiatives in the Nile Delta.[47] The Brotherhood does not seek to confront Western countries. According to Richard Mitchell, it has even praised Western countries for respecting individual freedoms and rights of workers, and the responsibility of rulers to their people.[48] The Brotherhood has appeared pragmatic and moderate by engaging in efforts to protect the environment.

Like the Brotherhood, Hizbullah has tried to reshape its image internationally. This effort began in the mid- to late 1990s. In a message addressed to Pope John Paul II upon his visit to Lebanon in May 1997, for example, Hizbullah claimed that 'no materialistic doctrine could persist as a socio-political system, the greater crises, hunger, poverty, pollution, corruption and wars, confirm the downfall of the materialistic doctrine generally and its failure in organising the human living so as to realize its safety and development'.[49] Following the end of the Lebanese civil war, Hizbullah sought to address issues of global concern that were at first sight unrelated to its core mission, namely the liberation of south Lebanon. The group has clearly condemned Western materialism but approached the Pope as a potential ally in view of his worldwide influence.

Moreover, Hizbullah has participated in several anti-globalisation conferences and meetings. In September 2004, for example, the group participated in a Beirut conference entitled 'Where Next for the Global Anti-War and Anti-Globalization Movements?'.[50] According to Abdel-Halim Fadlallah, vice-president of the Hizbullah-affiliated Centre for Strategic Studies, 'Hizbullah succeeded in incorporating the idea of resistance as part of the international anti-globalisation movements . . . [T]hrough our contacts with these groups, we have managed to challenge the idea that Hizbullah is a dogmatic terrorist Islamist organisation and convince part of the international Left that we can be a strong partner.'[51] As a result, Hizbullah's new manifesto, published in December 2009, spends a great deal of time attacking 'an economic system that only views the world as markets that have to abide by America's own view'.[52] Hence, environmental issues are understood as part of a greater problem, namely the failure of capitalism to achieve sustainable development with environmental protection.

Hizbullah's ideology is neither static nor unchanging. The group has problematised the relationship between the developed capitalist core countries and the peripheral countries of the Middle East. Immanuel Wallerstein's world-systems theory has explained how the spread of capitalist economy created unequal development in the world. In this way, Hizbullah has almost abandoned Ayatollah Khomeini's division between *mustakbirin* (oppressors) and *mustad'afin* (oppressed) for a neo-Marxist analysis of class conflict. In this new perspective, environmental problems are problems associated with unequal development and neo-imperialism.

Hizb ut-Tahrir's criticism, meanwhile, goes beyond the essence of capitalism. After all, capitalism is one of what the group calls 'man-made' ideologies that have developed in the West. The root cause of the environmental crisis lies in the very nature of Western societies, which have embraced secularism. From its point of view, '[Western] culture is materialistic and benefit-oriented, and its philosophy dictates that the Creator should be separated from the affairs of life . . . Western societies are described as consumer societies that do not take the environmental impact of superfluous consumption into account.'[53] In other words, the lack of spirituality and the culture of consumerism are the two main factors that can explain the failure of the West to protect the environment. Hizb ut-Tahrir's ideologues believe that godless liberal society has turned humans into greedy consumers who feel no responsibility towards nature. Hizb ut-Tahrir has argued that economics based on *riba* (usury) drives a desire for growth which has a destructive effect on the environment.[54]

This anti-consumerist stance perhaps traces its origins to Adam Smith's claim that the consumption of non-essential goods could corrupt morals.[55] Much later, during the 1970s, the Marxist group Socialisme ou Barbarie was established by the Greek-French philosopher Cornelius Castoriadis. He argued that the drive for economic progress 'transformed human beings into machines for production and consumption'.[56] The French philosopher Bernard Stiegler has expressed the opinion that contemporary capitalism is defined not by production but by consumption. In the hyper-industrial society, Stiegler argues, the individual is essentially a consumer without any individuation.[57] The rise of materialism has resulted in the alienation of man from nature.

The group has integrated Marx's metabolic-rift analysis of explaining capitalist contradictions, such as slash-and-burn agriculture.[58] Yet, Hizb ut-Tahrir has not endorsed the Marxist assertion that humanity is alienated from nature due to private ownership of land.[59] In fact, it has supported the right to own land under certain conditions, as mentioned earlier in Chapter 3. As a result, the group has been able to reach out to small farmers in Africa and south-east Asia.

Hizb ut-Tahrir's critique of the Western culture of consumerism has been shaped by greater debates on the evolution of capitalism and its consequences. This influence reflects an internal shift of power within the party. The European branches have benefited from the atmosphere of openness and tolerance, but they have become more exposed to new ideas. Indeed, the group has combined anti-consumerism with its own selective interpretation of Islamic environmental ethics. Hizb ut-Tahrir accepts the mainstream Islamic belief that humanity is accountable to God for its actions on the earth, but eventually it will blame only Western secularism for the ongoing environmental crisis.

The content of Hamas's environmentalism has been determined by its hostile relationship with Israel. Palestine is viewed by Hamas as a sacred land for Muslims that has been invaded by another religious group. Thus, it perceives the environment as a battlefield between the Palestinians and the Jews. It is impossible to separate the group's view on environmental issues from its perception of the Jewish State as an illegitimate state. The Israeli–Palestinian conflict is essentially about the control of territory. Therefore, the disputed land of Palestine/Israel constitutes a physical and cognitive battlefield between two competing nationalisms seeking dominance and expansion.

Hamas has focused on certain problems (for example, the water crisis and the destruction of trees) where the environment and security are linked in diverse ways. It has understood pollution as a technical issue and has used a nationalist rhetoric to address the question of offshore gas reserves. In this way, the group can take credit for improving the quality of life within the country and defending Palestinian interests against Israel. Religion is not the cause of the conflict, but an intellectual-spiritual instrument of conquest and counter-conquest. It serves more as a marker of identity than as a source of guidance. Consequently, the environmentalism of Hamas has strong nationalist overtones. The uncompromising stance against Israel defines its perspective on the environment. This can explain why Hamas's environmentalism has often contradicted Islamic principles and rules.

In contrast to Hamas's localised agenda, al-Qaeda has been keen to portray itself as an organisation seeking global justice. Although the concept of justice (*adl*) has been a fundamental concept of Islamic environmental ethics, al-Qaeda has structured its own version based on class analysis and conflict. In May 2007, Ayman al-Zawahiri, Osama bin Laden's then deputy and now successor, made the case for a global campaign to restore justice:

> I want blacks in America, people of colour, American Indians, Hispanics, and all the weak and oppressed in North and South America, in Africa and Asia, and all over the world, to know that when we wage Jihad in Allah's path, we aren't waging Jihad to lift oppression from the Muslims only, we are waging Jihad to lift oppression from all of mankind, because Allah has ordered us never to accept oppression, whatever it may be.[60]

This rationalisation of the social world based on class and race has prompted al-Qaeda to adopt an environmentalist approach that resonates with Muslims and non-Muslims, sympathisers and opponents.

Additionally, jihadi-Salafis have endorsed a narrative of anti-colonialism which is energy-specific. They have taken for granted the Western dependence on Middle Eastern oil and gas. Since hydrocarbons are perceived as the Achilles heel of Western economies, jihadi-Salafis have targeted energy infrastructure to inflict economic pain on them. Not surprisingly, they have followed an oil- and gas-centric approach to energy matters; they have largely ignored other sources of energy (for example, nuclear, renewables). However, the Middle East's energy reserves have become less important due to technological changes and the discovery of shale gas around the world. Energy remains a central theme of jihadi-Salafi propaganda, if only for one reason: the politicisation of oil and gas is an inherent element of Middle Eastern politics. Hence, jihadi-Salafi environmentalism takes the form of economic nationalism against the West.

In conclusion, ideological realignment can partly explain why Islamists have developed environmental agendas in recent years. Since capitalism is perceived as harmful, and perhaps ethically corrupt, a return to 'authentic' Islam could save the world from an environmental catastrophe. And yet, they do not support a form of environmentalism that utilises the wisdom of the Muslim faith in the form of rules and ethics. Instead, each group has embraced nationalism or neo-Marxism to rationalise the social world. This ideological realignment has a profound impact on Islamist environmentalist policies and approaches.

Notes

1. Bassam Tibi, *Islam: Between Culture and Politics* (Basingstoke: Palgrave, 2001), p. 3.
2. Peter L. Berger, *Facing Up to Modernity: Excursions in Society, Politics, and Religion* (Harmondsworth: Penguin Books, 1979), pp. 101–12.
3. Harvey Cox, *Religion in the Secular City: Toward a Postmodern Theology* (New York: Simon & Schuster, 1984), p. 183.
4. See, for example, David Zeidan, *The Resurgence of Religion: A Comparative Study of Selected Themes in Christian and Islamic Fundamentalist Discourses* (Leiden: Brill, 2003); Scott M. Thomas, *The Global Resurgence of Religion and the Transformation of International Relations: The Struggle for the Soul of the Twenty-First Century* (New York: Palgrave Macmillan, 2005).
5. Max Weber, *The Protestant Ethic and the Spirit of Capitalism* (Mineola, NY: Dover, [1905] 2003), p. 70.
6. See Peter L Berger (ed.), *The Desecularization of the World: Resurgent Religion and World Politics* (Grand Rapids, MI: William B. Eerdmans, 1999).
7. See Jürgen Habermas, 'Notes on Post-Secular Society', *New Perspectives Quarterly*, vol. 25, no. 4, 2008, p. 17–29.
8. Mariano Barbato, 'Postsecular Revolution: Religion after the End of History', *Review of International Studies*, vol. 38, no. 5, 2012, pp. 1079–97.
9. James S, Diamond, 'The Post-Secular: A Jewish Perspective', *CrossCurrents*, vol. 53, no. 4, 2004, pp. 580–606.
10. See, for example, Janine A. Clark, 'The Conditions of Islamist Moderation: Unpacking Cross-Ideological Cooperation in Jordan', *International Journal of Middle East Studies*, vol. 38, no. 4, 2006, pp. 539–60; Eva Wegner and Miquel Pellicer, 'Islamist Moderation without Democratization: The Coming of Age of

the Moroccan Party of Justice and Development?', *Democratization*, vol 16, no. 1, 2009, pp. 157–75; Günes Murat Tezcür, 'The Moderation Theory Revisited: The Case of Islamic Political Actors', *Party Politics*, vol. 16, no. 1, 2010, pp. 69–88; Jillian Schwedler, 'Can Islamists Become Moderates? Rethinking the Inclusion-Moderation Hypothesis', *World Politics*, vol. 63, no. 2, 2011, pp. 347–76.

11. In 2015, for example, a Pew Research opinion poll found that 67 per cent of Lebanese, 44 per cent of Jordanians and 38 per cent of Palestinians believed that climate change was a very serious problem. See Bruce Stokes, Richard Wike and Jill Carle, 'Global Concern about Climate Change, Broad Support for Limiting Emissions', Pew Research Center, 5 November 2015, https://www.pewresear ch.org/global/2015/11/05/1-concern-about-climate-change-and-its-consequen ces/ (accessed 24 June 2022).

12. 'Interactive: Full Egypt Election Results', Al Jazeera, 1 February 2012, http://www.aljazeera.com/indepth/interactive/2012/01/20121248225832718.html (accessed 24 June 2022).

13. برنامج حزب النور ('The Electoral Programme of the Al-Nour Party'), 2011, https://egyptianpartiesprograms.wordpress.com/النور-حزب-برنامج/ (accessed 24 June 2022).

14. Ibid.

15. The Salafis of al-Nour and the Ikhwan have maintained an antagonistic relationship following the overthrow of President Morsi by the military in June 2013. To the surprise of many, al-Nour supported General Sisi in the May 2014 presidential elections.

16. Hoda Baraka, 'The Future of Environmental Politics in Egypt', *Egypt Independent*, 29 March 2011, https://www.egyptindependent.com/future-environmental-po litics-egypt/ (accessed 24 June 2022).

17. Quinn Mecham, 'Islamist Parties as Strategic Actors: Electoral Participation and Its Consequences', in Quinn Mecham and Julie Chernov Hwang (eds), *Islamist Parties and Political Normalization in the Muslim World* (Philadelphia: University of Pennsylvania Press, 2014), p. 29.

18. Sarah Lynch, 'Nasrallah goes green', Now Media, 20 October 2010, https://now.media.me/lb/en/reportsfeatures/nasrallah_goes_green.

19. Ibid.

20. Sayyed Hassan Nasrallah, 'Victory (May 26, 2000)', in Nicholas Noe (ed.), *Voice of Hezbollah: The Statements of Sayyed Hassan Nasrallah* (London and New York: Verso, 2007), p. 238.

21. Karim Makdisi, 'The Rise and Decline of Environmentalism in Lebanon', in Alan Mikhail (ed.), *Water on Sand: Environmental Histories of the Middle East and North Africa* (New York: Oxford University Press, 2013), p. 173.

22. See, for example, Asma Ajroudi, 'Hezbollah, Amal and allies biggest winners in Lebanon elections', Al Jazeera, 8 May 2018, https://www.aljazeera.com/news /2018/05/hezbollah-amal-allies-claim-lebanon-election-sweep-1805071605244 02.html (accessed 24 June 2022).

23. Laura King, 'Palestinians ponder life under Hamas', *Los Angeles Times*, 6 February 2006, https://www.latimes.com/archives/la-xpm-2006-feb-06-fg-isla mic6-story.html (accessed 24 June 2022).

24. The IJAN has launched the Stop the Jewish National Fund Campaign to protest against tree plantings in 'Palestinian stolen land'. See 'Fight Greenwashing and Green Sunday', IJAN, no date, http://www.ijan.org/projects-campaigns/stopth ejnf/fight-greenwashing-and-green-sunday/ (accessed 24 June 2022).

25. Khaled Hroub, *Hamas: A Beginner's Guide* (London: Pluto Press, 2006), pp. 119–25.

26. 'First Conference', Tehran, 19–22 October 1991, https://en.parliran.ir/eng/en /Content/articles/First-Conference-International-Conference-on-Support-for -the-Islamic-Revolution-of-People-of-Palestine-Tehran-October-1922-1991 -20170903

27. Jack Shenker, 'Nile Delta: "We are going underwater. The sea will conquer our lands"', *The Guardian*, 21 August 2009, https://www.theguardian.com/envi ronment/ 2009/aug/21/climate-change-nile-flooding-farming (accessed 24 June 2022).

28. Roy Prosterman, 'Egypt's landless have no love for Mubarak', *The Guardian*, 8 February 2011, https://www.theguardian.com/global-development/poverty -matters/2011/feb/08/egypt-landless-mubarak (accessed 24 June 2022).

29. Magdi Abdelhadi, 'The Muslim Brotherhood connects with Egypt's rural major-ity', *The Guardian*, 25 June 2012, https://www.theguardian.com/commentisf ree/2012/jun/25/muslim-brotherhood-egypt (accessed 24 June 2022).

30. Sayyed Hassan Nasrallah, '"Hezbollah Is Not an Iranian Community in Lebanon" (September 11, 1992)', in Nicholas Noe (ed.), *Voice of Hezbollah: The Statements of Sayyed Hassan Nasrallah* (London and New York: Verso, 2007), p. 90.

31. Moshe Terdiman, 'The Environmental Message of Hizbullah', Green Compass Research, January 2012, http://web.archive.org/web/20120202105821/htt p://gc-research.org/the%20environmental%20message%20of%20hizbullah/ (accessed 24 June 2022).

32. Dion Nissenbaum and Nazih Osseiran, 'A row over trees could spark the next Israel–Lebanon war', *Wall Street Journal*, 28 June 2020, https://www.wsj.com /articles/a-row-over-trees-could-spark-the-next-israel-lebanon-war-1159334 5635 (accessed 24 June 2022).

33. Hassan Nasrallah, 'Speech on marking end of planting one million trees campaign', 9 October 2010, https://english.alahednews.com.lb/12511/385 (accessed 18 July 2022).

34. According to a 2017 Palestinian public opinion poll, 47 per cent of Palestinians in Gaza demanded that Hamas accept the conditions put forward by President Mahmoud Abbas (that is, that the unity government should operate in Gaza) to improve conditions in the enclave. See 'Palestinian public opinion poll – July 2017', Medium.com, 7 July 2017, https://medium.com/@thepalestinepro ject/palestinian-public-opinion-poll-july-2017-cbb7b11f55f9 (accessed 24 June 2022).

35. Baraa Hashem, 'The rapid degradation of Wadi Gaza', EcoMENA, 12 July 2021, https://www.ecomena.org/wadi-gaza/ (accessed 24 June 2022).

36. Interview with three members of Hizb ut-Tahrir, London, 13 December 2018.

37. Hizb ut-Tahrir has rejected democracy as a political system. Nonetheless, it has occasionally participated in elections. An-Nabhani ran for the Jordanian parliament in 1951, but he did not manage to get elected. Hizb ut-Tahrir participated in Jordan's parliamentary elections in 1954 and 1956, but its candidates stood as independents. Ahmad al-Daur won a seat in both elections, although he was expelled from the parliament in 1958 for alleged anti-government activities. See Amnon Cohen, *Political Parties in the West Bank under the Jordanian Regime, 1949–1967* (Ithaca, NY: Cornell University Press, 1982), p. 216.

38. 'New video release from Adam Gadahn, "The Tragedy of the Floods"', Jihadology, 29 September 2010, http://jihadology.net/2010/09/29/new-video -release-from-adam-gadahn-the-tragedy-of-the-floods/ (accessed 24 June 2022).

39. During the 1990s, the Taliban regime was diplomatically recognised by Pakistan, Saudi Arabia and the UAE.

40. There is a growing number of environmental NGOs in the country, such as the Wildlife Conservation Society of Afghanistan and the Ecology and Conservation Organisation of Afghanistan, that engage in environmental management and advocacy.

41. Clifford Geertz, *The Interpretation of Cultures* (New York: Basic, 1973), p. 193.

42. Valeriano Ramos, 'The Concepts of Ideology, Hegemony, and Organic

Intellectuals in Gramsci's Marxism', *Theoretical Review*, March–April 1982, available at https://www.marxists.org/history/erol/ncm-7/tr-gramsci.htm (accessed 24 June 2022).

43. John Wilson, *Introduction to Social Movements* (New York: Basic, 1973), pp. 91–2.

44. Nathan J. Brown, *When Victory Is Not an Option: Islamist Movements in Arab Politics* (Ithaca, NY: Cornell University Press, 2012), pp. 72–3.

45. Michael Billig, *Ideology and Opinions: Studies in Rhetorical Psychology* (London: Sage, 1991), p. 157.

46. See, for instance, Miranda Mockrin and Michelle Thieme, 'Nile Delta Flooded Savanna', no date, World Wide Fund for Nature, http://web.archive.org/web/20130501033854/https://www.worldwildlife.org/ecoregions/pa0904 (accessed 24 June 2022).

47. Volker Ahlemeyer, 'EBRD, EU and Juhayna support sustainable dairy farming in Nile Delta', European Bank for Reconstruction and Development, 3 March 2016, https://www.ebrd.com/news/2016/ebrd-eu-and-juhayna-support-sustainable-dairy-farming-in-nile-delta.html (accessed 24 June 2022).

48. Richard P. Mitchell, *The Society of the Muslim Brothers* (London: Oxford University Press, 1969), pp. 246–7.

49. Hizballah, 'A message addressed to the Pope upon his visit to Lebanon in May', Al-Manar TV, 20 June 1997, available at http://almashriq.hiof.no/lebanon/300/320/324/324.2/hizballah/

50. Nathan Guttman, 'Hezbollah among hosts of anti-war conference', *Haaretz*, 14 September 2004, https://www.haaretz.com/1.4838989 (accessed 24 June 2022).

51. Raed Rafei, 'Hezbollah finds left-leaning friends abroad', *Los Angeles Times*, 30 August 2008, https://www.latimes.com/la-xpm-2008-aug-30-fg-hezleft30-story.html (accessed 24 June 2022).

52. 'Full text of Hezbollah's new political document', Syrian News Station, 30 November 2009, http://web.archive.org/web/20100304182521/http://sns.sy/sns/?path=news/read/7187 (accessed 24 June 2022).

53. Hizb ut-Tahrir Denmark, *The Environmental Problem: Its Causes and Islam's Solution* (Copenhagen: Hizb ut-Tahrir Denmark, 2009), p. 9.

54. 'The state leads the people to destruction through the riba-based financing system', The Khilafah, 3 January 2019, http://www.khilafah.com/the-state-leads-the-people-to-destruction-through-the-riba-based-financing-system/ (accessed 24 June 2022).

55. Lisa Hill, 'Adam Smith and the Theme of Corruption', *Review of Politics*, vol. 68, no. 4, 2006, pp. 636–62.

56. Cornelius Castoriadis, *A Society Adrift, Interviews and Debates, 1974–1997* (New York: Fordham University Press, 2010), p. 8.

57. Bernard Stiegler, *Symbolic Misery, vol. 1: The Hyperindustrial Epoch* (Cambridge: Polity Press, 2014), p. 59.

58. On Marx's theory of metabolic rift see John Bellamy Foster, 'Marx and the Rift in the Universal Metabolism of Nature', *Monthly Review*, December 2013, https://monthlyreview.org/2013/12/01/marx-rift-universal-metabolism-nature/ (accessed 24 June 2022).

59. See Chris Williams, 'Marxism and the Environment', *International Socialist Review*, no. 72, 2010, http://isreview.org/issue/72/marxism-and-environment (accessed 24 June 2022).

60. 'Third Interview with Dr Ayman al-Zawahiri – 5/2007', As-Sahab, 5 May 2007, available at https://archive.org/details/Third-Interview (accessed 24 June 2022).

CONCLUSIONS

Although the rise of political Islam has attracted the attention of scholars since the early 1980s, most studies have focused on the militancy of certain groups and the proliferation of Islamist parties. This overemphasis on politically and emotionally charged issues has created a literature gap regarding less contested areas of Islamist engagement that this book has tried to bridge. Islamist environmentalism has gained considerable visibility in recent years but has remained understudied. This aspect of Islamism perhaps creates some perplexity among Western scholars because environmental protection is usually viewed as a noble cause.

Islamist environmentalism is a phenomenon that sits on the fringe between social sciences and humanities. The Muslim Brotherhood, Hizb ut-Tahrir, Hizbullah, Hamas and al-Qaeda/ISIS are groups and movements strive for power. Political science can certainly explain the policies and motives of such political actors. Yet Islamists make claims to religious authenticity that political science cannot assess. It does not have the theoretical tools to evaluate the validity of such claims. Islamic studies can offer an understanding of religious concepts and principles embedded in the different versions of environmentalism. In this way, this research has sought to expand the interdisciplinary study of political Islam as represented by Islamist environmentalists. More specifically, the book has addressed two research questions: 1) What is the environmental policy of Islamist groups? 2) What role does religion play in Islamist environmentalism?

Before answering the research questions, the book described the Islamic perspective on the environment. Since Islamists draw their legitimacy from religion, it is important to understand how the Muslim faith has approached certain environmental issues. Islam has been preoccupied with nature since the Prophet started preaching his messages to Arab communities in the mid-seventh century. Overall, Islam as a religion has favoured a balanced environmental approach that permits harmonious co-existence between humans and nature.

Since the 1960s, there has been a constant theological-intellectual effort to offer an Islamic alternative in line with modern environmentalist thinking. Islamic eco-theology is a contextual form of theology focusing on the relationship between faith and nature. The Qur'an and *Sunna* could offer spiritual and practical guidance through certain principles, such as *tawhid*, *khalifa* and *akhirah*. The unity of God implies the wholeness and interdependence of all creation. Moreover, human beings are obliged to act as God's viceregents on the earth. Believers are also accountable for their actions towards the natural world. In addition, the concepts of *adl*, *shura*, *mizan*, *rahman*, *maslaha*, *ihsan*, *fitra*, *wasatiyya* and *tahara* could define the ethical parameters of the Islamic environmental paradigm. The meaning of environmental ethics is not rigid and inflexible. It depends on political and social circumstances. Yet, as Celia Deane-Drummond has pointed out, eco-theology cannot be reduced to environmental ethics.[1]

Islamic eco-theology is foundational to faith in the sense that it seeks knowledge about the creation of the world. The entire earth is Allah's mosque. Water has a purifying effect on the believer through the ritual of prayer. Water belongs to both humans and non-humans, but humanity has the sole responsibility to conserve and protect it. Islam has also understood trees as autonomous beings. Trees of legendary or mythical origin carry great symbolic meaning in the Qur'an and *ahadith*. Therefore, Muslims have a religious obligation to protect them. From the Islamic point of view, animals are not soulless creatures that exist to serve mankind. They form their own communities and worship God like humans do. The pollution of land and water resources is not permitted; yet the Islamic perspective on energy is oil-centric.

Islamic eco-theology relies on textual sources of wisdom and authority as

Islamic law does. Shari'a dictates many rules which provide a historical-legal framework for environmental protection and management. Environmental policy in Shari'a has a broad spectrum, including land management and water use. At the same time, increased environmental awareness has compelled religious leaders to offer relevant fatwas. Thus, they have utilised the Qur'an and the *Sunna* to promote environmental solutions. The legalistic approach does not substitute the theological study of the environment; it rather supplements it by granting rights and obligations.

Against this background, the present book has examined the content of Islamist environmentalism. First, it described the environmental policies of the Muslim Brotherhood, Hizb ut-Tahrir, Hamas and Hizbullah, and the environmental approaches of al-Qaeda and ISIS. Each group has espoused a different scale of environmental engagement depending on its priorities and area of operations.

Despite their differences, Islamists have similar understandings and perceptions of nature and its components. Due to scarcity and mismanagement, water is probably the most important issue for Islamist environmentalists. From the Ikhwan's point of view, water scarcity is connected to external factors, such as the construction of dams by upstream countries. Hizb ut-Tahrir has also recognised the importance of water as a natural resource, accusing non-Muslim countries of mismanagement and theft. Hizbullah and Hamas have constantly addressed water management issues in Lebanon and Gaza respectively, focusing on the confrontation with Israel. ISIS has weaponised water in its effort to crush its perceived enemies, while al-Qaeda has overlooked the issue. In summary, Islamists have stressed the political importance of water resources. Thus, the management of rivers has been perceived as a source of great friction between Muslims and non-Muslims. At the same time, Islamist environmentalists do not deny the spiritual significance of water. In fact, they have used religious rhetoric to advance their water policy. Yet they have not abided by Shari'a rules regarding the efficient and equal distribution of water within Muslim communities.

Additionally, some Islamists have attached religious meaning to trees because they are important symbols of divine power and wisdom. Hence, Hizbullah and Hamas have used Islamic evidence from the Qur'an and the

Sunna to support its reforestation projects. Tree-planting activities have not deterred the simultaneous weaponisation of trees taking place in the embattled spaces of Lebanon and Palestine. In contrast, the Muslim Brotherhood and Hizb ut-Tahrir have paid little attention to trees. One can only speculate the reasons for omitting such an important issue. The Brotherhood has probably ignored tree-related questions and activities due to the desert geography of Egypt and the lack of public interest. Hizb ut-Tahrir has focused on environmental issues with political implications and trees have an insignificant role to play in this regard. Finally, there is no single jihadi-Salafi approach to trees: the al-Qaeda-allied Taliban view trees as vital for life, whereas ISIS perceives them as collateral damage.

Islamist representations of animals have reflected traditions and beliefs, motivational strategies and propaganda priorities. Despite a generic acknowledgement of humanity's duty to protect animal life, the Muslim Brotherhood has not developed any concrete proposals. The question of halal meat has been at the forefront of Hizb ut-Tahrir's approach to animal rights. The Islamic diet has become a symbolic battleground for Muslim self-expression and identity-building in the West. Additionally, African branches of Hizb ut-Tahrir have perceived poaching and smuggling of wildlife as proof of capitalist exploitation and human greed that require an Islamic response. Hizbullah has not addressed animal rights at all, for unknown reasons. Hamas has perceived animals as instruments of warfare. Jihadi-Salafis have attributed characteristics to animals which echo cultural and religious beliefs and bias. Overall, Islamists have perceived animals as passive objects of human agency. This approach deviates from the body of Islamic teachings defining mankind's relationship to the animal world as equal and respectful   .

Pollution has been another issue of environmental concern. The Muslim Brotherhood has offered solutions against land, water and air pollution in Egypt. Hamas has focused on sewage management and pollution control because such issues can affect the living conditions of the population in Gaza. Hizb ut-Tahrir has understood pollution as a failure of Western capitalism and secularism. Therefore, it has dismissed global initiatives (for example, the Kyoto Protocol, the Paris Accord) as unjust and Western-centric. Hizbullah has been involved in numerous efforts to reduce urban pollution, although the contamination of water is acknowledged as a perennial problem. Moreover, Hizbullah has not ignored the problem of climate change. Osama bin Laden's al-Qaeda also focused on the same problem to undermine Western capitalism and illustrate global reach.

The Islamic perspective on energy is centred on oil and gas, due to the large reserves of hydrocarbons that can be found in the Middle East. To start with, energy was utilised by the Morsi government as a bargaining chip to achieve foreign policy goals. The Brotherhood has also considered the use of renewable energy as an alternative way of generating electrical power. Hizb ut-Tahrir has focused on oil and gas, although it also advocates the use of nuclear energy for both peaceful and military purposes. Hizbullah has developed the concept of hydro-territoriality, concentrating on the exploitation of offshore energy resources. Likewise, Hamas has been preoccupied with the Eeastern Mediterranean gas fields. For jihadi-Salafis, energy is a zero-sum game between themselves and the enemy. Overall, energy is more than anything else a political issue for Islamist environmentalists.

The book assessed the degree of influence that Islamic texts, rulings and principles have on Islamist environmental policies. The Muslim Brotherhood came to formulate an environmental policy relatively recently. Hassan al-Banna and Sayyed Qutb touched on environmental matters without probing in depth the Islamic perspective. Contemporary leaders, such as Yusuf al-Qaradawi, Mohamed Badie and Mohamed Morsi, have acknowledged the importance of green issues because the environmental situation has grown more dire. Indeed, they have tried to insert religious meaning into policy. Nevertheless, the Brotherhood's environmental policy relies less on religion and more on science. The group has used green issues to build alliances and reach out to Egyptians outside of its traditional constituency. Following the fall of the Mubarak regime, the Ikhwan made proposals to improve water management and efficiency since many of its supporters live in the Nile Delta. Political expediency is an important factor explaining the formulation of the Brotherhood's environmental policy. Simultaneously, the Ikhwan have shown a growing interest in environmental issues for ideological reasons. Since they have endorsed both Egyptian nationalism and pan-Islamism, water and energy are perceived as political issues worth fighting for.

Although Hizb ut-Tahrir is a Palestinian-led group, it has managed to establish a presence in many countries around the world. The group has developed an environmental agenda that resonates with different audiences. The founder of Hizb ut-Tahrir offered a general perspective on the environment, but various branches have made their own contributions. Islamic theology and history sometimes serve as a source of guidance in the development of policy positions, albeit not always very explicitly articulated. It is the long quest for authenticity that can perhaps explain this approach. After all, Hizb ut-Tahrir claims to represent an authentic Islam that can lead to the establishment of a perfect society. In this way, it can gain legitimacy in the eyes of those Muslims seeking an Islamic answer to environmental challenges. Nevertheless, the use of religious rhetoric and references is not always indicative of piety and determination. In its statements and leaflets, Hizb ut-Tahrir has not usually mentioned Shari'a rules, which are complex and broad in scope. Moreover, the group has not been involved in acts of environmental activism, notwithstanding its activist character. It has only provided theoretical or policy-oriented analyses to reinforce its image as an environmentally friendly organisation, while deconstructing the appeal of its adversaries who claim environmental credentials and successes. It is an intellectual exercise driven by its ideological realignment because the group has been exposed to neo-Marxist ideas about capitalism and consumerism. Hizb ut-Tahrir has proposed an anthropocentric environmental policy to build an all-powerful caliphate that could achieve world hegemony.

Hizbullah has also developed its own environmental policy which has broad applications. Its environmentalism has little religious relevance, although sometimes the protection of the environment is portrayed as a religious duty. Hizbullah does not usually offer theological evidence and argumentation for its policy choices. Consequently, it can be argued that the Muslim faith has only partly dictated the content of its environmentalism. The group has built alliances with Muslim and non-Muslim political forces around shared goals, including environmental protection. Political expediency is another important factor explaining Hizbullah's environmentalism. The group is accountable to its constituency and the wider electorate because it plays a role in the legislative process and sometimes even in the government itself. Moreover, political expediency is manifested in the militarisation of the environment for the purpose of defeating Israel. Furthermore, Hizbullah's environmentalism is the product of ideological realignment based on a critical understanding of the relationship between the developed capitalist core countries and the peripheral countries of the Middle East.

Hamas has viewed the environmental situation via the lens of the political conflict with Israel. The group has elevated the religious status of Palestine, without strong Islamic justification. This religionisation of the environment is not synonymous with the sacralisation of nature. Despite its proclaimed adherence to Islamic principles, Hamas has used religion as a strategic resource to mobilise supporters for environmental purposes among others. The group has accused the Jews of waging ecological warfare against the Palestinian Muslims. Additionally, Hamas has engaged from time to time in dialogue with anti-capitalist groups. This occasional interaction is facilitated by its non-adherence to Shari'a rules. The environmentalism of Hamas is also the product of political expediency because it cannot afford to ignore the mounting problems of pollution, water shortages and energy security. Finally, ideological realignment to nationalism is a factor contributing to the emergence of Hamas's environmentalism.

Jihadi-Salafi groups have not formulated an environmental policy because they see themselves foremost as warriors. Yet they have indicated a growing interest in environmental matters. Jihadi-Salafis have embraced various notions of territoriality, depending on their orientations and strategies. This diversity of approaches can explain why only ISIS has weaponised water resources: the group has sought to control a specific territory after defeating local enemies. In the world of jihadi-Salafism, religion serves as an instrument of legitimacy rather than a source of inspiration. Taken as a whole, this form of Islamist environmentalism is defined by the reality of perpetual conflict.

In general, the level of influence of religion on Islamist environmental policies is usually weak. Although they claim to represent authentic Islam, Islamists tend to avoid faith-based solutions to environmental problems. Their views and responses are essentially anthropocentric because they focus on human needs. This does not mean that Islamist environmentalists do not have a genuine religious interest in protecting the environment. From time to time, they do seek guidance from Islamic sources.

The findings, although preliminary, show that Islamist groups are complex organisations. Not only do they confront authorities and foes, but they also proactively pursue policies for their communities. Islamist environmentalism connects pre-modern Islamic conceptions of environmental responsibility with modern perceptions of political legitimacy and postmodern realities of a fast-moving and unpredictable world.

* * *

The study of Islamist environmentalism can help us understand the evolution of political Islam as a social movement. Contemporary Islamism is adaptive and constantly changing, having a rather superficial connection to Islamic theology and ethics. Since political Islam is a product of its time, as Tariq Ramadan argues, principles and traditions serve the purpose of supporting a political struggle.[2] It is hardly a coincidence that Islamist groups do not participate in theological-legal debates about various aspects of the environmental crisis. But religion and politics can co-exist in Muslim societies without dilemmas and disputes. It is not because Islam is more political than other religions. Religion influences politics as much as politics allows it. It is a socially complex and adaptive process that involves many actors and interests.

The emergence of postsecularism could possibly explain this dialogic harmony between faith and reason in the form of environmental politics. The construction of the religious–secular dichotomy is largely (but not exclusively) a legacy of Western colonialism in the Muslim world. Malek Bennabi and Ali Shariati approached the issue from the same starting point: Islam was meant to be only a remnant of another era because it was perceived as a threat. Yet modernisation has not eliminated the public role of the Muslim faith. Aleksandr Kyrlezhev has observed that postsecularism includes the de-monopolisation of religion and the de-monopolisation of secularism.[3] Islamists make a claim to religious knowledge without abandoning the scientific achievements of secularism. They are aware of the rich ecological heritage of Islam, which incorporates principles and practices that could improve environmental conditions. Nonetheless, they have chosen to utilise them only selectively.

In any case, the rise of Islamist environmentalism challenges Western perceptions about contemporary Islamism. There is a widespread perception of political Islam as an anti-modern and traditionalist movement seeking to reassert 'Islamic values', notwithstanding their conceptual deficits. However, political Islam is more modern than it dares to admit.

Islamism seeks to propose solutions under any circumstances. Contextualising religion is a process of many layers, with each layer requiring its own application process in policy-relevant areas. Islamic concepts and principles are interpreted and applied broadly when they serve the purpose of supporting policies. Thus, the use of religious knowledge is an ongoing rather than a static process.

Irrespective of their individual circumstances, Islamists have addressed environmental problems mostly technocratically. While this may look like a paradox, it really is not. The nostalgic evocation of an idealised Islamic past does not imply a return to another era. Nostalgia is not necessarily anti-modern. On the contrary, the transformation of the present could pave the way for the development of an alternative future. The environment is more physical than spiritual space because Islamists have political agendas to further. Religious concerns are almost inevitably marginalised by the urgency of modern political life. Thus, it is fair to argue that Islamist environmentalists are political entrepreneurs with some religious sensitivities.

And yet, Islam is inherently friendly to nature due to the way it evolved theologically. The resacralisation of nature could end the dichotomy between humans and non-humans. The precondition for such radical departure is a new understanding of science. Unfortunately Islamist environmentalists have not advocated a model of development based on the unity of religion and science. Indeed, science guided by religion could serve humanity's needs better. It is an irony that Islamists, who claim to know Islam more and better than others, do not usually follow the teachings of the Qur'an and the example of the Prophet (pbuh).

Notes

1. Celia Deane-Drummond, *Eco-Theology* (London: Darton, Longman & Todd, 2008), p. xii.

2. Tariq Ramadan, *Islam and the Arab Awakening* (New York: Oxford University Press, 2012), p. 84.

3. Aleksandr Kyrlezhev, 'The Postsecular Age: Religion and Culture Today', *Religion, State and Society*, vol. 36, no. 1, 2008, pp. 21–31.

APPENDIX

Muslim Brotherhood

Egyptians Paying for Sisi's Selling Out of Egypt Historical Nile Water Share

To the patriotic people of Egypt and the great revolutionaries . . .

Almost thirty whole months have passed and you are still standing steadfast, in your prisons and in liberty squares across Egypt. The whole world solemnly applauds your determination and resolve.

You have trampled all the calculations of the putschist junta. Their end is approaching fast, God willing. Sisi is marching steadily from failure to failure, while powerful waves of revolutionary protests are coming to save the homeland and the people and stop the shameful concessions and betrayals.

Egypt's simple peasants are already paying for the Nile water loss, the crisis created by Sisi's recklessness. Indeed, all Egyptians, especially future generations, will pay for Sisi's mistake.

The junta-controlled media has misled the Egyptian people, as it celebrated the Ethiopian Renaissance Dam agreement signed by Sisi, and pictured it as a great achievement! Now, it has been revealed that with this agreement Sisi and his gang have forfeited the Egyptian people's right to Nile water. Evidently, the traitorous Sisi is implementing a Zionist plot to eliminate Egypt's historical achievements.

The whole world heard the words of Egypt's legitimate president, Mohamed Morsi: 'If Egypt's share of Nile water is decreased by one drop, we will sacrifice our blood to get it back.'

We assure the whole world that these words alone represent the Egyptian people in this matter. Only the traitorous Sisi and his gang take responsibility for any agreements signed by the murderous general. He only stands for his own cronies, the putschist traitors.

We are certainly not gloating, nor rejoicing, for that matter. For this crisis will not hurt Sisi and his regime alone, but all citizens of this country, including us. We, therefore, bitterly lament this situation as we appreciate the gravity of the loss.

Now, Sisi's army, the great warriors who recently slaughtered one Palestinian man who tried to escape the illegitimate and vicious blockade of Gaza, has not moved a finger to address this serious breach of the country's national security. The time to oust the putschist generals is surely upon us.

Muslim Brotherhood, 27 December 2015
Source: https://www.ikhwanweb.com/article.php?id=32383

Hizb ut-Tahrir

Only Khilafah Rashedah Can Solve the Problems of Water Resources on a Regional and International Level

During the Fourth Water Conference in Kabulon 6 March 2017, the president of Afghanistan asked countries in the region to support construction of water dams and a supply network in Afghanistan. He said, 'Water is a key element of regional cooperation. By establishing legal frameworks and bilateral and multilateral agreements, we can create better grounds for the use of waters.'

The media office of Hizb ut-Tahrir in Afghanistan would like to elaborate the following issues concerning water problems and the foundations for mechanisms of its management. Illegal ideas of 'nation state', 'national interests' and 'national borders' are the root cause and main challenge to proper management and use of water resources on a regional and international level. In such circumstances, establishment of legal frameworks to solve these problems is doomed to failure. Why? Because, such frameworks are designed within the limits and on the basis of pre-defined national interests. Such an outlook and mechanisms based on this vision disregards humans' right of access to water resources – proposed by Islam. Consequently, such frameworks not only fail to solve the problem of the right of use of water resources, but rather further complicate the problem.

Water resources that begin and end within the territory of Islamic lands – regardless of how many countries they pass through – are the common property of all Muslims. No single country or person can claim ownership of such public property of all Muslims. All Muslims can utilise such resources according to the rules of Islam (Ah'kaam) and in consideration of their needs, and there is no prohibition in utilizing water resources. Because, the Prophet (saw) has said: 'People are partners in three things, pastures, water and fire' (narrated in Abu-Daud).

It has become evident to intellectuals and leaders in the water resources management sector that man-made ideologies, and international laws based on such ideologies, have fallen short of giving comprehensive solutions to the issue of water resources. The only solution to these problems lies in Islam. Therefore, we should work for the establishment of Khilafah on the basis of the Prophethood to unite Islamic lands, spread ideas of one Ummah, one land, and one political system based on the Islamic Aqeedah, and consequently eliminate political and economic tensions caused by the problem of ownership of water resources in the region.

For a detailed understanding on how Islam solves the issue of water resources between countries, please refer to a detailed opinion by Ameer of Hizb ut Tahrir titled 'Shariah Principles on the issue of water resources' at the following link: http://hizb-ut-tahrir.info/en/index.php/qestions/jurispru dence-questions/11800.html

Media Office of Hizb ut Tahrir in Wilayah Afghanistan, 9 March 2017
Source: https://www.hizb-ut-tahrir.info/en/index.php/press-releases/afghanis tan/12649.html

Hizbullah

Excerpts from Hassan Nasrallah's Speech on Marking End of Planting One Million Trees Campaign, 9 October 2010

I welcome all of you in this blessed ceremony marking the wrap up of the blessed campaign – the kind tree campaign. In this occasion, I would like to tackle three issues: the first topic is the one million tree campaign and its backgrounds, horizons and the outlook to this issue; the second topic has to do with the anticipated visit of President Ahmadi Nejad to Lebanon in the coming few days; and the third topic is related to the developments in our country and region especially what is related to the Special Tribunal of Lebanon, the indictment, the false witnesses and the repercussions of this issue on the status quo.

As far as the first issue is concerned, I say that this is an ancient jihad for Jihad Al Binaa. However and praise be to Allah Almighty it was an ascending jihad. Perhaps the only period of time in which the agricultural and tree-planting side retreated was in 2006 when Jihad Al Binaa was occupied with a greater priority – namely facing the repercussions of July War in 2006.

This year the effort was advanced and made greater through the advertisement and the execution of the million tree campaign. Many campaigns partook in this campaign along Jihad Al Binaa. We took pains to generalise this culture so that it won't be a sheer act made by the Institution. We believe that this is a great national issue which needs participation, cooperation and the presence of everyone in the field.

No ministry or institution or society or region or group or party or movement or current may solely carry on this effort. Rather we must deal with it as an important great national issue which needs mustering all efforts. Hence was the cooperation between the Ministry of Agriculture in Lebanon, the various municipalities, the youths' societies and others. Here I would like to remind [you] of the special presence of the resistance fighters in the South and in Bekaa in particular. In fact they had their distinctive participation in broad tree-planting operations in various regions, mountains, hills and valleys especially in some regions where man is at risk such as some valleys, mountains and hills where scouts or municipalities may not have access due to mines and the like. The resistance men are thus more able and accurate in dealing with such areas due to their experience and skill.

Indeed I would like to address with special thanks our brethren in Syria. I recall that several years ago this issue took place with an initiation made by President Bashar Assad. There has been great cooperation with Jihad Al Binaa since several years. This cooperation developed with the Syrian brethren year after year until it reached this stage. I know that this issue is not limited to Jihad Al Binaa. There are other sides which asked for such aids and received them from Syria. I also know that the Syrian brethren are ready for endless cooperation in this perspective.

There are sequels to tree-plantations in every country and that is not special for Lebanon only. However there is something special as far as Lebanon is concerned. When we talk about health, environmental, climatic and aesthetic sequels and consequently how that influences the life of people on all perspectives: health, environmental, tourist, social and so on – this must be tackled with specialists – and I am not one of them – who must explain these issues to people so that the society would have a general education in this perspective whether in Lebanon or in other countries.

It is the education of finding motives that push people to assume national responsibilities in this domain. It is enough to mention briefly that the climatic threat today is one of the most serious threats which face humanity and its integrity, security, stability and very existence. Perhaps it is the most serious threat because this threat is about or has already been out of control even by great states.

Nuclear threat is a very great threat on human existence on Earth but it is under control and is still under control. However what the world is witnessing today such as earthquakes, floods, torrents, serious climatic changes and fires that threatened millions and what is taking place now in India, China and especially in Pakistan is a human catastrophe in the whole sense of the word. These are the results of climatic changes. Today humanity is confronting this great and serious climatic threat.

Indeed due to its small area, Lebanon might not be very influential in founding a change in face of this great threat. Still this does not make our country irresponsible. Regardless of the great threat on the level of the Globe, when we become concerned in this file nationally and popularly, we will pick all the blessings embodied in this kind tree – whether health, environmental, climatic, aesthetic, nutritive, social and all other blessings. This is on one hand.

On the other hand, we Lebanese always laud of Lebanon, the green. Indeed in a short period of time this will be part of history due to natural and unnatural desertification – i.e. cities and the conquest of cement. Thus the slogan of Lebanon, the green would be a mere slogan mentioned only in poetry. Well I say as Lebanon is green, this is part of its essential nature exactly as the freedom of expression, the freedom of faith, the freedom of practising human rituals are part of Lebanon's essential nature.

If these aspects stopped to exist and were detached this country will not be Lebanon anymore. It will be something else regardless of what this other thing is. The same applies to trees, greenery, verdure and bloom. These are part of Lebanon's essential existence. If Lebanon failed to be green and beautiful, it won't be Lebanon anymore. It will be something else. Consequently as we all laud of Lebanon and its beauty, greenery and climate, we must all assume this responsibility.

The third point is not special to Lebanon only, but Lebanon is most in need of. It is the need of dealing with trees, tree-planting, woods, forests and even trees on roads and in front of houses as part of the Lebanese national security. So it is not only an environmental, health, climatic, aesthetic aspect of a green country. Lebanon is in need of this tree. Lebanon protects it so that it protects Lebanon.

Notice that all around the world – even in military studies, military sciences, geography and demography – nature gives defensive characteristics which at times might be very important and can not be available through what man owns regarding equipments and capabilities. Thus combating in deserts differs from fighting in mountains which in its turn differs from battling in valleys. Thus when we once threatened saying that should five or six 'Israeli' squads break into our territories, we pledge to destroy them . . . We talked about the geographic nature of our territories, hills, valleys, trees and mountains. All of that gives very important defensive characteristics.

You might have noticed – as the Lebanese know – that since 1972, 'Israelis' in the occupied region or in the region they head to occupy resort to cutting trees off from roads and the various regions. They used to set on fire, shell and destroy trees because they are aware of this defensive characteristic the Lebanese people and resistance enjoy. I still remember – anyway Hajj Imad gained martyrdom and this is not a secret anymore – that following 25 May 2000 and the celebration we held in Bint Jbeil, I and brother martyr Hajj Imad Mughniyeh toured the coastal area from Naqura all through the border area until reaching Shebaa Farms and upwards until reaching near the 'Israeli' outposts in Shebaa Farms.

It was remarkable that when we stood on top of one of the high hills and looked towards inside occupied Palestine we noticed that everything was green: woods, trees and forests even in the surroundings and inside 'Israeli' settlements while from the border inwards towards the Lebanese territories we could see barren waste land with few trees which were kept and protected. During the occupation and especially since 1982 until 2000, 'Israelis' worked at exterminating the greater part of the national natural wealth which southern Lebanon and west Bekaa enjoy. The issue is not that of enmity with nature and enmity with goodness only, it is also part of the field struggle which took place all through these years. Even in [the] July War, they resorted to shelling many forests and orchids which had nothing militarily at all. That was only to seize the opportunity of destroying such capacities.

That means that we must all tackle this issue with great national responsibility on two levels: first, broadening the areas of such forests, woods and greeneries, and second, protecting what already exists and what will exist because it is not enough to plant as on the opposite side there exist those who blaze, cut off and destroy.

There is a positive thing which we must do which is more plantations and more efforts in this perspective. The second point is protecting what already exists but at times we lose what already exists due to negligence. Here the state assumes part of the responsibility. People also assume part of the responsibility especially the citizens who go to woods, eat, barbecue, have their hubble-bubbles and leave the fire on. Many fires took place for such reasons. Still I believe that some fires are set on deliberately and are schemed for. We must search for the 'Israeli' hands behind that especially in some areas. Anyway, there are very great and important responsibilities to be assumed in both directions.

I wrap up the first topic with special encouragement. We know that in national, civil and social education and mobilization and positive and not negative provocation, encouragement means finding the motives to do a definite thing. For that there are various speeches and means. However all through history, the religious and divine motive has been the strongest motive ever in moving man especially in the directions which do not seem to yield rapid results. That means that man usually likes quick gain and achievements.

Source: https://english.alahednews.com.lb/12511/385

Hamas

Excerpts from the 2017 Document of General Principles and Policies

Palestine is the land of the Arab Palestinian people, from it they originate, to it they adhere and belong, and about it they reach out and communicate. Palestine is a land whose status has been elevated by Islam, a faith that holds it in high esteem, that breathes through it its spirit and just values and that lays the foundation for the doctrine of defending and protecting it. Palestine is the cause of a people who have been let down by a world that fails to secure their rights and restore to them what has been usurped from them, a people whose land continues to suffer one of the worst types of occupation in this world. Palestine is a land that was seized by a racist, anti-human and colonial Zionist project that was founded on a false promise (the Balfour Declaration), on recognition of a usurping entity and on imposing a fait accompli by force. Palestine symbolises the resistance that shall continue until liberation is accomplished, until the return is fulfilled and until a fully sovereign state is established with Jerusalem as its capital. Palestine is the true partnership among Palestinians of all affiliations for the sublime objective of liberation. Palestine is the spirit of the Ummah and its central cause; it is the soul of humanity and its living conscience . . .

Palestine, which extends from the River Jordan in the east to the Mediterranean in the west and from Ras al-Naqurah in the north to Umm al-Rashrash in the south, is an integral territorial unit. It is the land and the home of the Palestinian people. The expulsion and banishment of the

Palestinian people from their land and the establishment of the Zionist entity therein do not annul the right of the Palestinian people to their entire land and do not entrench any rights therein for the usurping Zionist entity. Palestine is an Arab Islamic land. It is a blessed sacred land that has a special place in the heart of every Arab and every Muslim.

Source: https://hamas.ps/ar/uploads/documents/06c77206ce934064ab5a90
    1fa8bfef44.pdf

Al-Qaeda

Excerpts from Osama bin Laden's letter on implications of Climate Change

My Islamic nation
Peace, Allah's mercy and blessings be upon you
Congratulations on the arrival of the Holy Month of Ramadan, the month of both the Qur'an and fasting and the month of the nightly prayers, alms-giving and Jihad, so let's strive in worshipping and avoid what keeps us away from glorifying Allah Almighty. Effects associated with the enormous climate changes using such expression without mentioning the view of Shari'ah concerning earthquakes and discord seems purely Western. The secularists maintain that these are natural disasters we must confront. In other words, they are saying, we are able to stand up to Allah and confront His judgment and they have neglected what is stated in the Qur'an concerning these events.

Indeed, what our Ummah is experiencing, of effects associated with the enormous climate changes and the great suffering the natural disasters are leaving behind that now become prevalent throughout the Muslim countries, renders the traditional relief efforts insufficient. Relief work is mentioned as the only solution for these disasters, without warning that it is a plague or suffering from Allah Almighty, and the first solution is faith and correct deeds. One of the correct deeds is assisting Muslims.

Although the provision of tents, food and medicine will always be crucial, the afflictions are taking a larger shape and volume, hence the quality, method and timing of aid must be equally improved. Similarly, we are in need of making major efforts in our relief work, as those victimised by the current climate change is a very large number, expected to rise. According to the studies, this number is higher than the number of people victimised by wars, for which the states recruit their strongest men, offer their best training and slash major portions of their budgets . . .

Millions of children are left in the open, without a suitable living environment, including good drinking water, which has exposed them to dehydration, dangerous diseases and higher death rates. I pray to Allah Almighty to grant them both relief and mercy. And owing to the high frequency of such disasters caused by climate changes, the effort must not become merely one of providing temporary assistance, rather, to set up a distinct relief organization . . . It is therefore incumbent upon such an organization to shoulder the numerous tasks and major duties that would require the collaboration of those who are sincere. Among its duties, for example, would be:

First: To research the residential compounds built along the banks of rivers and valleys in the Islamic World and the prospects of future disasters as a result of climate changes. For what disastrous floods have befallen the city of Jeddah in the past was expected for a simple reason, Jeddah and many other cities were not only built over the banks of valleys, many of their structures and residential buildings were constructed over the entire valleys' paths. I am not pointing to whose responsibility that was, for such may be discussed in a different time. Yet I am attempting to portray what took place, to avoid similar flooding disasters and to find fundamental solutions for the dangers that threaten people's lives. Additionally, it is essential that all dam and bridge safety regulations be examined and revised.

Second: What is also required is to do what is needed towards the countries that are or may be afflicted with famines resulting from wars or climate changes, for the famine most likely gives early warning a year or more prior to taking place; delaying the relief and essential aid would result in a large number of deaths, in particular among children, while those who may not die may not escape malnutrition and some form of brain damage.

Third: The establishment of development projects in the ravaged and poor areas, as there is excellent opportunity for establishing such projects since only modest spending is required. For example, the construction of regulators and canals in the countries where rivers or seasonal valleys are flowing, such as in Sudan, Chad, Somalia and Yemen. Based on field work in Sudan, the cost of a regulator capable of irrigating tens of thousands of acres, together with the main and tributary canals, which also means providing assistance to tens of thousands of people, is about 200,000 euros, more or less, based on the proximity or remoteness of the required construction material.

Fourth: Work towards realizing food-security, as the reports stated that if a calamity befalls any major wheat-exporting country and causes a cease in exports, many countries worldwide, and in our region particularly, shall experience deadly famine in the full sense of the word. At that point, the money would not stave off the deadly hunger as long as the bread, the main nourishment, is lacking. Whereas Sudan is endowed with rain-irrigated agricultural land of an area estimated at 80 million hectares, only little of that area has been cultivated. So, it is essential to raise people's awareness about such dangers and to encourage the merchants and their families to entirely devote some of their sons to relief and agricultural work; the merchants today are the field knights who may rescue their nation from the predictable horrible famines. So, it is essential to focus on this aspect and avoid investment in unproductive sectors, while it is also wrong to rule out investing in agriculture based on the current circumstances and on the grounds that such requires great effort while the profits are small compared to other forms of investment – for the issue is not an issue of losses and profits, it is an issue of life and death . . .

Fifth: We need to raise Muslim awareness about the dangers associated with depleting the underground water used for agriculture that is not renewable, while it is crucial to establish a network of pipes that joins the agricultural wells with the main network of drinking water, in order to be used in times of necessity.

And last, I encourage my Muslim brothers to be kind and give out all they could to rescue the weak and relieve their suffering. Whoever relieves a believer's suffering, Allah will relieve an Afterlife of distress for. So, we should work for that and ponder Allah's words, Glorious and Almighty: And whatever good ye send forth for your souls ye shall find it in God's Presence – yea, better and greater, in Reward and seek ye the Grace of God. For God is Oft-Forgiving, Most Merciful.

Osama bin Laden

Source: https://www.dni.gov/files/documents/ubl/english/Letter%20Impl ications%20of%20Climate%20Change.pdf

SELECT BIBLIOGRAPHY

Primary Sources

Muslim Brotherhood

'The Muslim Brotherhood's program 2005', IkhwanWeb, 13 June 2007, http://www.ikhwanweb.com/article.php?id=811

'The role of Muslim Women in an Islamic society', IkhwanWeb, 10 June 2007, https://www.ikhwanweb.com/article.php?id=787

Mohsen Saleh, 'Hassan Al Banna's centenary . . . Attitude towards Palestinian cause', IkhwanWeb, 13 June 2007, http://www.ikhwanweb.com/article.php?id=820

'The electoral programme for Shura Council 2007', IkhwanWeb, 14 June 2007, http://www.ikhwanweb.com/article.php?id=822

'Muslim Brotherhood 2008 municipal election platform', IkhwanWeb, 9 March 2008, https://www.ikhwanweb.com/article.php?id=16257

'Muslim Brotherhood MP warns against pollution of Nile River', IkhwanWeb, 20 May 2008, http://www.ikhwanweb.com/article.php?id=17137

'MB MP: Against sabotage even if to halt gas exports to Israel', IkhwanWeb, 12 January 2009, http://www.ikhwanweb.com/article.php?id=19026

'MP: 400,000 pigs in Cairo threaten spread of human epidemic', IkhwanWeb, 27 April 2009, http://www.ikhwanweb.com/article.php?id=20015

'Letter from the MB new chairman Mohammed Badie', IkhwanWeb, 16 January 2010, http://www.ikhwanweb.com/article.php?id=22665

الإسلامي التراث في البيئة نظافة ('The cleanliness of the environment in Islamic heritage'),

Ikhwan Online, 24 February 2010, http://www.ikhwanonline.com/Mobi le/MArticle.asp?ArtID=60911&SecID=293

'MB chairman: Do no mischief on the earth, after it has been set in order', IkhwanWeb, 6 May 2010, http://www.ikhwanweb.com/article.php?id=24637

'MB MP requests ending of gas exports to Israel to accommodate Egypt's demands', IkhwanWeb, 24 August 2010, http://www.ikhwanweb.com/article.php?id=2 6148

'A conversation with Sheikh Yusuf Al-Qaradawi', IkhwanWeb, 27 December 2010, http://www.ikhwanweb.com/article.php?id=27682

Freedom and Justice Party, 'Election Program 2011', https://www.scribd.com/docu ment/73955131/FJP-Program-En

'Text of Selmi's controversial supra-constitutional principles', IkhwanWeb, 4 November 2011, http://www.ikhwanweb.com/article.php?id=29360

'FJP chair: 'FJP visions for Egypt's future', IkhwanWeb, 6 January 2012, http://www .ikhwanweb.com/article.php?id=29518

'Al-Shater outlines Egyptian renaissance project at first press conference', IkhwanWeb, 9 April 2012, http://www.ikhwanweb.com/article.php?id=29859

('Imam Hassan al-Banna writes about عن يكتب البنا حسن الشهيد الإمام سيناء والسودان: Sinai and Sudan') Ikhwan Online, 28 April 2012, https://www.ikhwanonline .com/Section/107234/Default.aspx

'"Clean Homeland" Campaign launched today in Cairo and other governorates', IkhwanWeb, 27 July 2012, http://www.ikhwanweb.com/article.php?id=30212

'Muslim Brotherhood: Official and popular diplomacy will resolve any water crisis', IkhwanWeb, 29 May 2013, http://www.ikhwanweb.com/article.php?id=30983

'Muslim Brotherhood: Egyptians paying for Sisi's selling out of Egypt historical Nile water share', IkhwanWeb, 30 December 2015, http://www.ikhwanweb.com/ar ticle.php?id=32383

('Brotherhood and the Nile River: a history والحماية الوفاء من تاريخ.. النيل ونهر الإخوان) of loyalty and protection'), Ikhwan Online. 22 October 2019, https://www.ikh wanonline.com/article/237266

('Egypt's Nile is a red line'), Ikhwan Online, 6 July 2020, www. أحمر خط.. مصر نيل ikhwanonline.com/article/240362/الإخوان-المسلمون-نيل-مصر-خط-أحمر

('Wheat supply prices جادو جلال بقلم:.. مصر في الفلاحين طحن وسياسة القمح توريد أسعار and the policy of grinding farmers in Egypt'), Ikhwan Online, 7 April 2021, www.ikhwanonline.com/article/244353/ أسعار-توريد-القمح-وسياسة-طحن-الفلاحين- في-مصر-بقلم-جلال-جادو

('Greetings to Palestine in memory of الأرض يوم ' ذكرى في.. فلسطين إلى تحية

Land Day'), Ikhwan Online, 30 March 2022, www.ikhwanonline.com/
article/253476/الأرض-يوم-ذكرى-في-فلسطين-إلى-تحية

Hizb ut-Tahrir

An-Nabhani, Taqiuddin, *Concepts of Hizb ut-Tahrir* (London: Al-Khilafah, no date)

Msellem, Masoud, 'Crime by Britain and America is greater than poaching', no date, http://www.hizb-ut-tahrir.info/en/index.php/2017-01-28-14-59-33/news-com ment/download/1635_765c33067ee80d8d1fa1cce4205965f2.html

An-Nabhani, Taqiuddin, *A Warm Call from Hizb ut-Tahrir to the Muslims* (London: Al-Khilafah, 1962)

Hizb ut-Tahrir, *Khilafah Is the Answer* (London: Al-Khilafah, 1989).

Ata Abu al-Rashta, 'The Manufacturing Policy and Building an Industrial State from the Viewpoint of Islam', Amman, 18 September 1990, http://www.hizb-ut-tah rir.org/PDF/EN/en_books_pdf/Siyasat_al-Tasnii_EN_26.05_.2015_1_.pdf

Hizb ut-Tahrir, *The Ruling System in Islam*, 5th ed. (London: Al-Khilafah, 1996)

An-Nabhani, Taqiuddin, *The Economic System of Islam* (London: Al-Khilafah, 1997)

An-Nabhani, Taqiuddin, *The Islamic State* (London: Al-Khilafah, 1998)

Hizb ut-Tahrir, *The Methodology of Hizb ut-Tahrir for Change* (London: Al-Khilafah, 1999)

Hizb ut-Tahrir, *The Inevitability of the Clash of Civilisation* (London: Al-Khilafah, 2002)

Hizb ut-Tahrir, *Science and Islam* (London: Al-Khilafah, 2002)

Hizb ut-Tahrir Bangladesh, *How the Khilafat Will Solve Bangladesh's Economic Crisis*, June 2003, https://www.systemofislam.com/pdf/khilafah_solve_bangladesh _economic_crisis.pdf

Hizb ut-Tahrir, *Foundations of the Education Curriculum in the Khilafah State* (Beirut: Dar al-Ummah, 2004)

Hizb ut-Tahrir Denmark, *The Environmental Problem: Its Causes and Islam's Solution* (Copenhagen: Hizb ut-Tahrir Denmark, 2009)

After the Arab Spring: The Islamic Khilafah – A Manifesto for Change, Hizb ut-Tahrir Britain, June 2012

Hizb ut-Tahrir, 'A Draft Constitution of the Khilafah State', *The Khilafah*, 18 January 2013, http://www.khilafah.com/a-draft-constitution-of-the-khilafah-state/

'The politics of evolution', Hizb ut-Tahrir Britain, 21 January 2013, http://www.hi zb.org.uk/viewpoint/the-politics-of-evolution/

'Cow slaughter ban in India – milking the democracy loophole', Ibn Ahmed blog,

14 April 2013, https://petraria.wixsite.com/ibnahmed/single-post/2013/04/14/cow-slaughter-ban-in-india-milking-of-the-democracy-loophole

'Haze chokes Singapore and Malaysia!', Hizb ut Tahrir Central Media Office, 28 June 2013, http://www.hizb-ut-tahrir.info/en/index.php/2017-01-28-14-59-33/news-comment/2303.html

'Halal meat on the chopping block again!', Hizb ut-Tahrir Britain, 10 March 2014, http://www.hizb.org.uk/viewpoint/halal-meat-on-the-chopping-block-again/

'Media statement regarding ISIS's declaration in Iraq', Hizb ut-Tahrir Britain, 12 July 2014, http://www.hizb.org.uk/current-affairs/media-statement-regarding-isiss-declaration-in-iraq

'Democratic rulers and politicians neglect to safeguard Kashmir from floods', Hizb ut-Tahrir Central Media Office, 25 September 2014, https://hizb-ut-tahrir.info/en/index.php/radio-broadcast/radio-broadcast/5791.html

'Report on the issues of the Ummah forum Hizb ut Tahrir stirs the Ummah's resolve to face the Three Wings of Death', 25 October 2014, http://www.hizb-ut-tahrir.info/en/index.php/multimedia/video/6151.html

Wadud, Fehmida Binte, 'Only under the leadership of a God-fearing Khaleefah will the future generation of Bangladesh be ready to tackle all kinds of environmental challenges', *The Khilafah*, 26 September 2015, http://www.khilafah.com/only-under-the-leadership-of-a-god-fearing-khaleefah-will-the-future-generation-of-bangladesh-be-ready-to-tackle-all-kinds-of-environmental-challenges/

Abu Yusuf, Wasif, 'Mars discovering water and covering other cracks in capitalism', 14 October 2015, http://www.hizb.org.uk/viewpoint/part-2-mars-discovering-water-and-covering-over-cracks-in-capitalism/

'Indonesian democratic government fails to end suffering of millions children [*sic*] due to forest fire', Hizb ut Tahrir Central Media Office, 18 October 2015, http://hizb-ut-tahrir.info/en/index.php/2017-01-28-14-59-33/news-comment/8772.html

Choudhry, Tanish, 'Was the 21st Climate Change Conference really a "monumental triumph"?', *The Khilafah*, 23 December 2015, http://www.khilafah.com/was-the-21st-climate-change-conference-really-a-monumental-triumph/

'Q&A: Pakistan's request to join the Nuclear Suppliers Group', *The Khilafah*, 12 June 2016, http://www.khilafah.com/qa-pakistans-request-to-join-the-nuclear-suppliers-group/

Nazia Rehman, 'Polluted air health emergency', *The Khilafah*, 2 October 2016, http://www.khilafah.com/polluted-air-health-emergency/

'The Shar'i principles for dealing with rivers', Hizb ut Tahrir Central Media Office, 12 November 2016, http://hizb-ut-tahrir.info/en/index.php/qestions/jurisprudence-questions/11800.html

'Only Khilafah "Caliphate" Rashedah can solve the problems of water resources on a regional and international level', Hizb ut Tahrir Central Media Office, 9 March 2017, http://www.hizb-ut-tahrir.info/en/index.php/press-releases/afghanistan/12649.html

'Through water talks, normalization picks up pace: the Khilafah will solve the water issue by destroying the "Greater India" plan', Hizb ut-Tahrir Pakistan, 22 March 2017, http://www.hizb-pakistan.com/home/press-releases/local-prs/water-talks-normalization-picks-pace/

Al-Rashta, Ata Abu, 'Britain's disruption of American interests', in 'From the Question & Answer of the Ameer of Hizb ut Tahrir, Ata Bin Khalil Abu al-Rashtah, Part 8', Hizb ut Tahrir Central Media Office, 30 April 2017, http://www.hizb-ut-tahrir.info/en/index.php/archives/speeches/13008.html

Amin, Imadul, 'Havoc in Bangladeshi swamplands due to uranium-mixed flood water from India', *The Khilafah*, 8 May 2017, http://www.khilafah.com/havoc-in-bangladeshi-swamplands-due-to-uranium-mixed-flood-water-from-india/

Salim, Mgeni J., 'Effects of rain is a result of corruption in the country', Hizb ut-Tahrir Kenya, 10 June 2017, http://hizb.or.ke/index.php/women-s-section/articless/item/403-effects-of-rain-is-a-result-of-corruption-in-the-country

'An-Nahdha (Grand Renaissance) Dam and the Threats of Water War; Negligence of the Rulers and the Duty of the Ummah', Hizb ut-Tahrir Wilayah of Sudan, September 2017, http://www.khilafah.com/images/images/PDF/Books/Sudan_Booklet_22.09.2017_EN.pdf

Nisbet, Yahya, 'Liberating the whole of Palestine is the Islamic solution for al-Quds', Hizb ut-Tahrir Britain, 6 December 2017, http://www.hizb.org.uk/media/press-releases/liberating-whole-palestine-islamic-solution-al-quds/

Nisbet, Yahya, 'School bullies to forcibly secularize young Muslim girls', Hizb ut-Tahrir Britain, 17 January 2018, http://www.hizb.org.uk/media/press-releases/school-bullies-forcibly-secularise-young-muslim-girls/

'The Danish crusade campaign in banning the niqab continues', Hizb ut-Tahrir, 4 May 2018, http://www.hizb-ut-tahrir.org/index.php/EN/nshow/3717

'Pakistan's constitution is anything but Islamic', Hizb ut-Tahrir Britain, 13 July 2018, http://www.hizb.org.uk/viewpoint/pakistans-constitution-is-anything-but-islamic/

Mwalimu, Shabani, 'Mau Forest crisis: poor management of natural resources by capitalist- secular governments', *The Khilafah*, 4 August 2018, http://www.kh ilafah.com/mau-forest-crisis-poor-management-of-natural-resources-by-capitali st-secular-governments/

'The elections law for the year 2018 contradicts Islam and enshrines falsehood', Hizb ut Tahrir Central Media Office, 23 November 2018, http://www.hizb-ut-tahrir .info/en/index.php/leaflet/sudan/16491.html

'Pakistan headlines 30/11/2018', Hizb ut Tahrir Central Media Office, 30 November 2018, http://www.hizb-ut-tahrir.info/en/index.php/2017-01-28-14-59-33/he adlines/16499.html##

'The state leads the people to destruction through the riba-based financing system', *The Khilafah*, 3 January 2019, http://www.khilafah.com/the-state-leads-the-people-to-destruction-through-the-riba-based-financing-system/

'The educational excellence and rights of women under the Khilafah', Hizb ut-Tahrir Britain, 7 March 2019, http://www.hizb.org.uk/viewpoint/educational-excellen ce-rights-women-khilafah/

'Secular democracy's new front: Islamic education, following to the investigation of Nieuwsuur and NRC Handelsblad's on Islamic education', Hizb ut Tahrir Central Media Office, 12 September 2019, http://www.hizb-ut-tahrir.info/en /index.php/press-releases/the-netherlands/18189.html

'O people! The price-hike of diesel-kerosene is manifestation of the tyrannical policy of Hasina regime, the agent of the capitalists', Hizb ut-Tahrir, 12 November 2021, http://www.hizb-ut-tahrir.org/index.php/EN/wshow/4740

Wahid, Abdul, 'Islam and the environmental challenge: part five – Islam's unique architecture and vision for humanity', Hizb ut-Tahrir Britain, 30 November 2021, https://www.hizb.org.uk/resources/in-depth/islam-the-environmental-ch allenge-part-five-islams-unique-architecture-and-vision-for-humanity

Hizbullah

'Agriculture', Jihad al-Binaa Development Association, no date, https://jihadbinaa .org.lb/english/essaydetails.php?eid=4&cid=274#.XFday1z7Q2w

'The Good Tree', Jihad al-Binaa Development Association, no date, https://jihad binaa.org.lb/english/essaydetails.php?eid=64&cid=384#.XFOJg1z7Q2w

'Introduction', Jihad al-Binaa Development Association, no date, https://jihadbinaa .org.lb/english/essaydetails.php?eid=14&cid=284#.XFOLqVz7Q2w

'Who We Are?', Jihad al-Binaa Development Association, no date, https://jihadbinaa .org.lb/english/essaydetails.php?eid=34&cid=273#.XFOD61z7Q2w

Hizballah, 'A message addressed to the Pope upon his visit to Lebanon in May',

Al-Manar TV, 20 June 1997, http://almashriq.hiof.no/lebanon/300/320/324 /324.2/hizballah/

Hizbullah, البرنامج الانتخابي لحزب الله في الانتخابات النيابية للعام 2000 (2000 Electoral Programme), https://www.moqawama.org/essaydetails.php?eid=11255&cid= 109

'Hizbullah's 1996 Parliamentary Elections Program', in Joseph Alagha, *The Shifts in Hizbullah's Ideology: Religious Ideology, Political Ideology, and Political Program* (Amsterdam: Amsterdam University Press, 2006)

Hizbullah, البرنامج الانتخابي لحزب الله للانتخابات النيابية 2009 (2009 Electoral Programme), https://www.moqawama.org/essaydetailsf.php?eid=14229&fid=45

'The New Hezbollah Manifesto', November 2009, available at http://www.lebanon renaissance.org/assets/Uploads/15-The-New-Hezbollah-Manifesto-Nov09.pdf

'Speech of Hezbollah secretary general Sayyed Hassan Nasrallah on Tuesday, August 24, 2010', The Saker, 27 August 2010, http://thesaker.is/speech-of-hezbollah- secretary-general-sayyed-hassan-nasrallah-on-tuesday-august-24-2010/

'One million tree campaign: culture of nature', 8 October 2010, http://www.english .moqawama.org/essaydetailsf.php?eid=12310&fid=55

Nasrallah, Hassan, 'Speech on marking end of planting one million trees campaign', 9 October 2010, https://english.alahednews.com.lb/12511/385

Khamenei, Imam, الخامنئي الإمام: تشكيل منع الإسلامية الأمة وعلى البحر إلى النهر من فلسطين الصهيوني للكيان أمن هامش ('Palestine from the river to the sea'), 17 January 2018, https://www.moqawama.org/essaydetails.php?eid=34738&cid=202&st=%D9 %86%D9%87%D8%B1

'Sayyed Nasrallah: We can disable Israel's offshore installations within hours', Al Manar TV, 16 February 2018, http://english.almanar.com.lb/447900

Hizb'allah, البرنامج الانتخابي لحزب لدورة انتخابات الله العام (2018 Electoral Programme), البرنامج الانتخابي لحزب لدورة انتخابات الله العام 2018, 22 March 2018

Moughnieh, Sara Taha, 'Sayyed Nasrallah: After every victory we will witness US chemical play', Al Manar TV, 15 April 2018, http://english.almanar.com.lb/48 6385

'Loyalty to resistance: Cabinet formation delay triggers new complications', Al Manar TV, 30 August 2018, http://english.almanar.com.lb/570953

'Hezbollah: Martyrdom of commanders in Yemen indicates imminent victor', Al Manar TV, 9 August 2019, https://english.almanar.com.lb/800417

'Hezbollah on Land Day: Israeli occupation gains no legitimacy, resistance to con- tinue', Al Manar TV, 30 March 2020, https://english.almanar.com.lb/982 676

'Hezbollah congratulates Palestine on historic victory: resistance has upper hand', Al Manar TV, 21 May 2021, https://english.almanar.com.lb/1347623

'Hezbollah denies claims its fighters were martyred in Israeli aggression on Syria', Al Manar TV, 21 August 2021, https://english.almanar.com.lb/1413480

El-Din, Hashem Safi, الدين صفي هاشم السيد: أهم أسباب المشكلات التي يعاني منها لبنان هي (سياسات الولايات المتحدة الأمريكية) ('The most important causes of the problems that Lebanon suffers from are the policies of the United States of America'), Al Manar TV, 23 November 2021, https://www.almanar.com.lb/8975353

Nasrallah, Hassan, كلمة الأمين العام لحزب الله في الله إحياء مهرجان ذكرى القادة الشهداء ('Speech of the secretary-general of Hezbollah at the festival commemorating the martyred leaders'), Al Manar TV, 16 February 2022, https://www.almanar.com.lb/9268668

Nasrallah, Hassan, نصرالله السيد: مشروعنا الحقيقي هو العدالة والسلام و'اسرائيل' كيان مؤقت سيزول ('Our real project is justice and peace, and "Israel" is a temporary entity that will disappear'), Al Manar TV, 23 February 2022, https://www.almanar.com.lb/9293649

بالفيديو | أبرز ما جاء في كلمة الأمين العام لحزب الله حول الإنتخابات ('Highlights of the speech of the secretary-general of Hezbollah about the elections'), Al Manar TV, 2 March 2022, https://www.almanar.com.lb/9319444

'Hezbollah: Resistance across Palestine "only way to victory"', Al Manar TV, 23 March 2022, https://english.almanar.com.lb/1566237

Hamas

'The Charter of Allah: The Platform of the Islamic Resistance Movement (Hamas)', translated and annotated by Raphael Israeli, Hebrew University, Jerusalem, 1988, https://fas.org/irp/world/para/docs/880818.htm

بيان صحفي حول إغراق الاحتلال حي الشجاعية بمياه بعضها عادمة ('A press release about the occupation of the Shajaiya neighbourhood by water, some of which is wastewater', Hamas, 27 March 2001, http://hamas.ps/ar/post/367/ بيان-صحفي-حول-إقدام-الاحتلال-على-إغراق-حي-الشجاعية-بالمياه-وبعضها-مياه-عادمة

'The Islamic Resistance Movement (Hamas)', memo prepared by Hamas Political Bureau in 2000, in Azzam Tamimi, *Hamas: Unwritten Chapters* (London: Hurst, 2007)

'On Hamas TV Friday sermon: calls to annihilate the Jews, who are compared to dogs', Memri TV, 3 April 2009, https://www.memri.org/tv/hamas-tv-friday-sermon-calls-annihilate-jews-who-are-compared-dogs/transcript

'Hamas MP and cleric Yunis al-Astal on swine flu and "the brothers of apes and pigs"', Memri TV, 15 May 2009, https://www.memri.org/tv/hamas-mp-and-cleric-yunis-al-astal-swine-flu-and-brothers-apes-and-pigs/transcript

حماس تهدف لاستزراع مليون شجرة زيتون في غزة ('Hamas aims to cultivate one million olive trees in Gaza'), *Islam Times*, 12 November 2010, http://islamtimes.org/ar/doc/news/43733/حماس-تهدف-لاستزراع-مليون-شجرة-زيتون-في-غزة

'Hamas MP Marwan Abu Ras: The Jews are behind every catastrophe on earth', Memri TV, 12 September 2012, https://www.memri.org/tv/hamas-mp-marwan-abu-ras-jews-are-behind-every-catastrophe-earth

'Hamas official Mahmoud al-Zahhar: The Qur'an tells us to drive the Jews out of Palestine in its entirety', Memri TV, 7 March 2017, https://www.memri.org/tv/hamas-official-mahmoud-al-zahhar-quran-tells-us-drive-jews-out-palestine-its-entirety

'Press release issued by Hamas on the 41st anniversary of Palestinian Land Day', Hamas, 31 March 2017, http://hamas.ps/en/post/601/press-release-issued-by-hamas-on-the-41st-anniversary-of-palestinian-land-day

'A Document of General Principles and Policies', Hamas, May 2017, https://hamas.ps/ar/uploads/documents/06c77206ce934064ab5a901fa8bfef44.pdf

نص خطاب رئيس المكتب السياسي لحركة حماس إسماعيل هنية ('The text of the speech of the president of the Political Bureau of Hamas Ismail Haniyeh'), 6 July 2017, http://hamas.ps/ar/post/7588/نص-خطاب-رئيس-المكتب-السياسي-لحركة-حماس-إسماعيل-هنية

تصريح صحفي حول العدوان الصهيوني علىغزة ('Press statement about the Zionist aggression on Gaza'), Hamas, 2 November 2019, hamas.ps/ar/post/11192/تصريح-صحفي-حول-العدوان-الصهيوني-على-غزة

تصريح صحفي حول استمرار الحصار وتفاقم أزمة الكهرباء ('A press statement about the continuation of the siege and the exacerbation of the electricity crisis'), Hamas, 18 August 2020, https://hamas.ps/ar/post/12370/تصريح-صحفي-حول-استمرار-الحصار-وتفاقم-أزمة-الكهرباء

تصريح صحفي حول تهرب الاحتلال من مسؤولياته تجاه معاناة قطاع غزة ('A press statement about the occupation evading its responsibilities towards the suffering of the Gaza Strip'), Hamas, 20 November 2020, https://hamas.ps/ar/post/12689/تصريح-صحفي-حول-تهرب-الاحتلال-من-مسؤولياته-تجاه-معاناة-قطاع-غزة

تصريح صحفي تضامنا مع ضحايا الفيضانات في أوروبا ('Press release in solidarity with the victims of the floods in Europe'), Hamas, 17 July 2021, https://hamas.ps/ar/post/13553/تصريح-صحفي-تضامنا-مع-ضحايا-الفيضانات-في-أوروبا

تصريح صحفي تضامنا مع الجزائر في مواجهة موجة الحرائق ('A press statement in solidarity with Algeria in face of the wave of fires'), Hamas, 11 August 2021, https://hamas.ps/ar/post/13619/تصريح-صحفي-تضامنا-مع-الجزائر-في-مواجهة-موجة-الحرائق

تصريح صحفي حول تشديد الاحتلال حصاره على غزة وتصاعد الإنسانية الأزمة') 'A press statement about the tightening of the occupation's siege on Gaza and the escalation of the humanitarian crisis'), Hamas, 29 August 2021, https//hamas.ps/ar/post/13679/ الإنسانية الأزمة وتصاعد غزة على حصاره الاحتلال تشديد حول صحفي تصريح

تصريح صحفي صادر عن رئيس المكتب السياسي للحركة') 'A press statement issued by the head of the movement's political bureau'), Hamas, 30 March 2022, https://hamas.ps/ ar/post/14738/للحركة-السياسي-المكتب-رئيس-عن-صادر-صحفي-تصريح

Al-Qaeda/ISIS

Abu Hamza al-Masri, *Allah's Governance on Earth*, 1999, https://www.kalamullah .com/Books/Allah%20Governance%20on%20Earth.pdf

Abu Bakr Naji, *The Management of Savagery: The Most Critical Stage through Which the Umma Will Pass* (Cambridge, MA: John M. Olin Institute for Strategic Studies, Harvard University, 2006)

'Al Qaeda in Saudi Arabia: Excerpts from "The Laws of Targeting Petroleum-Related Interests"', Global Terror Alert, March 2006, http://web.archive.org/web/201 11202105333/http://azelin.files.wordpress.com/2010/08/al-qaida-in-saudi-ara bia-excerpts-from-e2809cthe-laws-of-targeting-petroleum-related-interests.pdf

'"The Solution": a video speech from Usama bin Laden addressing the American people on the occasion of the sixth anniversary of 9/11 – 9/2007', SITE Intelligence Group, 7 September 2007, http://www.csun.edu/~hfspc002/442 /txt/20070911_OBL.pdf

'Message of Felicitation from Mulla Mohammed 'Umar, on the eve of 'Id al-Fitr', Jihadology, 8 September 2010, http://jihadology.net/2010/09/08/message-of -felicitation-from-mulla-mu%E1%B8%A5mmad-umar-on-the-eve-of-id-al-fi %E1%B9%ADr/

'New video release from Adam Gadahn: "The Tragedy of the Floods"', Jihadology, 29 September 2010, http://jihadology.net/2010/09/29/new-video-release-from -adam-gadahn-the-tragedy-of-the-floods/

'New statement from the Islamic Emirate of Afghanistan: "The greenery of Band-e-Sarda, fallen prey to the American terror"', Jihadology, 26 January 2011, http:// jihadology.net/2011/01/26/new-statement-from-the-islamic-emirate-of-afgha nistan-the-greenery-of-band-e-sarda-fallen-prey-to-the-american-terror/

'New statement from the Islamic Emirate of Afghanistan: "Destruction of trees will not turn American defeat into victory"', Jihadology, 2 February 2011, http://ji hadology.net/2011/02/02/new-statement-from-the-islamic-emirate-of-afghanis tan-destruction-of-trees-will-not-turn-american-defeat-into-victory/

'Letter from the editor', *Inspire Magazine*, Spring 2013

'Smashing the Borders of the Tawaghit', *Islamic State Report: An Insight into the Islamic State*, no. 4, 2013

Official Spokesman for the Islamic State, 'Indeed your Lord is ever watchful', *Dabiq*, no. 4, 2013

'A call to hijrah', *Dabiq*, no. 1, 2014

'Introduction', *Dabiq*, no. 1, 2014

'The capture of Division 17', *Dabiq*, no. 2, 2014

'Remaining and expanding', *Dabiq*, no. 5, 2014

Interviews

Interview with Hussam Abdulhadi, director of Foreign Media Unit, Hamas Information Office, 29 January 2018 (email correspondence).

Interview with Harfiyah Haleem, Islamic Foundation for Ecology and Environmental Sciences, London, 13 February 2018

Interview with Nur Khairiana, NGO Fitra, Singapore, 28 July 2018.

Interview with Professor Osman Bakar, Universiti Brunei Darussalam, Brunei, 31 July 2018

Interview with Professor Nurdeng Deuraseh, Sultan Sharif Ali Islamic University, Brunei, 1 August 2018

Interview with Dr Fachruddin Mangunjaya, Center for Islamic Studies, Universitas Nasional, Jakarta, 2 August 2018

Interview with Dr Hayu Prabowo, chairman of Environmental and Natural Resources Board, Indonesian Council of 'Ulama, Jakarta, 3 August 2018

Interview with three members of Hizb ut-Tahrir, London, 13 December 2018

Interview with Professor Ibrahim Özdemir, Åbo Akademi University, Turku, 22 May 2019 (email correspondence)

Interview with Egyptian former minister of planning and international co-operation Amr Darrag, 3 June 2019 (email correspondence)

Secondary Sources

Books

Abdelal, Wael, *Hamas and the Media: Politics and Strategy* (Abingdon: Routledge, 2016)

Abdul-Matin, Ibrahim, *Green Deen: What Islam Teaches about Protecting the Planet* (San Francisco: Berrett-Koehler Publishers, 2010)

Abdul-Rahman, Muhammad Saed, *Islam: Questions and Answers, vol. 17: Manners* (London: MSA, 2007)

Abdul-Raof, Hussein, *Schools of Qur'anic Exegesis: Genesis and Development* (Abingdon: Routledge, 2010)

Aboulela, Leila, *The Kindness of Enemies* (London: Weidenfeld & Nicolson, 2015)

Abu-Rabi', Ibrahim M., *Intellectual Origins of Islamic Resurgence in the Modern Arab World* (Albany: State University of New York Press, 1996)

Abu-Sway, Mustafa, *Islam: The Environment and Health* (Durban: Islamic Medical Association of South Africa, 1999)

Achcar, Gilbert and Michel Warschawski, *The 33-Day War: Israel's War on Hezbollah in Lebanon and Its Consequences* (Boulder, CO: Paradigm, 2007)

Adams, Charles C., *Islam and Modernism in Egypt* (Boston: Russell & Russell, 1968)

Al-e Ahmad, Jalal, *Occidentosis: A Plague from the West* (Berkeley, CA: Mizan Press, 1983)

Ahmad, Mirza Tahir, *Revelation, Rationality, Knowledge and Truth* (Tilford, England: Islam International, 1998)

Ahmed, Leila, *Women and Gender in Islam: Historical Roots of a Modern Debate* (New Haven, CT: Yale University Press, 1992)

Alagha, Joseph, *The Shifts in Hizballah's Ideology: Religious Ideology, Political Ideology, and Political Program* (Amsterdam: Amsterdam University Press, 2006)

Ali, Muhammad (tr.), *The Holy Quran*, 4th ed. (Lahore: Ahmadiyya Anjuman Isha'at Islam,1951)

Allawi, Ali A., *The Crisis of Islamic Civilization* (New Haven, CT: Yale University Press, 2009)

Allen, Douglas, *Myth and Religion in Mircea Eliade* (New York: Routledge, 2002)

Ammons, Elizabeth and Modhumita Roy (eds), *Sharing the Earth: An International Environmental Justice Reader* (Athens: University of Georgia Press, 2015)

Al-Anwar, Bihar, *The Promised Mahdi, vol. 13* (Mumbai: Ja'fari Propagation Centre, n.d.)

Aquinas, St Thomas, *Summa Theologica, vol. 3* (New York: Cosimo Classics, 2007)

Arkoun, Mohammed, *Islam: To Reform or to Subvert?* (London: Saqi, 2007)

Asad, Mohammad, *The Message of the Qur'an* (Gibraltar: Dar al-Andalus, 1984)

Asad, Talal, *Genealogies of Religion: Discipline and Reasons of Power in Christianity and Islam* (Baltimore: Johns Hopkins University Press, 1993)

Atwan, Abdel Bari, *After Bin Laden: Al-Qaeda, the Next Generation* (New York: New Press, 2013)

Atwan, Abdel Bari, *Islamic State: The Digital Caliphate* (London: Saqi, 2015)

Avon, Dominique and Anaïs-Trissa Khatchadourian, *Hezbollah: A History of the 'Party of God'* (Cambridge, MA: Harvard University Press, 2012)

Ayoob, Mohammed, *The Many Faces of Political Islam: Religion and Politics in the Muslim World* (Ann Arbor: University of Michigan Press, 2008)

Ayoub, Mahmoud M., *Islam: Faith and History* (London: Oneworld, 2004)

Azani, Eitan, *Hezbollah: The Story of the Party of God – From Revolution to Institutionalization* (New York: Palgrave Macmillan, 2011)

Bar, Shmuel, *The Muslim Brotherhood in Jordan* (Tel Aviv: Moshe Dayan Center, 2000)

Bakar, Osman, *Qur'anic Pictures of the Universe* (Petaling Jaya, Malaysia: Islamic Book Trust, 2016)

Al-Banna, Hasan, *Memoirs of Hasan al-Banna Shaheed* (Karachi: International Islamic Publishers, 1982)

Bartholomew, Ecumenical Patriarch, *On Earth as in Heaven: Ecological Vision and Initiatives of Ecumenical Patriarch Bartholomew* (New York: Fordham University Press, 2011)

Beblawi, Hazem and Giacomo Luciani, *The Rentier State* (New York: Croom Helm, 1987)

Beinin, Joel and Frédéric Vairel (eds), *Social Movements, Mobilization, and Contestation in the Middle East and North Africa* (Stanford, CA: Stanford University Press, 2011)

Bennett, Clinton, *Studying Islam: The Critical Issues* (London: Continuum, 2010)

Benstein, Jeremy, *The Way into Judaism and the Environment* (Woodstock, VT: Jewish Lights, 2006)

Berger, Peter L. (ed.), *The Desecularization of the World: Resurgent of Religion and World Politics* (Grand Rapids, MI: William B. Eerdmans, 1999)

Berger, Peter L., *Facing Up to Modernity: Excursions in Society, Politics, and Religion* (Harmondsworth: Penguin, 1979)

Billig, Michael, *Ideology and Opinions: Studies in Rhetorical Psychology* (London: Sage, 1991)

Black, Antony, *The History of Islamic Thought: From the Prophet to the Present*, 2nd ed. (Edinburgh: Edinburgh University Press, 2011)

Boden, Alison L., *Women's Rights and Religious Practice: Claims in Conflict* (Basingstoke: Palgrave Macmillan, 2007)

Bomberg, Elizabeth, *Green Parties and Politics in the European Union* (London: Routledge, 1998)

Bramwell, Anna, *The Fading of the Greens: The Decline of Environmental Politics in the West* (New Haven, CT: Yale University Press, 1994)

Brenner, Björn, *Gaza under Hamas: From Islamic Democracy to Islamist Governance* (London and New York: I. B. Tauris, 2017)

Brown, Daniel, *A New Introduction to Islam*, 2nd ed. (Chichester: Wiley-Blackwell, 2009)

Brown, Nathan J., *When Victory Is Not an Option: Islamist Movements in Arab Politics* (Ithaca, NY: Cornell University Press, 2012)

Buzan, Barry, Ole Wæver and Jaap de Wilde, *Security: A New Framework for Analysis* (Boulder, CO: Lynne Rienner, 1998)

Calvert, John, *Sayyid Qutb and the Origins of Radical Islamism* (London: Hurst, 2009)

Camosy, Charles A., *For Love of Animals: Christian Ethics, Consistent Action* (Cincinnati: Franciscan Media, 2013)

Capps, Walter H., *Religious Studies: The Making of a Discipline* (Minneapolis: Fortress Press, 1995)

Cardoso, Fernando Henrique and Enzo Faletto, *Dependency and Development in Latin America* (Berkeley, CA: University of California Press, 1979)

Caridi, Paola, *Hamas: From Resistance to Government* (New York: Seven Stories Press, 2012)

Castoriadis, Cornelius, *A Society Adrift, Interviews and Debates, 1974–1997* (New York: Fordham University Press, 2010)

Chapman, John Alexander, *Maxims of Ali* (Lahore: Sh. M. Ashraf, 1968)

Charbonneau-Lassay, Louis, *The Symbolic Animals of Christianity* (London: Stuart & Watkins, 1970)

Chehab, Zaki, *Inside Hamas: The Untold Story of the Militant Islamic Movement* (New York: Nation, 2007)

Choueiri, Youssef M., *Islamic Fundamentalism* (London: Pinter, 1990)

Chryssavgis, John and Bruce V. Foltz (eds), *Toward an Ecology of Transfiguration: Orthodox Christian Perspectives on Environment, Nature, and Creation* (New York: Fordham University Press, 2013)

Cloutier, David, *Walking God's Earth: The Environment and Catholic Faith* (Collegeville, MN: Liturgical Press, 2014)

Cockburn, Patrick, *The Rise of Islamic State: ISIS and the New Sunni Revolution* (London and New York: Verso, 2015)

Cohen, Amnon, *Political Parties in the West Bank under the Jordanian Regime, 1949–1967* (Ithaca, NY: Cornell University Press, 1982)

Copleston, Frederick Charles, *Aquinas: An Introduction to the Life and Work of the Great Medieval Thinker* (London: Penguin, 1991)

Cox, Harvey Gallagher, *Religion in the Secular City: Toward a Postmodern Theology* (New York: Simon & Schuster, 1984)

Crone, Patricia and Michael Cook, *Hagarism: The Making of the Islamic World* (Cambridge: Cambridge University Press, 1977)

Dabashi, Hamid, *Theology of Discontent: The Ideological Foundations of the Islamic Revolution in Iran* (New Brunswick, NJ: Transaction, 2006)

Daher, Joseph, *Hezbollah: The Political Economy of Lebanon's Party of God* (London: Pluto Press, 2016)

Dalai Lama, *Freedom in Exile: The Autobiography of His Holiness the Dalai Lama of Tibet* (London: Hodder & Stoughton, 1990)

Dalton, Russell J., *The Green Rainbow: Environmental Groups in Western Europe* (New Haven, CT: Yale University Press, 1994)

Al-Dawoody, Ahmed, *The Islamic Law of War: Justifications and Regulations* (New York: Palgrave Macmillan, 2011)

Deane-Drummond, Celia, *Eco-Theology* (London: Darton, Longman & Todd, 2008)

DeLong-Bas, Natana J., *Wahhabi Islam: From Revival and Reform to Global Jihad* (Oxford: Oxford University Press, 2004)

Denzin, Norman K., *Sociological Methods: A Sourcebook*, 2nd ed. (New York: McGraw-Hill, 1978)

Deuraseh, Nurdeng, *Islam: Faith, Shari'ah and Civilization – An Interpretation for Better Civilization* (Kuala Lumpur: Attin Press, 2015)

Dowie, Mark, *Losing Ground: American Environmentalism at the Close of the Twentieth Century* (Cambridge, MA: MIT Press, 1995)

Egerton, Frazer, *Jihad in the West: The Rise of Militant Salafism* (Cambridge: Cambridge University Press, 2011)

Eliade, Mircea, *Images and Symbols: Studies in Religious Symbolism* (Princeton, NJ: Princeton University Press, 1991)

Ernst, Carl W. and Richard C. Martin, *Rethinking Islamic Studies: From Orientalism to Cosmopolitanism* (Columbia: University of South Carolina Press, 2010)

Esposito, John L., *The Islamic Threat: Myth or Reality?*, 3rd ed. (New York: Oxford University Press, 1999)

Al-Faruqi, Ismail, *Islam and Other Faiths* (Leicester: Islamic Foundation, 1998)

Faruqui, Naser J., Asit K. Biswas and Murad J. Bino (eds), *Water Management in Islam* (Tokyo: United Nations University Press, 2001).

Fitzpatrick, Coeli and Adam Hani Walker, *Muhammad in History, Thought, and*

Culture: An Encyclopedia of the Prophet of God (Santa Barbara, CA: ABC-CLIO, 2014)

Foltz, Richard C., *Animals in Islamic Traditions and Muslim Cultures* (London: Oneworld, 2014)

Foltz, Richard C., Frederick M. Denny and Azizan Baharuddin (eds), *Islam and Ecology: A Bestowed Trust* (Cambridge, MA: Harvard University Press, 2003)

Fox, Stephen, *The American Conservation Movement: John Muir and His Legacy* (Madison: University of Wisconsin Press, 1986)

Gaard, Greta, *Ecological Politics: Ecofeminists and the Greens* (Philadelphia: Temple University Press, 1998)

Gade, Anna M., *Muslim Environmentalisms: Religious and Social Foundations* (New York: Columbia University Press, 2019)

Gambetta, Diego and Steffen Hertog, *Engineers of Jihad: The Curious Connection between Violent Extremism and Education* (Princeton, NJ: Princeton University Press, 2016)

Geertz, Clifford, *The Interpretation of Cultures* (New York: Basic, 1973)

Gerges, Fawaz A., *The Rise and Fall of Al-Qaeda* (New York: Oxford University Press, 2011)

Gould, Kenneth A., Allan Schnaiberg and Adam S. Weinberg, *Local Environmental Struggles: Citizen Activism in the Treadmill of Production* (Cambridge: Cambridge University Press, 1996)

Graham, Otis L. Jr (ed.), *Environmental Politics and Policy, 1960s–1990s* (University Park, PA: Pennsylvania State University Press, 2000)

Al-Gulpaygani, Ayatullah Lutfullah as-Safi, *Discussion Concerning al-Mahdi* (Qum: Ansariyan, 2001)

Gunning, Jeroen, *Hamas in Politics: Democracy, Religion, Violence* (London: Hurst, 2007)

Haddad, Fanar, *Sectarianism in Iraq: Antagonistic Visions of Unity* (London: Hurst, 2011)

Hafez, Mohammed M., *Suicide Bombers in Iraq: The Strategy and Ideology of Martyrdom* (Washington, DC: United States Institute of Peace, 2007)

Haider, Najam, *Shi'i Islam: An Introduction* (New York: Cambridge University Press, 2014)

Hak, Gordon, *Locating the Left in Difficult Times: Framing a Political Discourse for the Present* (Cham: Palgrave Macmillan, 2017)

Haleem, Harfiyah Abdel (ed.), *Islam and the Environment* (London: Ta-Ha, 1998)

Hallaq, Wael B., *The Impossible State: Islam, Politics, and Modernity's Moral Predicament* (New York: Columbia University Press, 2013)

Hamzeh, Ahmad Nizar, *In the Path of Hizbullah* (Syracuse, NY: Syracuse University Press, 2004)

Hancock, Rosemary, *Islamic Environmental Activism in the United States and Great Britain* (Abingdon: Routledge, 2017)

Haq, Gary and Alistair Paul, *Environmentalism since 1945* (London: Routledge, 2011)

Harik, Judith Palmer, *Hezbollah: The Changing Face of Terrorism* (London: I. B. Tauris, 2004)

Hegghammer, Thomas (ed.), *Jihadi Culture: The Art and Social Practices of Militant Islamists* (Cambridge: Cambridge University Press, 2017)

Helmy, Mustafa Mahmud, *Islam and Environment 2: Animal Life* (Kuwait: Environment Protection Council, 1989)

Hokayem, Emile, *Syria's Uprising and the Fracturing of the Levant* (Abingdon: Routledge, 2013)

Holman, John, *The Return of the Perennial Philosophy: The Supreme Vision of Western Esotericism* (London: Watkins, 2008)

Hroub, Khaled, *Hamas: A Beginner's Guide* (London: Pluto Press, 2006)

Hroub, Khaled, *Hamas: Political Thought and Practice* (Washington, DC: Institute of Palestine Studies, 2000)

Hughes, Aaron, *Theorizing Islam: Disciplinary Deconstruction and Reconstruction* (Durham, England: Acumen, 2014)

Huntington, Samuel P., *The Clash of Civilizations and the Remaking of World Order* (New York: Simon & Schuster, 1996)

Husaini, S. Waqar Ahmad, *Islamic Environmental Systems Engineering* (London: Macmillan, 1980)

Ibrahim, Gehan S. A., *Virtues in Muslim Culture: An Interpretation from Islamic Literature, Art and Architecture* (London: New Generation, 2014)

Ignatow, Gabriel, *Transnational Identity Politics and the Environment* (Lanham, ND: Lexington, 2007)

Inoue, Takashi, *Public Relations in Hyper-globalization: Essential Relationship Management – A Japan Perspective* (Abingdon: Routledge, 2018)

Izzi Dien, Mawil, *The Environmental Dimensions of Islam* (Cambridge: Lutterworth Press, 2000)

Jasper, James M. and Dorothy Nelkin, *The Animal Rights Crusade: The Growth of a Moral Protest* (New York: Free Press, 1991)

Al-Jibouri, Yasin T., *Kerbala and Beyond* (Qum: Ansariyan, 2002)

Jones, James W., *Can Science Explain Religion? The Cognitive Science Debate* (New York: Oxford University Press, 2016)

Kalechofsky, Roberta, *Judaism and Animal Rights: Classical and Contemporary Responses* (Marblehead, MA: Micah, 1992)

Kartanegara, Mulyadhi, *Essentials of Islamic Epistemology* (Bandar Seri Begawan: Universiti Brunei Darussalam, 2014)

Kepel, Gilles, *Muslim Extremism in Egypt: The Prophet and the Pharaoh* (Berkeley, CA: University of California Press, 1984)

Kersten, Carool, *Cosmopolitans and Heretics: New Muslim Intellectuals and the Study of Islam* (London: Hurst, 2011)

Khadduri, Majid, *The Islamic Conception of Justice* (Baltimore: Johns Hopkins University Press, 1984)

Khalil, Fazlun M. and Joanne O'Brien, *Islam and Ecology* (London: Cassell, 1992)

Khan, Muhammad Akram, *Islamic Economics and Finance: A Glossary*, 2nd ed. (London: Routledge, 2003)

Khomeini, Imam, *Islam and Revolution: Writings and Declarations* (Berkeley, CA: Mizan Press, 1981)

Khomeini, Imam, *Islamic Government: Governance of the Jurist* (Tehran: Institute for Compilation and Publication of Imam Khomeini's Works, 2002)

Kohlenberger, John R. (ed.), *NIV Interlinear Hebrew-English Old Testament* (Grand Rapids, MI: Zondervan, 1979)

Lawrence, Bruce, *Defenders of God: The Fundamentalist Revolt against the Modern Age* (London: I. B. Tauris, 1990)

Lawrence, Bruce (ed.), *Messages to the World: The Statements of Osama Bin Laden* (London and New York: Verso, 2005)

Leaman, Oliver, *The Qur'an: An Encyclopedia* (Abingdon: Routledge, 2006)

Leeuw, G. van der, *Religion in Essence and Manifestation: A Study in Phenomenology* (New York: Macmillan, 1938)

Lefèvre, Raphaël, *Ashes of Hama: The Muslim Brotherhood in Syria* (New York: Oxford University Press, 2013)

Leifer, Michael, *Dictionary of the Modern Politics of Southeast Asia* (London: Routledge, 1995)

Lesch, David W., *Syria: The Fall of the House of Assad* (New Haven, CT: Yale University Press, 2012)

Levitt, Matthew, *Hamas: Politics, Charity, and Terrorism in the Service of Jihad* (New Haven, CT, and London: Yale University Press, 2006)

Levitt, Matthew, *Hezbollah: The Global Footprint of Lebanon's Party of God* (Washington, DC: Georgetown University Press, 2013)

Lewis, Bernard, *What Went Wrong? The Clash between Islam and Modernity in the Middle East* (London: Weidenfeld & Nicolson, 2002)

Lijphart, Arend, *Thinking about Democracy: Power Sharing and Majority Rule in Theory and Practice* (Abingdon: Routledge, 2008)

Lincoln, Bruce, *Holy Terrors: Thinking about Religion after September 11*, 2nd ed. (Chicago: University of Chicago Press, 2006)

Linzey, Andrew, *Animal Rights: A Christian Assessment of Man's Treatment of Animals* (London: SCM Press, 1976)

Linzey, Andrew, *Christianity and the Rights of Animals* (Eugene, OR: Wipf & Stock, 2016)

McCormick, John, *The Global Environmental Movement*, 2nd ed. (Chichester: Wiley, 1995)

McCutcheon, Russell T., *Manufacturing Religion: The Discourse on Sui Generis Religion and the Politics of Nostalgia* (New York: Oxford University Press, 1997)

Al-Mallah, Hashim Y., *The Governmental System of the Prophet Muhammad: A Comparative Study in Constitutional Law* (Beirut: Dar al-Kotob al-Ilmiyah, 2011)

Martin, Richard C., *Approaches to Islam in Religious Studies* (Oxford: Oneworld, 1985)

Martin, Richard (ed.), *Encyclopedia of Islam and the Muslim World* (New York: Macmillan, 2004)

Masri, B. A., *Islamic Concern for Animals* (Petersfield, England: Athene Trust, 1987)

Maududi, Abul Ala, *Islamic Law and Constitution* (Lahore: Islamic Publications, 1960)

Mavani, Hamid, *Religious Authority and Political Thought in Twelver Shi'ism: From Ali to Post-Khomeini* (Abingdon: Routledge, 2013)

Mecham, Quinn and Julie Chernov Hwang, *Islamist Parties and Political Normalization in the Muslim World* (Philadelphia: University of Pennsylvania Press, 2014)

Mernissi, Fatima, *The Veil and The Male Elite: A Feminist Interpretation Of Women's Rights In Islam* (New York: Basic, 1992)

Milton-Edwards, Beverley and Stephen Farrell, *Hamas: The Islamic Resistance Movement* (Cambridge: Polity, 2010)

Mishal, Shaul and Avraham Sela, *The Palestinian Hamas: Vision, Violence, and Coexistence* (New York: Columbia University Press, 2006)

Mitchell, Richard P., *The Society of the Muslim Brothers* (London: Oxford University Press, 1969)

Moghadam, Assaf (ed.), *Militancy and Political Violence in Shiism: Trends and Patterns* (Abingdon: Routledge, 2012)

Mohamed, Yasien, *Fitrah: The Islamic Concept of Human Nature* (London: Ta-Ha, 1996)

Monshipouri, Mahmood, *Muslims in Global Politics: Identities, Interests, and Human Rights* (Philadelphia: University of Pennsylvania Press, 2009)

Müller, F. Max, *Introduction to the Science of Religion*, new ed. (London: Longmans, Green, 1882)

Nasr, Seyyed Hossein, *Man and Nature: The Spiritual Crisis of Modern Man*, new ed. (London: Unwin Paperbacks, 1990)

Nasr, Seyyed Hossein, *Religion and the Order of Nature* (New York: Oxford University Press, 1996)

Nasr, Seyyed Vali Reza, *Islamic Leviathan: Islam and the Making of State Power* (New York: Oxford University Press, 2001)

Nasr, Vali, *The Shia Revival: How Conflicts within Islam Will Shape the Future* (New York: W. W. Norton, 2007)

Nejima, Susumu (ed.), *NGOs in the Muslim World: Faith and Social Services* (Abingdon: Routledge, 2016)

The New English Bible, 2nd ed. (Oxford: Oxford University Press, 1970)

Noe, Nicholas (ed.), *Voice of Hezbollah: The Statements of Sayyed Hassan Nasrallah* (London: Verso, 2007)

Northcott, Michael S., *The Environment and Christian Ethics* (Cambridge: Cambridge University Press, 1996)

Nüsse, Andrea, *Muslim Palestine: The Ideology of Hamas* (Amsterdam: Harwood Academic, 1998)

O'Brien, Kevin J., *An Ethics of Biodiversity: Christianity, Ecology, and the Variety of Life* (Washington, DC: Georgetown University Press, 2010)

Oliver, Anne Marie and Paul F. Steinberg, *The Road to Martyrs' Square: A Journey into the World of the Suicide Bomber* (New York: Oxford University Press, 2006)

O'Neill, Michael, *Green Parties and Political Change in Contemporary Europe: New Politics, Old Predicaments* (Brookfield, VT: Ashgate, 1997)

Osman, Mohamed Nawab Mohamed, *Hizbut Tahrir Indonesia and Political Islam: Identity, Ideology and Religio-Political Mobilization* (Abingdon: Routledge, 2018)

Osman, Tarek, *Egypt on the Brink: From Nasser to the Muslim Brotherhood* (New Haven, CT, and London: Yale University Press, 2013)

Özdemir, Ibrahim, *The Ethical Dimension of Human Attitude towards Nature: A Muslim Perspective* (Istanbul: Insan, 2008)

Palmer, Tim, *Endangered Rivers and the Conservation Movement*, 2nd ed. (Lanham, MD: Rowman & Littlefield, 2004)

Pankhurst, Reza, *Hizb ut-Tahrir: The Untold History of the Liberation Party* (London: Hurst, 2016)

Al-Qaradawi, Yusuf, *Education and Economy in the Sunnah* (Cairo: Al-Falah Foundation, 2005)

Al-Qaradawi, Yusuf, *Faith and Life* (Cairo: Al-Falah Foundation, 2004)

Al-Qaradawi, Yusuf, *Fiqh al-Jihad* ('The Jurisprudence of Jihad') (Cairo: Wehbe Press, 2009)

Al-Qaradawi, Yusuf, *Fiqh al-Zakah: A Comparative Study of Zakah, Regulations and Philosophy in the Light of the Qur'an and Sunnah* (Jeddah: Scientific Publishing Centre, n.d.)

Al-Qaradawi, Yusuf, *The Lawful and Prohibited in Islam*, http://www.usislam.org/pdf/Lawful&Prohibited.pdf

Al-Qaradawi, Yusuf, *Priorities of the Islamic Movement in the Coming Phase* (Cairo: Al-Dar, 1992)

Qassem, Naim, *Hizbullah: The Story from Within* (London: Saqi, 2005)

Qutb, Sayyid, *A Child from the Village* (Syracuse, NY: Syracuse University Press, 2004)

Qutb, Sayyid, *Milestones*, rev. ed. (Chicago: American Trust, 2005)

Radical Islam in Central Asia: Responding to Hizb ut-Tahrir, International Crisis Group, 30 June, 2003, https://d2071andvip0wj.cloudfront.net/58-radical-islam-in-central-asia-responding-to-hizb-ut-tahrir.pdf

Ramadan, Tariq, *Introduction to Islam* (New York: Oxford University Press, 2017)

Ramadan, Tariq, *Islam and the Arab Awakening* (New York: Oxford University Press, 2012)

Ramadan, Tariq, *Radical Reform: Islamic ethics and Liberation* (Oxford: Oxford University Press, 2009)

Ramadan, Tariq, *Western Muslims and the Future of Islam* (New York: Oxford University Press, 2004)

Rand, Ayn, *Return of the Primitive: The Anti-Industrial Revolution* (New York: Meridian, 1999)

Rashid, Ahmed, *Taliban: Militant Islam, Oil and Fundamentalism in Central Asia*, 2nd ed. (New Haven, CT: Yale University Press, 2010)

Ratzinger, Joseph, *Salt of the Earth: The Church at the End of the Millennium – An Interview with Peter Seewald* (San Francisco: Ignatius Press, 1997)

Al-Raysuni, Ahmad, *Imam al-Shatibi's Theory of the Higher Objectives and Intents of Islamic Law* (Herndon, VA: International Institute of Islamic Thought, 2013)

Rheingold, Howard, *The Virtual Community: Homesteading on the Electronic Frontier* (Reading, MA: Addison-Wesley: 1993)

Rouse, Carolyn Moxley, *Engaged Surrender: African American Women and Islam* (Berkeley, CA: University of California Press, 2004)

Roy, Sara, *Hamas and Civil Society in Gaza: Engaging the Islamist Social Sector* (Princeton, NJ: Princeton University Press, 2013)

Rubin, Barry (ed.), *The Muslim Brotherhood: The Organization and Policies of a Global Islamist Movement* (New York: Palgrave Macmillan, 2010)

Ryan, Michael W. S., *Decoding Al-Qaeda's Strategy: The Deep Battle against America* (New York: Columbia University Press, 2013)

Saad-Ghorayeb, Amal, *Hizbu'llah: Politics and Religion* (London: Pluto Press, 2002)

Sachedina, Abdulaziz Abdulhussein, *The Just Ruler (al-suktan al-adil) in Shi'ite Islam: The Comprehensive Authority of the Jurist in Imamite Jurisprudence* (New York: Oxford University Press, 1988)

Al-Sadr, Mohammad Baqir, *Our Economics, vol. 2*, 2nd ed. (Tehran: World Organization for Islamic Services, 1994)

Sadri, Mahmoud and Ahmad Sadri (eds), *Reason, Freedom, and Democracy in Islam: Essential Writings of Abdolkarim Soroush* (New York: Oxford University Press, 2000)

Al-Safa, Ikhwan, *The Case of the Animals versus Man before the King of the Jinn: A Tenth-Century Ecological Fable of the Pure Brethren of Basra* (Boston: Twayne, 1978)

Sageman, Marc, *Leaderless Jihad: Terror Networks in the Twenty-First Century* (Philadelphia: University of Pennsylvania Press, 2008)

Said, Edward W., *Orientalism* (New York: Penguin, 2003)

Salmoni, Barak A., Bryce Loidolt and Madeleine Wells, *Regime and Periphery in Northern Yemen: The Huthi Phenomenon* (Santa Monica, CA: RAND, 2010)

Sardar, Ziauddin (ed.), *The Touch of Midas: Science, Values and the Environment in Islam and the West* (Manchester: Manchester University Press, 1984)

Sato, Tsugitaka, *State and Rural Society in Medieval Islam: Sultans, Muqta's, and Fallahun* (Leiden: Brill, 1997)

Sayeed, Khalid Bin, *Western Dominance and Political Islam*: Challenge and Response (Albany: State University of New York Press, 1995)

Sayyid, S., *Fundamental Fear: Eurocentrism and the Emergence of Islamism* (London: Zed, 2003)

Schaeffer, Francis, *Pollution and the Death of Man: The Christian View of Ecology* (Wheaton, IL: Crossway, 1970)

Scheffer, Victor B., *The Shaping of Environmentalism in America* (Seattle: University of Washington Press, 1991)

Schimmel, Annemarie, *Deciphering the Signs of God: A Phenomenological Approach to Islam* (Albany: State University of New York Press, 1994)

Scott, Peter, *A Political Theology of Nature* (Cambridge, Cambridge University Press, 2003)

Sears, David, *The Vision of Eden: Animal Welfare and Vegetarianism in Jewish Law and Mysticism* (Spring Valley, NY: Orot, 2003)

Sedgwick, Mark, *Muhammad Abduh* (London: Oneworld, 2009)

Shari'ati, Ali, *What Is to Be Done? The Enlightened Thinkers and an Islamic Renaissance* (North Haledon, NJ., Islamic Publications International, 1986)

Sharma, Jyotirmaya, *Hindutva: Exploring the Idea of Hindu Nationalism* (New Delhi: Viking, 2003)

Sharpe, Eric J., *Understanding Religion* (London: Duckworth, 1983)

Siegel, Seth M., *Let There Be Water: Israel's Solution for a Water-Starved World* (New York: St Martin's Press, 2015)

Silber, Mitchell D., *The Al Qaeda Factor: Plots against the West* (Philadelphia: University of Pennsylvania Press, 2012)

Singer, Peter, *Ethics into Action: Henry Spira and the Animal Rights Movement* (Lanham, MD: Rowman & Littlefield, 1999)

Sivan, Emmanuel, *Radical Islam: Medieval Theology and Modern Politics* (New Haven, CT: Yale University Press, 1985)

Smart, Ninian, *The Science of Religion and the Sociology of Knowledge: Some Methodological Questions* (Princeton, NJ: Princeton University Press, 1973)

Smith, Jonathan Z., *Map is not Territory: Studies in the History of Religions* (Chicago: University of Chicago Press, 1993)

So, Alvin Y., *Social Change and Development: Modernization, Dependency, and World-System Theories* (Newbury Park, CA: Sage, 1990)

Stern, Jessica and J. M. Berger, *ISIS: The State of Terror* (London: William Collins, 2015)

Stiegler, Bernard, *Symbolic Misery, vol. 1: The Hyperindustrial Epoch* (Cambridge: Polity Press, 2014)

Swanborn, Peter, *Case Study Research: What, Why and How?* (London: Sage, 2010)

Tadros, Mariz, *The Muslim Brotherhood in Contemporary Egypt: Democracy Redefined or Confined?* (Abingdon: Routledge, 2012)

Taji-Farouki, Suha, *A Fundamental Quest: Hizb al-Tahrir and the Search for the Islamic Caliphate* (London: Grey Seal, 1996)

Al Tamamy, Saud M. S., *Averroes, Kant and the Origins of the Enlightenment: Reason and Revelation* (London and New York: I. B. Tauris, 2014)

Tamimi, Azzam, *Hamas: A History from Within* (Northampton, MA: Olive Branch Press, 2011)

Thomas, Scott M., *The Global Resurgence of Religion and the Transformation of International Relations: The Struggle for the Soul of the Twenty-First Century* (New York: Palgrave Macmillan, 2005)

Tibi, Bassam, *Islam: Between Culture and Politics* (Basingstoke: Palgrave, 2001)

Tirosh-Samuelson, Hava, *Judaism and Ecology: Created World and Revealed World* (Cambridge, MA: Center for the Study of World Religions, Harvard Divinity School, 2002)

Toperoff, Shlomo Pesach, *The Animal Kingdom in Jewish Thought* (Northvale, NJ: Jason Aronson, 1995)

Van Houtan, Kyle S. and Michael S. Northcott (eds), *Diversity and Dominion: Dialogues in Ecology, Ethics, and Theology* (Eugene, OR: Cascade, 2010)

Wach, Joachim, *Sociology of Religion* (London: Kegan Paul, Trench, Trubner, 1947)

Walker, Gordon, *Environmental Justice: Concepts, Evidence and Politics* (Abingdon: Routledge, 2012)

Wansbrough, John, *Quranic Studies: Sources and Methods of Scriptural Interpretation* (New York: Prometheus, 2004)

Warrick, Joby, *Black Flags: The Rise of ISIS* (New York: Doubleday, 2015)

Watt, William Montgomery, *Islamic Fundamentalism and Modernity* (London: Routledge, 1988)

Weber, Max, *The Protestant Ethic and the Spirit of Capitalism* (Mineola, NY: Dover, [1905] 2003)

Weiss, Michael and Hassan Hassan, *ISIS: Inside the Army of Terror* (New York: Regan Arts, 2015)

Wellman, David J., *Sustainable Diplomacy: Ecology, Religion, and Ethics in Muslim–Christian Relations* (New York: Palgrave Macmillan, 2004)

Whitehouse, Bill, *Reality without a Name: A Critique of 'Sufism: A Short Introduction'* (Bangor, ME: Interrogative Imperative Institute, 2009)

Wickham, Carrie Rosefsky, *The Muslim Brotherhood: Evolution of an Islamist Movement* (Princeton, NJ: Princeton University Press, 2013)

Wiebe, Donald, *The Politics of Religious Studies: The Continuing Conflict with Theology in the Academy* (New York: Palgrave, 1999)

Wilkinson, Katharine K., *Between God and Green: How Evangelicals Are Cultivating a Middle Ground on Climate Change* (New York: Oxford University Press, 2012)

Wolf, Anne, *Political Islam in Tunisia: The History of Ennahda* (London: Hurst, 2017)

Yaffe, Martin D, *Judaism and Environmental Ethics: A Reader* (Lanham, MD: Lexington, 2001)

Zeidan, David, *The Resurgence of Religion: A Comparative Study of Selected Themes in Christian and Islamic Fundamentalist Discourses* (Leiden: Brill, 2003)

Zollner, Barbara H. E., *The Muslim Brotherhood: Hasan al-Hudaybi and Ideology* (Abingdon: Routledge, 2009)

Book Chapters

Aftab, Tahera, 'Text and Practice: Women and Nature in Islam', in Alaine Low and Soraya Tremayne (eds), *Custodians of the Earth? Women, Spirituality and the Environment* (New York and Oxford: Berghahn, 2001)

Ahmed, Rumee, 'Islamic Law and Theology', in Anver M. Emon and Rumee Ahmed (eds), *The Oxford Handbook of Islamic Law* (Oxford: Oxford University Press, 2018)

Alagha, Joseph, 'Hezbollah's Conception of the Islamic State', in Sabrina Mervin (ed.), *The Shi'a Worlds and Iran* (London: Saqi, 2010)

Altman, Israel Elad, 'Egypt', in Barry Rubin (ed.), *Guide to Islamist Movements* (Armonk, NY: M. E. Sharpe, 2010), vol. 1

Antonsich, Marco, 'Territory and Territoriality', in Douglas Richardson (ed.), *The International Encyclopedia of Geography: People, the Earth, Environment and Technology* (New York: Wiley-Blackwell, 2017)

Arjomand, Said Amir, 'Social Movements in the Contemporary Near and Middle East', in Said Amir Arjomand (ed.), *From Nationalism to Revolutionary Islam* (London: Macmillan, 1984)

Al-Banna, Hassan, 'Our Mission', in International Islamic Federation of Student Organizations, *Majmu'at Rasa'il al-Imam al-Shahid Hasan al-Banna* (Kuwait City: International Islamic Federation of Student Organizations, 1996)

Al-Banna, Hassan, 'Toward the Light', in Roxanne L. Euben and Muhammad Qasim Zaman (eds), *Princeton Readings in Islamist Thought: Texts and Contexts from al-Banna to Bin Laden* (Princeton, NJ: Princeton University Press, 2009)

Bazzano, Elliott, 'Research Problems and Methods', in Clinton Bennett (ed.), *The*

Bloomsbury Companion to Islamic Studies (London and New York: Bloomsbury, 2013)

Boase, Roger, 'Ecumenical Islam: A Response to Religious Pluralism', in Roger Boase (ed.), *Islam and Global Dialogue: Religious Pluralism and the Pursuit of Peace* (Farnham: Ashgate, 2010)

Al-Din al-Afghani, Sayyid Jamal, 'An Islamic Response to Imperialism', in John J. Donohue and John L. Esposito (eds), *Islam in Transition: Muslim Perspectives* (New York: Oxford University Press, 1982)

Foltz, Richard C., 'Islam', in Roger S. Gottlieb (ed.), *The Oxford Handbook of Religion and Ecology* (New York: Oxford University Press, 2006)

Foltz, Richard C., 'Islamic Environmentalism: A Matter of Interpretation', in Richard C. Foltz, Frederick M. Denny and Azizan Baharuddin (eds), *Islam and Ecology: A Bestowed Trust* (Cambridge, MA: Harvard University Press, 2003)

Foltz, Richard C., 'Mawil Izzi Dien', in Bron R. Taylor (ed.), *Encyclopaedia of Religion and Nature* (London: Thoemmes, 2005)

Gleave, Robert, 'Political Aspects of Modern Shi'i Legal Discussions: Khumayni and Khu'i on *ijtihad* and *qada''*, in B. A. Roberson (ed.), *Shaping the Current Islamic Reformation* (London: Frank Cass, 2003)

Heck, Paul L., 'Knowledge', in Gerhard Bowering (ed.), *Islamic Political Thought: An Introduction* (Princeton, NJ: Princeton University Press, 2015)

Irwin, Robert, 'Political Thought in the Thousand and One Nights', in Ulrich Marzolph (ed.), *Arabian Nights in Transnational Perspective* (Detroit: Wayne State University Press, 2007)

Izzi Dien, Mawil Y., 'Islamic Environmental Ethics: Law and Society', in J. Ronald Engel and Joan G. Engel (eds), *Ethics of Environment and Development* (London: Belhaven, 1990)

Johnston, Hank, 'New Social Movements and Old Regional Nationalisms', in Enrique Larana, Hank Johnston and Joseph R. Gusfield (eds), *New Social Movements: From Ideology to Identity* (Philadelphia: Temple University Press, 1994)

Khalid, Fazlun, 'Islam, Ecology and Modernity: An Islamic Critique of the Root Causes of Environmental Degradation', in Richard C. Foltz, Frederick M. Denny and Azizan Baharuddin (eds), *Islam and Ecology: A Bestowed Trust* (Cambridge, MA: Harvard University Press, 2003)

Khalid, Fazlun, 'Islamic Basis for Environmental Protection', in Bron R. Taylor (ed.), *Encyclopedia of Religion and Nature* (London: Thoemmes, 2005)

Makdisi, Karim, 'The Rise and Decline of Environmentalism in Lebanon', in Alan

Mikhail (ed.), *Water on Sand: Environmental Histories of the Middle East and North Africa* (New York: Oxford University Press, 2012)

Masri, Al-Hafiz, 'Animal Experimentation: The Muslim Viewpoint', in Tom Regan (ed.), *Animal Sacrifices: Religious Perspectives on the Use of Animals in Science* (Philadelphia: Temple University Press, 1986)

Mavani, Hamid, 'Analysis of Khomeini's Proofs for *al-Wilaya al-Mutlaqa* (Comprehensive Authority) of the Jurist', in Linda S. Walbridge (ed.), *The Most Learned of the Shi'a: The Institution of the Marja' Taqlid* (New York: Oxford University Press, 2001)

Mecham, Quinn, 'Islamist Parties as Strategic Actors: Electoral Participation and its Consequences', in Quinn Mecham and Julie Chernov Hwang (eds), *Islamist Parties and Political Normalization in the Muslim World* (Philadelphia: University of Pennsylvania Press, 2014)

Meijer, Roel, 'Introduction', in Roel Meijer (ed.), *Global Salafism: Islam's New Religious Movement* (London: Hurst, 2009)

Mernissi, Fatima, 'A Feminist Interpretation of Women's Rights in Islam', in Charles Kurzman (ed.), *Liberal Islam: A Sourcebook* (New York: Oxford University Press, 1998)

Molen, Irna van der and Nora Stel, 'Multi-Stakeholder Partnerships in Fragile Political Contexts: Experiences from the Palestinian Water and Waste Sector', in Cheryl de Boer, Joanne Vinke-de Kruijf, Gül Özerol and Hans Bressers (eds), *Water Governance, Policy and Knowledge Transfer: International Studies on Contextual Water Management* (Abingdon: Routledge, 2013)

Naguib, Shuruq, 'Horizons and Limitations of Feminist Muslim Hermeneutics: Reflections on the Menstruation Verse', in Pamela Sue Anderson (ed.), *New Topics in Feminist Philosophy of Religion: Contestations and Transcendence Incarnate* (Dordrecht: Springer Press, 2010)

Nasr, Seyyed Hossein, 'The Ecological Problem in Light of Sufism: The Conquest of Nature and the Teachings of Eastern Science', in *Sufi Essays*, 2nd ed. (Albany: State University of New York Press, 1991)

Nasr, Seyyed Hossein, 'Islam, the Contemporary Islamic World, and the Environmental Crisis', in Richard R. Foltz, Frederick M. Denny and Azizan Baharuddin (eds), *Islam and Ecology: A Bestowed Trust* (Cambridge, MA: Harvard University Press, 2003)

Nasr, Seyyed Hossein, 'Sacred Science and the Environmental Crisis: An Islamic Perspective', in Harifyah Abdel Haleem (ed.), *Islam and the Environment* (London: Ta-Ha, 1998)

Ostovar, Afshon, 'The Visual Culture of Jihad', in Thomas Hegghammer (ed.), *Jihadi Culture: The Art and Social Practices of Militant Islamists* (Cambridge: Cambridge University Press, 2017)

Pusch, Barbara, 'The Greening of Islamic Politics: A Godsend for the Environment?', in Fikret Adaman and Murat Arsel (eds), *Environmentalism in Turkey: Between Democracy and Development?* (Abingdon and New York: Routledge, 2016)

Raji al-Faruqi, Ismail, 'Islam and Zionism', in John L. Esposito (ed.), *Voices of Resurgent Islam* (New York: Oxford University Press, 1983)

Roy, Olivier, 'The Impact of the Iranian Revolution on the Middle East', in Sabrina Mervin (ed.), *The Shi'a Worlds and Iran* (London: Saqi, 2010)

Salvatore, Armando, 'Modernity', in Gerhard Bowering (ed.), *Islamic Political Thought: An Introduction* (Princeton, NJ: Princeton University Press, 2015)

Şen, Mustafa, 'Transformation of Turkish Islamism and the Rise of the Justice and Development Party' in Birol Yeşilada and Barry Rubin (eds), *Islamization of Turkey Under the AKP Rule* (London: Routledge, 2011)

Siddiq, Mohammad Yusuf, 'An Ecological Journey in Muslim Bengal', in Richard C. Foltz, Frederick M. Denny and Azizan Baharuddin (eds), *Islam and Ecology: A Bestowed Trust* (Cambridge, MA: Harvard University Press, 2003)

Soage, Ana Belén, 'Yusuf al-Qaradaqi: The Muslim Brothers' Favourite Ideological Guide', in Barry Rubin (ed.), *The Muslim Brotherhood: The Organization and Policies of a Global Islamist Movement* (New York: Palgrave Macmillan, 2010)

Söderbaum, Fredrik, 'Comparative Regional Integration and Regionalism', in Todd Landman and Neil Robinson (eds), *The Sage Handbook of Comparative Politics* (London: Sage, 2009)

Swartz, Daniel. 'Jews, Jewish Texts, and Nature: A Brief History', in Roger S. Gottlieb (ed.), *This Sacred Earth: Religion, Nature, Environment* (New York: Routledge, 1996)

Sykiainen, Leonid, 'Democracy and the Dialogue between Western and Islamic Legal Cultures: The Gülen Case', in Robert A. Hunt and Yüksel A. Aslandoğan (eds), *Muslim Citizens of the Globalized World* (Somerset, NJ: The Light, 2007)

Timm, Roger E., 'The Ecological Fallout of Islamic Creation Theology', in Mary Evelyn Tucker and John A. Grim (eds), *Worldviews and Ecology: Religion, Philosophy, and the Environment* (Lewisburg, PA: Bucknell University Press, 1993)

Tirosh-Samuelson, Hava, 'Judaism', in Roger S. Gottlieb (ed.), *The Oxford Handbook of Religion and Ecology* (New York: Oxford University Press, 2006)

Voll, John, 'Fundamentalism in the Sunni Arab World: Egypt and the Sudan', in Martin E. Marty and R. Scott Appleby (eds), *Fundamentalisms Observed* (Chicago: University of Chicago Press, 1992)

Waardenburg, Jacques, 'The Study of Islam in German Scholarship', in Azim Nanji (ed.), *Mapping Islamic Studies: Genealogy, Continuity, and Change* (Berlin and New York: Mouton de Gruyter, 1997)

Yang, Tongjin, 'Towards an Egalitarian Global Environmental Ethics', in Henk A. M. J. ten Have (ed.), *Environmental Ethics and International Policy* (Paris: UNESCO, 2006)

Zonis, Marvin and Daniel Brumberg, 'Shi'ism as Interpreted by Khomeini: An Ideology of Revolutionary Violence', in Martin Kramer (ed.), *Shi'ism, Resistance, and Revolution* (Boulder, CO: Westview Press, 1987)

Journal Articles

Abderrahman, Walid A., 'Water Demand Management and Islamic Water Management Principles: A Case Study', *International Journal of Water Resources Development*, vol. 16, no. 4, 2000, pp. 465–73

Afrasiabi, Kaveh L., 'The Environmental Movement in Iran: Perspectives from Below and Above', *Middle East Journal*, vol. 57, no. 3, 2003, pp. 432–48

Ahmad, Ali, 'Islamic Water Law as an Antidote for Maintaining Water Quality', *University of Denver Water Law Review*, vol. 2, no. 2, 1999, pp. 170–88

Alaaldin, Ranj, 'The Islamic Da'wa Party and the Mobilization of Iraq's Shi'i Community, 1958–1965', *Middle East Journal*, vol. 71, no. 1, 2017, pp. 45–65

Alpay, Savaş, Ibrahim Özdemir and Dilek Demirbaş, 'Environment and Islam', *Journal of Economic Cooperation and Development*, vol. 34, no. 4, 2013, pp. 1–22

Amery, Hussein A., 'Islamic Water Management', *Water International*, vol. 26, no. 4, 2001, pp. 481–9

Al-Azm, Sadik J., 'Islamic Fundamentalism Reconsidered: A Critical Outline of Problems, Ideas and Approaches', part 1, *Comparative Studies of South Asia, Africa and the Middle East*, vol. 13, no. 1–2, 1993, pp. 93–121

Barbato, Mariano, 'Postsecular Revolution: Religion after the End of History', *Review of International Studies*, vol. 38, no. 5, 2012, pp. 1079–97

Bos, Abraham P., 'Aristotle on the Differences between Plants, Animals, and Human Beings and on the Elements as Instruments of the Soul', *Review of Metaphysics*, vol. 63, no. 4, 2010, pp. 821–41

Bouzenita, Anke Iman, 'Early Contributions to the Theory of Islamic Governance: 'Abd al-Rahman al-Awza'i', *Journal of Islamic Studies*, vol. 23, no. 2, 2012, pp. 137–64

Bulaç, Ali, 'On Islamism: Its Roots, Development and Future', *Insight Turkey*, Fall 2012, pp. 67–85

Callaghan, John, 'Environmental Politics, the New Left and the New Social Democracy', *Political Quarterly*, vol. 71, no. 3, 2000, 300–8

Dalacoura, Katerina, 'The 2011 Uprisings in the Arab Middle East: Political Change and Geopolitical Implications', *International Affairs*, vol. 88, no. 1, 2012, pp. 63–79

Al-Damkhi, Ali Mohamed, 'Environmental Ethics in Islam: Principles, Violations, and Future Perspectives', *International Journal of Environmental Studies*, vol. 65, no. 1, 2008, pp. 11–31

Deshen, Shlomo, 'The Emergence of the Israeli Sephardi Ultra-Orthodox Movement', *Jewish Social Studies*, vol. 11, no. 2, 2005, pp. 77–101

Deuraseh, Nurdeng, 'Earth in the Holy Qur'an: How to Protect and Maintain It?', *Jurnal Hadhari*, vol. 2, no. 2, 2010, pp. 73–88

Diamond, James S., 'The Post-Secular: A Jewish Perspective', *CrossCurrents*, vol. 53, no. 4, 2004, pp. 580–606

Ebtekar, Massoumeh, 'Iran's Environmental Policy in the Reform Period (1997–2006)', *International Journal of Environmental Studies*, vol. 66, no. 3, 2009, pp. 289–96

Eisenberg, Laura Zittrain, 'Israel's South Lebanon Imbroglio', *Middle East Quarterly*, vol. 4, no. 2, 1997, pp. 60–9

Erdur, Oğuz, 'Reappropriating the "Green": Islamist Environmentalism', *New Perspectives on Turkey*, vol. 17, 1997, pp. 151–66

Fahmy, Ninette S., 'The Performance of the Muslim Brotherhood in the Egyptian Syndicates: An Alternative Formula for Reform?', *Middle East Journal*, vol. 52, no. 4, 1998, pp. 551–62

Foster, John Bellamy, 'Marx and the Rift in the Universal Metabolism of Nature', *Monthly Review*, vol. 65, no. 7, 2013, https://monthlyreview.org/2013/12/01/marx-rift-universal-metabolism-nature/

Habermas, Jürgen, 'Notes on Post-Secular Society', *New Perspectives Quarterly*, vol. 25, no. 4, 2008, pp. 17–29

Hamed, Safei El-Deen, 'Seeing the Environment through Islamic Eyes: Application of *Shariah* to Natural Resources Planning and Management', *Journal of Agricultural and Environmental Ethics*, vol. 6, no. 2, 1993, pp. 145–64

Hill, Lisa, 'Adam Smith and the Theme of Corruption', *Review of Politics*, vol. 68, no. 4 2006, pp. 636–62

Islam, Muhammad Muinul, 'Towards a Green Earth: An Islamic Perspective', *Asian Affairs*, vol. 26, no. 4, 2004, pp. 44–89

Izzi Dien, Mawil, 'Islam and the Environment: Theory and Practice', *Journal of Beliefs and Values*, vol. 18, no. 1, 1997, pp. 47–57

Izzi Dien, Mawil, 'Islam and the Environment: Towards an "Islamic" Ecumenical View', *Qur'anica*, vol. 5, no. 2, 2013, pp. 33–52

Jacobus, Robert J., 'Understanding Environmental Theology: A Summary for Environmental Educator', *Journal of Environmental Education*, vol. 35, no. 3, 2004, pp. 35–42

Jeenah, Na'eem, 'Towards an Islamic Feminist Hermeneutic', *Journal for Islamic Studies*, vol. 21, 2001, pp 36–70

Johnston, David L., 'Intra-Muslim Debates on Ecology: Is Shari'a Still Relevant?', *Worldviews*, vol. 16, no. 3, 2012, pp. 218–38

Al-Jumah, Khaled Mohammed, 'Arab State Contract Disputes: Lessons from the Past', *Arab Law Quarterly*, vol. 17, no. 3, 2002, pp. 215–40

Kaufman, Asher, 'Who Owns the Shebaa Farms? Chronicle of a Territorial Dispute', *Middle East Journal*, vol. 56, no. 4, 2002, pp. 576–95

Kay, Jeanne, 'Concepts of Nature in the Hebrew Bible', *Environmental Ethics*, vol. 10, no. 4, 1988, pp. 309–27

Kersten, Carool, 'From Braudel to Derrida: Mohammed Arkoun's Rethinking of Islam and Religion', *Middle East Journal of Culture and Communication*, vol. 4, no. 1, 2011, pp. 23–43

Kortenkamp, Katherine V. and Colleen F. Moore, 'Ecocentrism and Anthropocentrism: Moral Reasoning about Ecological Commons Dilemmas', *Journal of Environmental Psychology*, vol. 21, no. 3, 2001, pp. 261–72

Kyrlezhev, Aleksandr, 'The Postsecular Age: Religion and Culture Today', *Religion, State and Society*, vol. 36, no. 1, 2008, pp. 21–31

Lucas, Ernest, 'The New Testament Teaching on the Environment', *Transformation*, vol. 16, no. 3, 1999, pp. 93–9

MacDonald, Matthew A., 'What is a Salafi Reformist? Tariq Ramadan and Sayyid Qutb in Conversation', *Political Theology*, vol. 15, no. 5, 2014, pp. 385–405

Martin, Luther H. and Donald Wiebe, 'Religious Studies as a Scientific Discipline: The Persistence of a Delusion', *Journal of the American Academy of Religion*, vol. 80, no. 3, 2012, pp. 587–97

Martinez-Alier, Joan, Leah Temper, Daniela Del Bene and Arnim Scheidel, 'Is There a Global Environmental Justice Movement?', *Journal of Peasant Studies*, vol. 43, no. 3, 2016, pp. 731–55

Matin-asgari, Afshin, "Abdolkarim Sorush and the Secularization of Islamic Thought in Iran', *Iranian Studies*, vol. 30, no. 1–2, 1997, pp. 95–115

Nasr, Vali, 'Politics within the Late-Pahlavi State: The Ministry of Economy and Industrial Policy, 1963–69', *International Journal of Middle East Studies*, vol. 32, no. 1, 2000, pp. 97–122

Özdemir, Ibrahim, review of Muhammad Hussaini Shirazi, *Fiqh al-Bi'ah* (Islamic Environmental Law), *Worldviews*, vol. 7, no. 3, 2003, pp. 356–8

Rahman, Zaizul Ab., 'The Role of Fitrah as an Element in the Personality of a Da'i in Achieving the Identity of a True Da'i', *International Journal of Business and Social Science*, vol. 3, no. 4, 2012, pp. 165–75

Ranstorp, Magnus, 'The Strategy and Tactics of Hizballah's Current "Lebanonization" Process', *Mediterranean Politics*, vol. 3, no. 1, 1998, pp. 103–34

Reat, Noble Ross, 'The Tree Symbol in Islam', *Studies in Comparative Religion*, vol. 9, no. 3, 1975, pp. 1–19

Saniotis, Arthur, 'Muslim and Ecology: Fostering Islamic Environmental Ethics', *Contemporary Islam*, vol. 6, no. 2, 2012, pp. 155–71

Savage, Allan M., 'Phenomenological Philosophy and Orthodox Christian Scientific Ecological Theology', *Indo-Pacific Journal of Phenomenology*, vol. 8, no. 2, 2008

Siavoshi, Sussan, 'Cultural Policies and the Islamic Republic: Cinema and Book Publication', *International Journal of Middle East Studies*, vol. 29, no. 4, 1997, pp. 509–30

Sinclair, Kirstine, 'Islam in Britain and Denmark: Deterritorialized Identity and Reterritorialized Agendas', *Journal of Muslim Minority Affairs*, vol. 28, no. 1, 2008, pp. 45–52

Sindawi, Khalid, 'The Donkey of the Prophet in Shi'ite Tradition', *Al-Masaq*, vol. 18, no. 1, 2006, pp. 87–98

Singer, Morris, 'Atatürk's Economic Legacy', *Middle Eastern Studies*, vol. 19, no. 3, 1983, pp. 301–11

Springborg, Robert, 'The Political Economy of the Arab Spring', *Mediterranean Politics*, vol. 16, no. 3, 2011, pp. 427–33

Wersal, Lisa, 'Islam and Environmental Ethics: Tradition Responds to Contemporary Challenges', *Zygon*, vol. 30, no. 3, 1995, 451–59

Wescoat, James L., Jr, 'The "Right of Thirst" for Animals in Islamic Law: A Comparative Approach', *Environment and Planning D: Society and Space*, vol. 13, no. 6, 1995, pp. 637–54

White, Lynn, Jr, 'The Historical Roots of Our Ecological Crisis', *Science*, 10 March 1967, pp. 1203–7

Wilkinson, John C., 'Muslim Land and Water Law', *Journal of Islamic Studies*, vol. 1, no. 1, 1990, pp. 54–72

Yanitsky, Oleg Nikolaevich, 'From Nature Protection to Politics: The Russian Environmental Movement 1960–2010', *Environmental Politics*, vol. 21, no. 6, 2012, pp. 922–40

Yavuz, M. Hakan, 'Understanding Turkish Secularism in the 21st Century: A Contextual Roadmap', *Southeast European and Black Sea Studies*, vol. 19, no. 1, 2019, pp. 55–78

Yildirim, A. Kadir, 'Between Anti-Westernism and Development: Political Islam and Environmentalism', *Middle Eastern Studies*, vol. 52, no. 2, 2016, pp. 215–32

Yilmaz, Ihsan, 'The Varied Performance of Hizb ut-Tahrir: Success in Britain and Uzbekistan and Stalemate in Egypt and Turkey', *Journal of Muslim Minority Affairs*, vol. 30, no. 4, 2010, pp. 501–17

Zaidi, Iqtidar H., 'On the Ethics of Man's Interaction with the Environment: An Islamic Approach', *Environmental Ethics*, vol. 3, no. 1, 1981, pp. 35–47

Conference Proceedings

Dedeoglu, Cagdas, 'From Radical Islamism to Radical Environmental Transformism', Conference Proceedings of POLITSCI '13 (Istanbul: DAKAM, 2013), pp. 234–5

Fahm, Abdul Gafar Olawale, 'Factors Contending with Environmental Sustainability in Nigeria: An Islamic Approach', Proceedings of the Social Sciences Research, 9–10 June 2014, Kota Kinabalu, Malaysia

YouTube Videos

'Hamas' children TV with a terrorist Jew eating rabbit', The Evil Israel, no date, https://www.youtu.be/0YU__vFw_0E

Hamas Mickey Mouse teaches terror to kids', MediaMayhem, 8 May 2007, https://youtu.be/gi-c6lbFGC4

'Hamas Bee Abusing Animals', *MEMRI TV*, 10 August 2007, https://www.youtube.com/watch?v=GXHSCgSN5zg

'Islam wants to kill Mickey Mouse', inei9j43710hd83k34, 27 December 2009, https://www.youtu.be/6cTZ9-TCvMc

'Israel, Lebanon battle over a tree', Associated Press, 3 August 2010, https://www.youtu.be/eGHCFfpV4Q4

'Pakistan flood victims receive aid from Jamaat-e-Islami (FRANCE24 report)', RightseXclusive, 14 August 2010, https://www.youtu.be/uT1TdlDPQGc

'Hezbollah leader Hassan Nasrallah plants in Beirut's suburbs', Hasan Almustafa, 8 October 2010, https://www.youtu.be/dZZsM_Tj-CE

'Hamas says Israel deliberately flooded Gaza', dahast de, 16 February 2011, https://www.youtu.be/mxGei2NdHfY

'"Clean Homeland Campaign" in Giza', Egyptindependent, 29 July 2012, https://www.youtu.be/D8FsL8LB_TI

'Islam and the preservation of the natural environment – Seyyed Hossein Nasr', Center for International and Regional Studies, 5 March 2013, https://www.youtu.be/lTHGZpu1rP4

Abu Hamza Al-Ansari (Water Department official), الحياة نبع هو الماء [Water is the spring of life], ISIS-Raqqa Media Office, April 2014

حملة لغرس نصف مليون شجرة بغزة ('A campaign to plant half a million trees in Gaza'), سكاي نيوز عربية (Sky News Arabia), 5 December 2014, https://www.youtu.be/eIsdCgEHwoA

'Islam and ecology: Dr Mustafa Abu Sway', Interfaith Center for Sustainable Development, 3 January 2015, https://www.youtu.be/VOByKmTyPfU

'Islam and climate change', Islamic Educational Center of Orange County, 24 June 2015, https://www.youtu.be/7dYy_SBoVgU

'Thousands of Hamas members take on massive cleaning up of streets', AP Archive, 30 July 2015, https://www.youtu.be/k3WWssNsGYo

نبع الحجير ('Al-Hujair spring'), تحاد بلديات جبل عامل (Federation of Jabal Aamel Municipalities), 4 June 2019, https://www.youtu.be/ZqgnJ_fgi3I

'Environmental justice in Islam – Sheikh Faiyaz Jaffer', Thaqlain, 19 September 2019, https://www.youtu.be/BB7YzPZl6SY

'Hizbullah Sec.-Gen. Hassan Nasrallah threatens Israeli ammonia storage facility', MEMRI TV, 5 August 2020, https://www.youtu.be/ZtbI4YEH6dA

كيفية #زراعة_الثوم_البلدي في الحاكورة ('How to cultivate garlic in Hakoura'), تحاد بلديات جبل عامل (Federation of Jabal Aamel Municipalities), 10 November 2020, https://www.youtu.be/X1EG2xkC9HM

'Islam and the environment', East London Mosque & London Muslim Centre, 2 July 2021, https://www.youtu.be/pdnb_qK27xI

'Environment: where is the voice of Islam?', Hizb Britain, 3 November 2021, https://www.youtu.be/K_iX0kTJNIo

'COP26: unearthing the agenda', Hizb Britain, 7 November 2021, https://www.youtu.be/dIY_GCL_lIA

'Environment: individual efforts vs systemic change', Hizb Britain, 13 November 2021, https://www.youtu.be/Iil_O2T6aBE

INDEX